My Dream of Fatherhood

AN UNCONVENTIONAL JOURNEY

A Memoir

By
Rami Aizic

Dedicated to all those unacknowledged and under-acknowledged individuals who are tenacious strivers.

Regardless of the final destination or the length of time there, embrace and value the journey.

Table of Contents

1

IN THE BEGINNING

⟡

Little girls often dream of their weddings. Little boys do not. As the girls get older, they talk about the perfect color scheme and agonize over the food. They worry about the music and plan a guest list, usually made up of all of their friends and a smattering of family members. I remember my cousins, the girls, sharing these dreams with me, as well as my friends who were girls. Over the years, I was a guest at many of their celebrations, which turned out to be as gorgeous as they had imagined. But this was never going to be my life. It wasn't that I didn't think of my wedding—well, actually, I really never did think of my wedding, not in terms of flowers or music or guests. What I did think about was knowing I was different in some way. I didn't know how or why I was different; I just knew I was. But there *was* something I was sure of and thought about all the time: being a dad. I knew I was going to have a child. I didn't think it would be a big deal. Everyone, it seemed to me, grew up, got married, and had children. I would just skip the "getting married" part. After all, was that *so* important? How hard could it be? Almost every boy grew up to be a father. And I would, too. Somehow.

This is the story of somehow.

I was five years old and living in Israel. It was 1967, and Dad was away in the army. My mother, my brother Gil, and I were living in a one-bedroom apartment, the bedroom housing my bed and Gil's crib, and the living room had a pullout couch that served as my parents' bed at night. Gil had just turned a year old, and I remember much tension in the house. It made sense. Mom was at home with two small children, not knowing when—or if—she would see her husband again. Which, as far as I understood things, left me being the "man" of the house.

Mom worked as a seamstress. From all the stories I was told, she was extremely talented. I remember the whirring of her sewing machine, which helped lull me to sleep. I don't think there was ever a night when I didn't hear the machine at work or when I was still awake when Mom stopped. For all I knew, Mom was up all night, attending to her handiwork. And then she would work all day. Every morning, she would drop Gil off at a day-care center on her way to work, leaving the house shortly after I did. The morning routine involved all three of us waking up and getting ready for the day. Once fed, I would be kissed on the cheek and wished a good day. Then I walked down the four half-flights of stairs and on my way to nursery school. We lived in a building in the middle of a block on a fairly busy street.

"Remember, when you get downstairs, wait for someone to help you cross the street." Mom reminded me every time I left the house without her.

"I know."

"And make sure that person is an adult."

"I know."

"And tell them that your mother said that you aren't allowed to cross the street alone."

"I know."

Reaching the curb outside our building, I did as I was told. I always did as I was told. I don't think I *ever* crossed that street alone.

Inevitably, I wound up where I needed to be and began the trek up the hill. I would see other kids and mothers walking together and wonder why I was doing this alone. I could rationalize why: my daddy was away fighting in the army, and my mommy had to go to work. But why did these mommies not have to go to work? Why did these other boys and girls have company climbing the hill to school, whereas I had to amuse myself? Since I had no answer, what I did was sing. I would sing various songs, sometimes to myself and sometimes out loud, with the lyrics and melodies as my companions. At the end of the school day, I reversed course, but this time, instead of panting uphill, I would run, run fast, all the way down the hill until I once again reached the curb of the main street. Whipping my head from side to side, I would spot the first adult I could see and ask them to take my hand, explaining that I lived across the street and my mommy wouldn't let me cross alone. A good Samaritan always escorted me, and as I reached the other side, I would shout, "Thank you!" and bolt up the stairs back into the safe space of my home.

I was also responsible for the "provisions" bag. In Israel in the late 1960s, and maybe still today, every family had a small, carry-on-sized bag with their necessities should the air raid sirens go off. This bag would ensure that no matter when it might be, the family would have blankets, canned food, water, any needed medications, and anything else that might help pass the time and keep people comfortable for the indefinite stretch they would spend in the bomb shelters. Our green and black plaid bag, with one big compartment on top and two small pockets, one on either side, rested against the wall to the left of the front door. A white blanket always peeked out the top. When the sirens went off, Mom would scoop Gil into her arms and call for me to come, assuming I was in the house. This routine was well choreographed. She would run out the door and down the stairs into the basement of the apartment building and save space for us. I was responsible for seeing that she and Gil were out, at which time I would grab the provisions bag, ensure the front door was shut behind me, and only then descend the stairs and find my family.

Even back then, at such a young age, with air raid sirens wailing, I remember thinking this was what it must be like to be responsible for a family and responsible for a child. I wasn't afraid. I actually felt good knowing I was somehow in charge and was capable of doing this. Somehow, being the "dad" felt right.

The shelter was a depressing space: dark, cramped, and smelly. Every family had their little area, but it still felt very crowded. My aunt and three cousins joined us, which made our corner seem insufferable. My mom, my aunt, and my baby brother would sit on the white blanket that came out of the provisions bag while my cousin Danny joined another family who had kids his age. And my twin girl cousins had each other for company. They would stand near our mothers and either entertain Gil or play a series of clapping games. They would stand face to face, mirroring each other, and create a sequence of moves with their hands, along with singing rhymes, which would take them through routine after routine. Each of them would make an identical move, yet because they were standing one in front of the other, it looked like a perfectly composed dance. These rhymes and hand movements seemed to go on and on. Whenever one of them would miss a beat or a move, they would laugh, stop for a few seconds, and then begin again. It was funny to me that between routines, they would shake their arms out and rotate from foot to foot like athletes, releasing the tension from their bodies before they began their next endeavor. Then they would count, *one . . . two . . . three,* and the contest would start anew. How I wanted to participate! Not so much for the game but to feel like I, too, had a mirror image, someone who was there for me, with me, to reflect what I was doing, thinking and feeling. But I would watch—my mom had her sister, the girls had each other, Danny had his friends. I had only my thoughts to keep me company.

Shortly after the war, in July of 1967, my father, who had not been around very much, no longer came home. I later learned he and my mother had decided it was time for them to leave Israel and go to "America" to make a better life for themselves and their children. "America," at that time, meant anywhere other than Israel. Ideally, it would have actually been the United States of America. In our case, it turned out to be Canada. The plan was for my dad to get to the new promised land, set up work for himself and a home for the family, and then send for us. Just like that, no more dad. I vaguely remember asking about him and being told he went on a trip and we would see him soon. But I was five years old, and my concept of time was not exactly realistic. What did "soon" mean? Where did he go? Why didn't he want us to go on this trip with him? Days went by, and I became more and more comfortable with no dad in the house. In fact, I became more and more comfortable with the role I assumed, *being* the dad of the house.

The routine of the days for Mom, Gil, and me, still in our apartment, was comfortable and familiar. Mom, Gil, and me. Mom was the mom. Gil was the baby. And then there was me. I was the "big boy." I was the "grocery-getter." I was the "provisions bag keeper." And I was still the "man" of the house. I went to school in the morning and then to the nearby park on my own in the afternoon. Sometimes, Mom would give me a list for the grocer, and again, with the help of an adult, I would cross the street, go to the local grocer, hand him the list, and sit on a stool while he collected the items. He would put them in a bag and tell me to be careful walking home, especially crossing the street. Back, I would trudge, bag or bags in hand, often stopping along the way to rest my arms. Across the street, up the stairs, and finally back home, I would help my mother put things away or amuse Gil while she did that.

In the evening, I remember helping Mom get the bath ready for Gil. It was my task to bring together two chairs from the kitchen and put them in the bedroom. I would place them one in front of the other, seats touching. Then, from the bathroom, I would drag the big metal washbasin and put it on the two chairs, ensuring it was secure. Mom would bring in kettles of hot water and fill the basin with enough water to give Gil a proper bath. I would stand next to Mom, keeping Gil entertained, chitchatting with Mom until bath time was over. Mom would wrap a towel around Gil, and I would hold him while she emptied the water from the basin; it was too heavy for me. Then we switched. She took Gil, got him diapered, put him in his pajamas, and got ready for bed. And I would heave the empty metal tub off the chairs and back into the bathroom or onto the balcony to dry. The chairs were returned to the kitchen, around the table, and I would wipe up any water that spilled onto the floor so as to prevent any one of us from slipping. With that done, Gil in his crib, it was time for me to get myself ready for bed. Mom would read me a story, kiss me goodnight, and relocate to the sewing machine while I sang myself to sleep. There we were, one happy little family.

Something I do not remember, but I was told many times, was that I missed my dad very much. Mom would say that on numerous nights, she would wake up hearing noises at our front door. She would inevitably find me standing there half-asleep, with my blanket over one shoulder, trying to unlock the door. When she would ask me what I was doing, I would tell her,

"I'm going to see Daddy."

She told me it would break her heart when she heard that and would shepherd me back to my bed. In the morning, she would ask me if I remembered the scene of the night before; I had, and still have, absolutely no recollection of it.

Nearly one year after he left, my dad sent for us to join him in Toronto. He started off in Montreal but later moved to Toronto. He would tell me later that it had been hard for him to learn *two* new languages, English *and* French, so he moved to Toronto. Many immigrants were settling there, taking on one or more jobs during the day and going to school at night to learn the language. Dad's first job was at a nearby cemetery, where he swept leaves and dirt off the gravestones, but that job did not last long. Once winter arrived and the snow came, there was nothing to sweep. Dad ultimately found a job working in a clothing factory, doing a myriad of odd jobs and learning the trade. He rented a two-bedroom apartment in a nice suburb, furnished it with the basics, and sent a telegram to Mom for us to join him. And again, just like that, Mom, Gil, and six-year-old me said goodbye to the only home we knew and traveled to parts unknown.

In Toronto, I learned English, went to school, and eventually became a happy, well-adjusted kid. At age thirteen, I had a small but promising group of friends. We met every morning as we walked to the bus stop on our way to school and then again in the afternoon at the end of the day. We would talk about homework, the bad lunches our moms packed for us that day, and the usual things. The girls would eventually talk about boys and dating, fantasizing about being brides and moms. The boys, on the other hand, would talk about sports and girls and wanting to be successful athletes or businessmen. And then there was me. I didn't relate to what the boys were discussing. I wasn't interested in girls the way they were, and what *I* wanted to talk about was growing up and having a family. Not giving birth to a baby, but being a father to one. Raising one. Educating one. Playing with one. That's what was important to me. How exactly was this going to play out if I wasn't interested in girls? And how was I going to get this baby? I chose to address this situation head-on—by way of denial. I brushed my dreams aside and continued to work hard in school, hold down part-time jobs to help earn money, and put off thinking in any realistic way about my future.

By the time I was twenty-one, this much-repressed, oft-ignored baby situation of mine was a full-blown crisis. I knew how babies were made, and I knew mine was not going to come about that way, but that didn't change my desire, my *need*, to be a daddy. I was living at home, going to the University of Toronto. I would go to class, take notes, study for tests, do well on my exams, and bring home good grades. I was, after all, the good boy who did as he was told. I didn't have much of a social life, mostly because I didn't seek one out. I had a few friends, but I always kept some distance from them. I was hiding a secret from them and from everyone. I wasn't ready to acknowledge this secret, not to myself and certainly not to family and friends. So I lived with the pain of feeling different, and I lived with the aloneness.

It all came to a head on August 26, 1983, when Anita, one of my closest friends—who had dreamed of pink roses and white lilies for her wedding flowers, gray tuxedos for the groomsmen, and pink dresses for the bridesmaids, and disco music to dance to—was getting married. She was the first among us to do so. All new and very exciting. She was, to me, a trailblazer of sorts. I was asked to be in the wedding party, which was both an honor and an expectation for me. On the day, I dressed in my rented gray tuxedo, pink bowtie, and shiny black shoes. The required ensemble. I knew this might be the closest I ever got to having my own wedding, standing next to the bride and groom.

The banquet hall of our synagogue served as the wedding venue. Inside, the tables were set just as Anita had wanted them: white tablecloths, gray cloth napkins, and pink and white baby roses as centerpieces. Tables were arranged in a U shape around the parquet dance floor, which lay before the head table, where Anita would sit with Elliott, her groom, and both of their immediate family members. On that long table were more pink and white flowers, taller than the others, making a bolder statement. They were beautiful: long-stemmed pink roses and white and pink lilies cascaded down the sides of the clear glass vases that housed them. The music speakers were placed well off to the sides, so no table was right in front of them, and they were not blocking anything in the room. Anita did not want any of her guests to feel slighted that they were seated in a less-than-desirable location.

A table with the guests' name cards was positioned just outside the main room so people could find their names in pristine black ink calligraphy on a pale gray card, with a small pink rose in the upper right corner. A bar was set up just inside the main doors to the left, away from the head table. Anita had thought about everything. No detail had not been addressed, covered, and instituted. And why not? Anita had been thinking of this day since she was a little girl. I do not mean this figuratively. No. Anita, by her admission, knew since she was five years old that she wanted a particular type of wedding, with specific colors, a traditional Jewish service, a long white "princess dress," as she called it (both in childhood and at age twenty-one), and a great party, with lots of music and dancing. That's what she was going to have. August 26, 1983, and Anita's childhood dream was about to come true.

The ceiling in the main room was outfitted with chandeliers and dimmers so Anita could create the ambiance that suited each part of the wedding. I stood at the light switch and played with the brightness in the room, from complete darkness, slowly increasing the light, and I thought about God. In the Bible, in Genesis, I read the story of the creation of the world. "In the beginning . . . the earth was formless and empty, darkness was over the surface of the deep . . . And God said, 'Let there be light,' and there was light. God saw that the light was good, and he separated the light from the darkness." In one slow, methodical movement, very purposefully, something was created out of nothing. Where there was darkness, now there is light. Where there was chaos, now there is order. Where there was emptiness, now there is completion. I thought about my life, the darkness and lack of order I felt inside, juxtaposed with the lightness I showed those around me on the outside. Was this what it was like? Would I have to create my world out of the void that lived inside me? Just as Anita had?

As I stood there, surveying the room, all I could think of was that Anita was getting everything she wanted. And, it was easy for her. I was so happy for her, creating the life she wanted. Without knowing it, she was my role model. She showed me that I, too, could do whatever I wanted. But the difference would be that all she had to do was grow up and just *be*. She was a girl who grew up to be a young woman marrying a young man. No fuss. Nothing out of the ordinary. For me, it would be different. I would have to *do*, not just *be*. But the problem was I didn't even know what had to be done to get *my* dream realized. I thought about the lighting again. I wished there was a way to put a dimmer switch on me so I could turn *my* darkness into light, make *my* chaos into order, and fill *my* emptiness with *my* dream of completion.

From the outside looking in, I seemed to be one of the gang. A friend of Anita's, standing up for her and Elliott on their wedding day in front of family, friends, and other well-wishers. Although they were young, we were seemingly all on track for this same experience. But on the inside, I was so different. I was an immigrant. I had to attend English as a Second Language classes to learn how to communicate with my peers. I was the one who translated mail and wrote out checks and made phone calls in our house until my parents learned how to write and speak better English. I was the one who had a paper route and lifeguarding jobs and babysitting gigs and tutoring assignments in order to have some additional pocket money while my friends were going off to summer camps and family vacations to Florida and Europe. While Anita dated various boys, and my other friends dated too, I was the "pal," the "buddy," the one who would be the third, fifth, or seventh wheel on their outings. And while we all sat together in class, on the bus, or at a movie, talking and laughing and sharing our dreams, I sheltered a piece of myself. I protected that part of myself that felt so singular, so unusual from my friends, so I would not have to feel the pain. I was terribly lonely, and I couldn't imagine how I would ever get past what I was hiding. But deep inside, I had hope. Somehow, someday in the future, just as I had found a way to learn English, hold down jobs, and advance academically, I would find a way to make *my* family happen.

2
A CHILDHOOD INTERRUPTED

G rowing up in Toronto, one of my cousins, Dalia, one of the twins, lived nearby. By this time, she was an adult, newly married to David, and starting her family. Dalia was always a very sweet and loving cousin. She was a devoted daughter, a good sister, and a hard worker. She and David made a wonderful couple. He was from a family where hard work and dedication to the family were of primary importance, and his devotion to Dalia was impressive. He adored her and showed her every chance he could with flowers, with compliments, and with pure love. He worked long hours, as did she, and within a few years of being married, they decided to start their family.

During Dalia's first pregnancy, I was in my early teens and spent considerable time with her. Besides the fact that I really loved her, I was intrigued by the concept of being close to someone who was growing a baby inside her. I would often ride my bike to her house and shadow her around for hours. We didn't go anywhere or do anything special. I just enjoyed being with her. She would make me tea and serve me cake. We would talk about my school, my friends, and any family event happening around that time, including any and all information that either of our mothers had revealed to us about our relatives living back in Israel.

"Do you remember how you would come over and only want to do what we were doing?" Dalia would ask, smiling.

"Vaguely. I do remember your brother not letting me play with him and his friends."

"Me too. He always thought of you as the pesky little brother he never had."

"Was I pesky?" I asked, wondering if that were the reality.

"To him, sure. Just like he was to me. And just like your little brother is to you."

"Hmmm, I guess that makes sense." I didn't like thinking of myself this way, but Dalia did have a point.

I was always at ease with Dalia. With her, I felt safe. Comfortable. I felt nurtured by her. In some ways, she was mothering me as if practicing for her offspring, soon to arrive. She didn't quite dote on me, but she really seemed to see me. And to talk to me. She didn't have an agenda. I never sensed that she was looking for a particular answer to any of her questions, nor that she judged me about anything I shared. She was genuinely interested. This kind of relationship was wholly unfamiliar because Dalia, to me, was the only close family member in my life who did not lead me to believe I was expected to "be" anything or anyone specific. It would have no real consequence for her if I had done well in school. It would not have affected her in any way if I was a good role model for my brother. She knew me from the time I was born. She knew I was inherently kind, gentle, respectful, and ethical. She did not seem to want to do anything other than to love me.

Whenever I saw her, we would talk about her latest doctor's appointment; I wanted to know everything.

"The doctor said that the baby is in exactly the right position. He wants me to keep taking the prenatal supplements because, according to my latest bloodwork, my folic acid and iron are a bit low."

Some of what Dalia shared with me went right over my head. But I didn't care because I was richer for the story and more knowledgeable about the concept of babies.

When we received the phone call that Dalia had a little girl, I remember *needing* to see the baby. And also Dalia. In that order. It seemed like forever until we got there and laid eyes on that baby. There she was, behind that glass, in a transparent cube, wrapped up in a traditional cozy-looking hospital blanket, white with a blue and pink stripe. She had a full head of dark hair; she was asleep, slightly stirring. Her little hands were formed into fists, and she was moving them around. Not her arms, just her hands. I remember noticing that, but I'm not sure what it meant if anything at all. It made me take notice. Her head was cocked to one side and ever so slightly moved up and down, almost as a subtle nodding, as if to say, *Yes, it's me, the one you've been waiting to meet.* It was strange to see activity behind the glass but hear virtually nothing.

As I looked around that room, a room full of babies, some bigger than others, some longer than others, some dark-skinned, some fair, I felt a pang of sadness. For all the joy and excitement of a new life in the world and in our family, the future generation happening right before me, I still felt sad. I didn't really feel a part of it. I was watching it, but I was not a participant in it. I was in close enough proximity to all of these events but still observing from the other side of the glass. I could see it all and had feelings about it, but if I were to reach out and try to actually hold it, there was a barrier between me and the object of my desire. I really was behind that glass, literally and figuratively, still trying to join in the genuine events occurring around me. I could see them. I could hear them. But I was not actually sharing in them. I knew I was still young, only a teenager, way too young to be thinking about starting my own family. But would this ever happen for me?

Something was different about me, that much I knew. But what was unknown. I did not allow myself to identify what that difference was. Would it always keep me behind the glass wall, able to see the life I wanted but not actually have it?

Dalia came home with the baby, whom they named Shirley, and I continued to spend as much time there as I could. I learned by watching how to feed a baby, holding the bottle at a particular angle so the flow of the milk would get directly to the baby, but not too quickly. I learned how to pick her up while supporting her neck since her muscles were still underdeveloped and pliable. When Shirley cried, I learned to listen for which cry it was. Dalia taught me so much, not intentionally, but by doing. And I watched, soaking it all in.

After what seemed like only a few months, Dalia announced she was pregnant again, and Iris arrived eighteen months after Shirley. She, too, was a love. She looked different from her big sister, much more like her father's side of the family than Shirley, who had the coloring and mannerisms of her mother's (and my) family. Iris was darker skinned, with soulful eyes. Now there were two of them for me to play with! That made me happy. Sometimes while I was there, I would spend more time with Shirley, and other times, with Iris. Sometimes with both girls. In my mind and in my fantasy, I was not a high school kid visiting my cousin but a father to two wonderful children. A father who changed diapers took the babies out in their strollers, fed them, burped them, played with them, taught them things, learned from them, and satisfied a core need of my own.

One game I used to play with the girls that we still remember to this day was Superman. This involved me scooping them up in both arms and holding them as if they were flying in the air. We would make up fantastic and far-fetched scenarios, how the girls, and they alone, were needed to fly overhead and save the day. Once the stories began, they just kept going.

"In the big city of Shirleyville, people were losing their candy. One minute, it was in their lunchbox, and the next . . . poof! Gone!"

"Where did it go?" Shirley would ask, providing me the opportunity to continue my story.

"We'll have to wait to find out. It's a mystery! Parents were shocked. Children were sad. And nobody knew what to do about it."

"Oh no! Everyone was sad?" Shirley would ask.

"Yes, everyone, kids and parents. The only thing the people of Shirleyville could think of was to get something, someone, to fly overhead and keep an eye out over the entire city."

"They knew someone who could fly?!" The amazement in her query was always so genuine, so sincere.

"This would be the only way the candy thief would be found. With hope almost lost, the city called on the only person who might possibly help."

"Who? Who? Who is it?!" Shirley would shout, half smiling, half serious.

"It's Shirley to the rescue!"

While in my arms, she would utter funny noises like "ooooooooohhhh" and "waaaaaaaaaaahhhhh," but mostly, there was laughter. And, when I felt like I was reaching the end of my ability to hold on for much longer, we would unquestionably find the culprit. We discovered who was stealing all the candy, and our hero let him know he was not allowed ever to do it again, or he would be removed from Shirleyville, foooohhhr . . . ehhhhh . . . verrrrrrr. At that point, I would slowly bring Shirley's body from the flying position to an upright one and put her back on her feet. Before I knew it, there were shouts of "Again! Again! Again!" If Iris were around, it would be her turn. And I would, on the spot, have to come up with an entirely different story, unique to her, so she didn't feel as if she were Super-Shirley's sidekick but a full-fledged superhero of her own: Super-Iris.

This continued for several years, from Shirley through Iris and into Naomi, who came along approximately two years after Iris—followed by two more girls, Michelle and Ashley. I continued to see Dalia and spend time with her and her family. Mostly her family. Superman remained a staple in our interactions, and I enjoyed doing it. I wanted something distinctive, something exclusive I could have with these girls. Thinking about it now, it wasn't just for them—it was equally, maybe even more, for me. This was proof of all those things I needed to believe were true. Oh, how I wished I could be Superman, with superhero powers, able to make the world a safer, happier, kid-filled place. Was this as close as I would get to having my own children? Would I always have to be "Cousin Rami" or "Uncle Rami," yet never get to be "Daddy"? Although I was still a teenager, I fretted about this, worried about how to make it happen. It became my central preoccupation. And somehow, I would have to transcend the "maybe" and create a reality. I *would* be Daddy. Someday. Somehow.

My high school was not too different from what I imagine most high schools are like. It was a medium-sized school with about 1,100 students, grades 10 through 13. The school had the usual mix of immigrants, as in most schools in Toronto: Israeli, Italian, Greek, Armenian, and Asian. Students were Jews, Catholics, Christians, Buddhists, Muslims, as well as atheists, although, to be honest, I didn't know of any. Some kids came from more affluent families, and some from lower socioeconomic backgrounds. Some kids were very sports-oriented, some more academic. Some were known as the "stoners," while others were referred to as the "brainiacs." Tall, short, thin, fat, light- and dark-skinned, they all walked the halls of William Lyon Mackenzie Collegiate Institute, or Mackenzie as we called it. Many clubs and organizations existed: the Photography Club, the Chess Club, a host of sports teams, the drama contingent, the Band, and several others. The one club that seemed to be missing was the "Am I Attracted to Other Boys?" Club.

Always having been a good student, I found myself taking classes with other smart kids. I liked that; it kept me stimulated and challenged. And while I was not a particularly competitive creature, I did want to feel accomplished in some area of my life. I was never incredibly athletic, and I definitely did not like team sports. I enjoyed running, swimming, tennis . . . all solitary sports. I had lots of time to be inside my head and think. I did play piano, but not well enough to be able to sit down and "jam" with others. I can carry a tune when it comes to singing, but I am in no way a "singer." So, for me, my area to shine was academics, languages, and humanities, more than math or science. I worked hard to do well, trying to finish near or at the top of the class. Deep down, I wanted to impress others, to show them I had value, that I was worthy of their attention and their love. I wanted to prove that even though I struggled with this one area of my life that was not acceptable, certainly not then. I had enough other redeeming features, so the unacceptable part could be overlooked.

The "meet me at my locker" drama was in full bloom. Girls met up at their lockers between classes to reapply lip gloss and gossip about who looked at whom in French class. Boys sidled up to each other between classes to check in and see who actually talked to whom in chem. Mini summits took place at lunch and during "spares" to advise and consult on who would ask whom out, where they would go, what they would wear, and if they would be picked up at home or meet at the venue. Boys declared their fantasies in the form of a fait accompli: what they would accomplish sexually with the girl during and after the date. Girls discussed strategies for looking their very best, wanting to look good but not too slutty, and how far they were willing to go sexually without coming back to school with a reputation. There was so much drama, and all of it excluded me. I was drama-adjacent, participating in some of the meetings with both the boys and the girls; I had friends in both camps. But the conversation was never about me asking a girl out. And not because I didn't like any of them—I wasn't sure what I was supposed to be feeling to qualify for "asking out" status. When I looked at friends who were girls, I could appreciate their appearance, their fashion sense, their makeup application, their humor. If I thought about being sexual with them intellectually, I could see it unfolding in my mind. . . but I didn't feel that feeling that lurks deep in the gut and in the groin. I wasn't sure what I was supposed to be feeling, but I did know that I didn't have it.

Every once in a while, when talking with my friends who were boys and listening to what they wanted to do with the girls they liked, there was a tiny, almost nonexistent . . . almost . . . tingling that occurred deep, deep inside me. Again, I wasn't sure what it was. Sometimes, I thought it was envy that they had these feelings, yet I was nowhere near any of that. Other times, when I allowed myself to feel my truest feelings fully, I wondered what it would be like for me to be the one these boys wanted to kiss, to touch, to be with. But, as soon as any of those feelings bubbled up, heading toward the surface, I shut them down. There was no room in my life even to consider these feelings.

Since I was never a "jock" by any means, I participated in almost no physical exercise at school; therefore, I had little reason to ever go into the locker room. As we got into the higher grades, P.E. classes became electives rather than required, and I opted out of them. When I was younger and was mandated to go to gym class, I was nearly always chosen last to be on the football team, or the baseball team, or the soccer team. I wasn't even chosen to be partners in wrestling because the other boys in my division knew I was an easy target who put up very little competition. For the boys who took this activity seriously, there was no value for them to pin me down in the first few seconds. Yet, when I did end up in the gym locker room during my high school years, for whatever reason, I was titillated. Would there be any boys in there? Would they be showering? Would I catch a glimpse of them in some stage of undress? And while titillated, I would also panic. What if I liked what I saw? What if I gawked? What if one of the boys saw me being too interested in what I was seeing? I couldn't take such a risk. Yet I wanted to. And so I struggled for years with the duality of my feelings, the conflict between my groin and my head, always making sure my head won out.

When it came time for high school prom, I asked Shani to be my date. She was bright, pretty, and understated. She was not part of the cool kids, yet she was certainly no nerd either. I joined in the conversations with those around me, looking forward to what would happen—that it was going to be the night, presumably, I would lose my virginity—but I knew such a thing would in no way take place.

I took a deep breath one night at home, picked up the phone, and dialed the seven numbers that led to Shani's phone.

"Hello?" Whew! She answered and not one of her parents.

"Hi Shani, it's Rami."

"Oh. Hi."

I chatted with her for a few minutes about our math class, especially our math teacher, whom few of us liked, but Shani, being a math genius, had more compassion for him, probably because he was trying his best to teach the rest of us numbskulls concepts that she picked up the first time.

"I was wondering if you were planning on going to the prom?" I considered waiting for a response but didn't want to lose my nerve, so I bulldozed my way forward.

"If you were and don't have a date yet, I would love to take you as *my* date."

There, I said it. It's now out in the open and cannot be taken back.

"Sure, I'd like that. Thanks."

"Great!" I might have shouted that a bit louder than I wanted to, but I hoped that she would find it endearing, as opposed to suspecting that my ears were ringing so loudly and my heart beating so quickly that I thought I was having a stroke.

Now what? Do we continue our conversation? I had no idea what to do. So, I defaulted to the old familiar refrain.

"Ok, I'm gonna get back to homework. We can talk about this more at school tomorrow."

"Ok. Bye." And before I realized what was going on, the deed had been done, and Shani had hung up.

I declared my excitement and happiness that Shani said yes, that she was all the things a guy wanted in a girl, and I sounded very convincing to others. But to me, it was all an act. I wanted to go to prom and participate in a rite of passage, but I didn't want the pressure that went along with the expectations. This was not at all about Shani. But, again, these thoughts remained buried deep, deep inside, far away from everyone's view, sometimes even from mine.

I preordered a pink corsage to match the fuchsia dress Shani would be wearing, picked her up at the appointed time, and off we went to our high school senior prom. We danced, ate, laughed, and spent time with our friends and classmates. Once the scheduled events of the official party were done, we joined a group of friends at someone's house for an after-party of sorts. Snacks, soft drinks, sitting up all night reminiscing about our four years that were coming to an end. Shani and I had fun. We were comfortable together. Outwardly, all looked right. I knew how to do that quite well. But the internal feelings of that night were sad for me. I was closing a chapter of my life that was no more settled at the end than at the start. Shani never knew of my angst; I never would have wanted her to think she was responsible in any way for it. She and I made a memory that would be ours for life; unfortunately, a portion of that memory was more melancholy than mirth for me.

3
WHEN DREAMS COLLIDE
WITH TRADITION

Many of the kids I grew up with went to sleepaway camp during the summers. This was a foreign concept to me as an immigrant; a place kids went without their parents, for a month or two at a time to participate in a multitude of activities. Boating, water-skiing, camping, rock climbing, tennis, archery, horseback riding—so many leisure interests and hobbies all in one place, all while being away from everything routine. It sounded like heaven to me! I went to a day camp when I was nine—we made lanyard key rings and tie-dyed T-shirts.

Instead, from the time I was ten, I took on part-time jobs during the summer. My first job was to deliver newspapers. This was not the *Toronto Star* or *The Sun*; I was delivering *The Mirror*, a free paper that was a cross between a throwaway supplement and a second-rate publication. None of that mattered to a ten-year-old boy who was earning four cents per paper delivered, with an expectation of delivering five hundred papers—that was big money! Each week, I received twenty dollars. I was so proud of myself. What did not occur to me was the amount of time and energy it would take every Wednesday to walk up and down the streets in my neighborhood and to place, toss, or throw this weekly rag at or near the front doors of the houses. Summers are hot and humid in Toronto. It often rains. And this delivery often took all day to complete.

Still, this was a learning experience, and it spurred me to find an easier way to make money the next summer, which I did. I worked as an assistant lifeguard. My primary duties were to make the lifeguard look good. That meant *I* cleaned the deck of all trash and vacuumed the bottom of the pool every morning before it officially opened. I then tested the chlorine levels of the water throughout the day to ensure the hygiene of the water and the safety of the swimmers. The lifeguard was responsible for flirting with the girls, pretending to be interested in the stories told by the elderly patrons, and signing off on the daily log sheets indicating the pool was being kept up according to health and safety codes. I didn't care because I was paid a dollar per hour. This gave me eight dollars a day and forty-eight dollars per week. By the end of the summer, I had a tan, complete knowledge of pool care, and $480.00 in my bank account. I never went to sleepaway camp as a camper, but I never stopped fantasizing about the idea.

The summer of 1981, shortly after high school graduation, I managed to secure a position as a camp counselor in California. This made me a bit of a "rock star" to my friends and fellow students. Some of my peers were going away to Europe in groups of three or four, some were taking long family vacations, and some were getting their first "real" jobs. I wanted to do something unique, too. I had done some sleuthing during the previous year and found out about a Jewish summer camp, Camp Ramah. There were several campsites, one on a lake not far from Toronto and one out west, north of Los Angeles, in Ojai, California. Getting there was my goal. I made phone calls to various offices until I found the right number and the appropriate person to interview me on the phone for the position of lifeguard and bunk counselor. This was to be in a facility I had never visited, in a state I had never been to, three thousand miles from home, and away from anyone who knew me. This was a dream opportunity for me. Once the Admissions Director and I started talking about my interests, how I had taught afternoon Hebrew school, and how I had always had a strong affinity to being around kids, as well as Judaism, she was sold. A few months later, I was at Toronto International Airport, saying goodbye to my parents.

"I promise that I will call when I can," I assured them.

"We want to make sure that you will be ok." My mother said.

"I will be. This place has been around for a long time. Nothing bad is going to happen." All I wanted was to be done with the goodbyes and get on the plane.

I flew Air Canada, which arrived at Terminal 2 at Los Angeles International Airport. A white van pulled up, and a very nice-looking young guy, about my age, introduced himself as Danny. He was medium height, slim, with a mop of curly blondish hair, tanned skin, and a big, broad, white-toothed smile. He was wearing a white T-shirt with a geometric design in blues and reds, cream-colored Ocean Pacific shorts with a blue stripe down both sides and flip-flops. This, to me, looked like the quintessential surfer outfit on a quintessential, stereotypical California boy. If this was what I was in for, let me at it!

Danny introduced himself to three other kids who were looking nearly as lost as I was and helped us with our duffel bags, throwing them into the back of the van. On the ride to Ojai, the radio played Steve Winwood's "While You See a Chance Take It," and I hoped this was a harbinger, an omen, for me to make the most of these next few months. We drove in whatever direction Ojai was from the airport: north, south, east, west . . . parallel to the Pacific Ocean. Far, far away from Toronto and my "regular" life.

Looking out the window, I saw a lot of brown, dried-out foliage along the hillsides on both sides of the highway or, as I was corrected, the *freeway*. Danny explained that Southern California was, after all, a desert, and without irrigation, especially in the summer months, plant life would die. The good news, he continued, was that throughout the winter months, the rain revived the deadened shrubbery to luscious green vegetation.

"You'll have to come back in the winter, Rami," he said, "and see the difference." Wow. Here was a stranger, so friendly that he was already inviting me back. Of course, this might have meant nothing other than Danny, who was an affable, gracious young man whose job was to make the new staff feel welcome. But I didn't hear it that way. For me, this was an invitation to be the most genuine, the most honest *me* there was. My problem was I didn't really know who that was. I knew who I thought I wanted it to be—someone more outgoing, more adventurous. More brash in my interactions with others. Able to admit that I have feelings for certain people.

"Invitation accepted. Thanks." I said with all the confidence that I wanted to feel.

"Who knows?" Danny continued. Maybe this will become a yearly thing. You can come here every summer and then again in the winter."

"Yeah, sure, all this sounds great, but let's see how I do after my first summer here." A part of the real me was beginning to seep through.

"Oh, you're gonna love it here. And we're gonna love having you here." With that, Danny smiled broadly, which I could see from where I was sitting in the rear-view mirror.

I listened to the chatter among the others in the van with me, all from the Portland, Washington area, and they were excited about being the counselors-in-training that summer. The previous year, they had been campers. Camp, Danny explained, was like the family you always *wanted* to have. Fun, carefree, loose, and "totally awesome." I had only been in California for about an hour and had already heard the word "awesome" so many times. At the airport. From the Portland campers. From Danny. Of course, I knew what the word meant, but I liked how they used it in California. Awesome. Larger than life. Breathtaking. Full of wonder.

We pulled off the main road and traveled down a gravelly one, and within minutes, I was standing inside the rustic tent that would be my home. A plywood floor measured approximately forty feet by thirty feet. The "walls" were made of dark green canvas and had been rolled up and tied to allow for ventilation. Overhead, more dark green canvas was held up by three thick wooden poles inside the tent, causing peaks in the roof, similar to the top of a circus tent. Abutting the walls along the perimeter of the tent were eight bunk beds made of old metal that housed the thinnest mattresses I had ever seen. Two other twin beds were placed side by side near the front entrance of the tent, separated by four dark blue plastic milk crates, two on the ground and two on top of those. The only other accouterments in the tent were dust and dirt, small lizards, and the intermittent bird that flew through. I was in heaven. I didn't know a soul, and that did not matter in the least. I was away from home, able to be whoever I wanted to be, with no history of any kind. True liberation.

As I put my duffel bag down on one of the single beds, I heard voices just outside. I looked over my left shoulder and saw a girl about my age directing two others up toward the main dining hall.

She nodded and smiled. "Hi, I'm Robin."

"Hi. I'm Rami."

"Are you new?"

Is it that obvious? I didn't know whether to say that out loud or just to keep it in my head. Either way, it was how I felt.

"Yeah, my first time here. Actually, it was my first time at a sleepaway camp."

"Well, welcome," Robin said. "I've been coming to this camp for years now, so if you need any help or have questions, feel free to ask me."

She was so sweet. And so sincere. Robin looked like many of the girls I went to school with:she was of average height, big brown eyes, olivey-tanned skin, and dark wavy hair pulled back in a ponytail. She was wearing a white T-shirt, a pair of light blue Ocean Pacific shorts, and the requisite flip-flops.

"Do you know what these milk crates are for?" I asked.

"Ohhhhh," she said. "You'll quickly learn how valuable those are! Your co-counselor must have brought these to your tent. Make sure you thank him. We use the milk crates as cubbies to put our clothes in so we don't have to live out of our duffel bags. But because there are so many counselors and so few milk crates, they're like gold around here."

Already, someone was treating me nicely, taking care of me. Three people, actually. Danny, who made me feel so welcome. Robin, by taking me into her confidence and giving me the inside scoop, and my co-counselor, who didn't even know me but thought enough of me to bring milk crates for both of us, not just for himself.

I walked around the boys' area. Like the tent, the bathrooms were rustic, only with a ceramic tile floor rather than plywood. The showers were in a long room with two rows of showerheads, one along each wall. "Rustic" was too sophisticated a word for this room. "Primitive" was too sophisticated a word for it. Mildly rusted-out showerheads jutted out of the walls. No stalls. No curtains. No dividers of any kind between one shower and the next. And a few drains in the floor.

When I got back to my tent, a tall guy, about my age was standing near the single beds.

"Hi, you must be Rami," he said. "I'm Jamie."

He was a longtime former camper, now a second-year counselor. A year older than I, he was in college in California on a baseball scholarship. His brothers went to this camp, his sister was currently at the camp as a counselor-in-training, and he wished me a great first experience. Jamie took great pride in describing the significance and value of the milk crates and said he hoped to be able to "snag another couple" before the campers arrived, but that had to stay between the two of us.

The rest of that first day was a whirlwind, in a good way. I met many people, most of whom were between the ages of seventeen and twenty-five, boys and girls, locals and foreigners, mostly returning staff, and a few first-timers. They were *all* friendly and very nice to me. They offered to introduce me to their friends and the inside tricks of the camp experience. They volunteered to take me with them on days off into Los Angeles proper, Santa Barbara, and the beach. They suggested I meet their non-camp friends and perhaps meet up during the school year in Toronto, where I could host them and show *them* around. All I could think was, "Wow, they're treating me so nicely, and I haven't had to do *anything* to them or for them!" They're just being nice to me for *me*! Not an image of me. *Me*!

I went to bed that night on a rickety old cot with a mattress about one inch thick, in a tent where I had rolled down the walls to keep *some* of the bugs out amidst dust and dirt, away from anyone familiar, feeling happier than I had felt in longer than I could remember. I lay there, taking stock of my first day. Robin was my first friend at the camp; Jamie, my co-counselor, my second; then David, Sharon, Jeff, Carla, Janet, Ron, and dozens of others. These were kids from California, Arizona, and Colorado, but I was the only Canadian—a bit of a novelty. I was also one of the few new faces at camp in the summer of 1981, and the genuine friendliness and true camaraderie were so unfamiliar and so welcome that I was thrilled to soak it all in. Every drop. Because of that summer and the two that followed, I knew California would eventually be my home. Six years and four months after my first flight to the Golden State, I returned with two large suitcases and had no intention of using my return ticket.

As the days went by and I became more accustomed to the schedule, I also became aware that I was feeling something strange. I should be *doing* more. Not in terms of my counselor duties but related to being a friend. I knew how to be a friend to the friends I had back home, often feeling the need to hide part of myself. There, I needed to be the Rami who needed to please others. In Toronto, I was a good son, according to what my parents expected of me. I was a good student, based on the demands of the school. I was a good friend, defined by what I was able to give and do for those around me. I was the good brother, cousin, kid in the neighborhood. Presenting all of *those* elements of Rami allowed me a diversion from going inside my head for too long a period and ruminating about all the life I was not experiencing. From the time of my earliest memories, I had images of helping out, doing for, and stepping in, but not of insisting on, demanding for, or being unrelenting about. I was so comfortable with being the sidekick or the buddy that it was extremely anomalous, even jarring, for me to be the center of attention. Here at camp, I was seen for who I was, not for what I did. I was pursued by others for *my company*, not for *their needs*. I remember the word used as soon as I arrived in Los Angeles: awesome. This was truly an astonishing occurrence for me. It was wonderful, at times a bit breathtaking, and overall, just plain good.

As the weeks progressed, the campers arrived, settled in, and became part of the tableau, and I continued to enjoy my time more and more. The campers in my bunk, *my kids*, were boys ages thirteen and fourteen. They ranged from withdrawn to spunky, but overall, they were happy to be at camp, to see their friends again, and to create memories for the summer of 1981. For many of them, this was their last year as campers. Beyond this age, they either leave the camp experience or return the following summer in a counselors-in-training program. For the majority of these campers, it was their fourth, fifth, maybe even sixth year of camp. Some had been coming even longer. This was the place they congregated after a long year of school, routine, and parents. Here, they reconnected with their "summer selves," something I was learning about myself too. This was a place they, we, could bring out the self that, for whatever reason, did not live in the open air during the year. Here, in the hills of Ojai, California, far enough away from home, wherever home happened to be, one could bring one's most faithful, most authentic self, no questions asked.

I made quick friends with the campers, walking the fine line between disciplinarian and buddy. Some days, I was their worst nightmare, while other days, I was their greatest ally. I was a big brother to these boys, a father figure, a guide, a mentor, a friend, a drill sergeant, a dictator, and a provider. Maybe even more. I often thought about Dalia and her kids throughout the summer and wondered if this was what the next phase of parenting was like. Raising boys, as opposed to Dalia's girls, I became sensitive to the fact that they have some of the same needs; they just look different. For example, just as the girls enjoyed my full attention at times and did not want to share me, so was the case with my campers. On some occasions, they were thrilled to be with their peers, oblivious to any adult figure around them. And other times, they, as individuals, seemed to need some additional notice and a little greater attention. Individual rather than communal. At those times, I applied an adolescent version of the Superman game, where I would sit with the boy and focus all of my attention on him and his needs of the moment. And most times, by the end of the "game," he would reach the equivalent of saving the world from the dreaded candy-stealing villain. In this version, he would reconcile the issues troubling him, maybe glean a greater understanding related to an incident, and ultimately feel better about going back out into the fold to resume his shared camp experience. Jamie often told me that when one of the boys seemed sad or was acting aloof, he would go to them, put his arm around them, and say, "Boy, you sure look like you could benefit from a talk with Rami right about now." That was one of the nicest compliments I had ever been paid.

Session One ended after a little more than five weeks, and it was a bittersweet occasion. I was happy to see myself thriving as a counselor to a group of adolescent boys, the boys leaving, having amassed experiences I would be permanently connected to. All of us counselors stood together in two rows, one on either side of that dirt road I initially arrived on, arms around one another's shoulders, singing songs that have become camp staples, waving goodbye to the kids, some of whom were crying, watching the buses trail away as they climbed the dusty dirt road, back toward the real world. In another month, I will be on one of those buses, too. I would be heading back into *my* real world, the one where I knew, more than ever, was not where I felt whole.

We had almost two full days off between sessions, and I took full advantage of them. Several of the counselors decided to drive to Los Angeles to sleep, do laundry, and eat what they called "real" food. Robin, my first-day-at-camp friend, and another girl, Sharon, who had also become a very good friend and was close with Robin's sister Janice, invited me to join them at Robin's house. She lived in the very trendy, fashionable, and popular area of Melrose Avenue. Sharon, who was from Tucson, Arizona, and had been to camp for years, told me to prepare myself for the family antics that went on in Robin's household. "They're really great people, but they are unique." And she was right. Robin's family took me in as if I were their long-lost son, a son they had loved and longed to see again.

I was welcomed into the home by Bernice and Dave, who sized me up immediately as Robin's "friend," a euphemism for "their future son-in-law." Nothing was explicitly said, but all actions pointed in the direction of "making this boy feel at home so he will want to come back and eventually be part of our family." The three-bedroom, one-bath house was modest and homey. Robin's bedroom had a trundle bed, but I was not allowed to sleep there. Bernice was concerned that if I slept on the bed and Robin slept on the trundle, I might "roll off the bed and onto Robin" in the night. And if Robin slept on the upper portion, and I slept on the trundle, Bernice was afraid I might "roll *up* during the night, onto Robin." This was so bizarre to me, not the "rolling up" part, but the notion that I might want to "be" with Robin. Not that she wasn't attractive. We had been together at camp for the past month. If we wanted things to "happen," they would have happened there. Then again, I can understand parents don't want to appear as if they condone their children having sex in their home. What was most peculiar to me about this entire conversation was that it never occurred to *me* that Robin and I would be sexual. Never. And I never thought about whether Robin wanted us to be more than friends.

Finally, it was decided Janice would give up her room for me, and she and Sharon would sleep in the living room on the couch. Janice was not as unhappy about this arrangement as I would have expected, losing her room to a stranger. Her condition was that as part of the deal, I would spray some of my Polo cologne in her room before I left so it would smell like a man had slept there.

I was not sexually attracted to Robin—nor, as far as I could tell, was she to me—but that didn't mean I had been lacking in female attention. I had very direct, straightforward offers from several of the female counselors. I chose to take some of them up on their offers, aware it was part of the growth I wanted to go through. Happily, I found myself enjoying physical contact with these girls much more than I had in the past when I experimented. Kissing had become more fun and sexually charged. Mutual touching of each other's bodies was highly arousing. And even oral sex, which I was terrified to practice but thrilled once I did, felt genuinely enjoyable. I wasn't ready yet for intercourse, so I decided to forgo those opportunities, even though they were complimentarily offered.

But something was wrong. Maybe "wrong" isn't the right word. But something did not make sense to me. While all of these options and prospects presented themselves, I was conscious of something else: boys. While I took in the girl counselors at camp—the shape of their bodies, the size of their breasts, the curves of their hips—I also noticed the boy counselors. The broad shoulders. The slim waists. The hairy chests. I found myself not knowing what to do about it, but very much conscious... far more conscious than I wanted to. And in a strange way, I really liked it. I enjoyed looking at these bodies but dreaded doing so. I didn't want to be caught staring. I didn't want anyone to know I even had those thoughts. As for the feelings, I didn't understand them myself. It wasn't that I wanted to reach out and touch any of these boys. Sort of. I certainly didn't know what I would do if I *did* touch any of them. I couldn't even fabricate a scenario that would put me in a position to *accidentally* put me in direct contact with any of these bodies. When I thought of the girls, I could fantasize about touching, kissing, caressing, and exploring them. What didn't join those fantasies was a deep-seated feeling of desire. I knew I liked the feeling of sex, but I didn't yearn for the touch of a girl. My core was reaching out for something. It was like a hunger for something unknown. I knew I wanted—I *needed*—something, but I just did not know what it was.

Throughout the summer, at the pool, in the showers, on days off, being around naked boys, I wrestled with what that meant. I saw so many of the guys being physical with one another: hugging, walking with arms around each other's shoulders, and it was all so agonizing for me. They did it with me, too, and it took all the fortitude I had to reciprocate, knowing that for me, that contact was torture. I was hypersensitive about not reaching out for a hug and only responding to one. If a buddy came by and put his arm around me as we walked around the camp, I would put my arm around his neck, trying to avoid the shoulders so as not to arouse any suspicions or anything else. And during shower time, in the stall showers open to all, I would find an equilibrium. I didn't want to avoid all eye contact, nor did I want to ogle. Other counselors were always clowning around, talking about penis sizes, mocking each other about their bodies, teasing each other about what action they'd had and with whom, thrusting their pelvises forward and back to simulate that action, and the usual verbal and physical banter that went on. It all made for a particularly uncomfortable time for me.

Nights could be difficult, too. Once all the activities of the day were over, a wonderful calm was carried through the breeze over the camp. The girls would go up the hill to their tents, and the boys came down to ours. This was often a time when the kids were all asleep. Some of the counselors had also turned in for the night, and the remaining few splintered into clusters, walking and talking, usually about more serious and intimate topics as opposed to raucous ones. This was when I felt the greatest connection with some of these new friends and felt a great affection for them. In some of those moments, that affection stirred within me, and deep, deep inside of me, I actually *felt* a tenderness for another boy that allowed me to romanticize a coming together of the physical and the emotional. It was fleeting, but it did happen.

The general procedure was that every night, on a rotating basis, two or three counselors were on night duty. From 10 p.m. until 1 a.m., we stayed put, sitting in the tent areas, ensuring the boys did not act up and helping out with any potential emergencies. We could not leave the campgrounds nor go off with a group of others to another part of the camp and play games, drink, or socialize. On one particular night, when I was assigned to night duty with a fellow counselor, some of those uncomfortable feelings I would feel deep inside of me fluttered to the surface. I was always careful to shut down any potential for exposure to those feelings, and I was usually successful. Except for one boy, one time.

He and I were on night duty together. It was very late and very still. The campers were all asleep, and the other counselors were either in bed or off doing whatever they were doing. He invited me to join him for a walk. He was handsome, had a great smile, very introspective and philosophical. He was wonderful with the kids, making them laugh and keeping them in line. And I had a little crush on him, to the extent I allowed myself to acknowledge it. On our walk, he asked me if I had feelings for any of the girls at camp. I gave my standard response: I liked a lot of people, but because I lived in another country, there was no use in starting a relationship that would have to end at the conclusion of the summer. He nodded his head, paused for a bit, and then shared a very intriguing notion with me. He said that he, too, liked many of the people at camp but did not want to commit to any one person in particular. "After all, it's the soul of the person I'm attracted to, not their gender."

Wow! I had never heard that before. I had never considered such a concept. Was he telling me he might not be attracted only to girls? Was there an insinuation, a whisper of some sort, that he was talking about me?

"Wait. What?" That was all I could come up with. Part of me wanted, *needed*, to continue this conversation. And the other part of me wanted to run as far away as possible.

"For me, it's the whole person. Their energy. Their values. If they are good people in the world or not."

"But what if the person who has all those qualities…" I hesitated to continue that question because I wanted to stay away from the "G" word. Fortunately, he picked up where I left off.

"Look. Guys and girls have been getting together forever. But so have guys and guys. And girls and girls. It must mean that those are options too." He said this so matter-of-factly that for a second or two, I felt convinced that any combination of two people was perfectly acceptable.

"Yeah, but…" Again, I was slow to finish that thought, but this time, he did not help me out.

"But what?" He challenged.

"I guess I never thought of it that way. I always thought, and think, about a guy liking a girl and her qualities, and a girl liking a guy for his qualities." I lied.

"Really? Hmmm…" was his response. He shrugged, and we both fell silent again as we continued to walk.

Whatever he said after that is lost to me. All I knew and felt was that I had to get away from him. I had to erase this incident from my consciousness. This was far too distant from my comfort zone, and I needed to get back to the Rami of Camp Ramah, the happy-go-lucky Rami from Canada who was funny and smart and engaging and all those mainstream, traditional and widely accepted things. That nice Jewish boy who loved kids and was good with them and was friendly to everybody and did not ruffle feathers or create controversy. As big as this world was, it still bound me to the precepts and guidelines and expectations of growing up, going to college, graduate school, choosing a profession, getting married, having children, and living happily ever after, whatever that meant. The sad reality was that I did want some of those things. I did want to go to college and probably law school after that. I did want to choose a profession that made me feel good about the work I did in the world, and I most certainly did want to have children. But getting married did not speak to me. It was something expected of me. And to think about anything different was simply a conduit to wasted time and sadness.

After saying our goodnights, tiptoeing into our respective tents, and tucking ourselves into our respective beds, I was left with a profound sadness. I asked myself if I would ever have a merging of what I wanted. Would I ever understand what those feelings were trying to tell me? Was there a way to make sense of that and still be the admired, pursued, lovable Rami who existed here at camp? For the first time, I formed the thought, *Does this mean I am gay?*

I never thought of myself, until that night, as being gay. "Gay" was not a word I liked to consider because deep down, I always knew it described me, and if that were the case, it would define me. And that definition was not one I could live with. I could not fathom a life without children, my children. I could not and would not create a life where I would be an onlooker, an "uncle" to my friends' children, yet never be a dad to my own. I could, and would, make my life as full as I could to create the life I wanted and envisioned.

That first summer at Camp Ramah showed me so much. I had value. If, in the future, I would have to manipulate and contrive my life in order to feel whole internally, then I would do that. Since being gay was in direct conflict with being a dad, I would choose the latter. I saw no other way.

4

BECOMING THE MAN I NEVER KNEW

⸺ ⁌ ⁍ ⸺

Between summers when I was back home, attending the University of Toronto, trying, like the vast majority of undergraduate students, to figure out what I wanted to be when I grew up, life was different than it was before I went to Camp Ramah. I brought back with me a more grounded sense of myself. I felt more confident. But only on the inside. At home, while I did have Debbie and Anita, my two closest friends whom I love to this day, I did not have the collection of friends I did in California. I did, however, keep in contact with them. Those were the days of "long-distance calling," with the best rates after 7 p.m. and on Sundays. What worked well for me, being on East Coast time, was to call friends late at night for me, which was still a decent time for them. My parents worried I would upset my friends' parents if I called too late. After all, I needed to be the good boy who was not rude and not insensitive. Once I was done with my homework and had sat with my parents in the family room of our three-story house, watching whatever 10 p.m. show we watched together, they would either flip the channel to the news or get ready to go to bed. I would go down to our basement, sit on one of the tall pleather barstools at the wet bar, and dial 1, plus the 10-digit number with the foreign area code. I was like a vampire, in a way. I waited until the dark of night to come to life, drinking in the lifeblood I needed to survive another day. Talking to one of my camp friends on the phone recalibrated me and helped me remember that the Rami of the West Coast still existed. It had not all been a dream that faded as soon as the Air Canada flight touched down on the tarmac in Toronto at the end of August. The version of me that lived in California was still there, very much alive in the history made by my very existence at camp. All it took was hearing the voice of one of those friends on the other end of the phone, and I was more than just transported back in time—I was *wanted* there. One of those friends was Judy.

Judy was a camper the first summer I met her. She is a few years younger than me, but we hit it off right away. While I stood at six feet four inches, Judy was about five feet tall. I was lanky, and she was plump. I was soft-spoken, and Judy . . . well, Judy had, and still to this day has, a raspy voice that carries quite a distance. From the outside, we looked a bit like "Mutt and Jeff," two total opposites; we were instant kindred spirits. We were both funny, quick, sharp, and just self-deprecating enough that those around us found us magnetic. The subject matter did not make a difference; we always had so much to talk about.

Judy was diagnosed with juvenile diabetes as a child. She had to keep insulin on hand and give herself shots several times each day to keep her blood sugar stable. Once, on one of our group outings, Judy had a sudden drop in sugar, and she seized. One minute, we were all walking on a dirt road alongside orange groves, and the next minute, I heard someone calling out for help. Judy had fallen to the ground and was convulsing. Fortunately, she did not hit her head on anything hard and had her syringe and medication with her. One of the other counselors stabbed Judy in the upper arm with the liquid extracted from the tiny glass vial. Judy's body almost immediately settled, and she opened her eyes. Once she found her bearings, one of the first things she said was, "Damn, now I won't get the exercise of finishing the hike!" Judy learned that living with a chronic illness, one that could be lethal, made life that much more important to *live*. Have fun. Laugh. Eat. Travel. Be your truest self. She didn't know it at the time, and maybe I didn't either, but I adopted that lifestyle and hoped that someday, somehow, I would be the valedictorian of the Judy School of Life Lessons.

Judy and I maintained our friendship through my years at the University of Toronto and then at Leeds University in the north of England, where I studied law. Judy came to visit me in both cities and each time we saw each other, it was as if no time had passed. When we imagined, in a half-fantasy, half-romanticized way, what our futures looked like, our future spouses were inevitably described.

"I think your husband, Jerry, will be a university professor." I posited.

"Yeah, that sounds right. With brown, curly hair, right?" Judy continued as if we were recounting something that had existed forever.

"Wild, curly brown hair!" I specified.

"And he wears those corduroy blazers with the patches at the elbows." Judy did not sound happy about Jerry's style choices, but here, it seemed as if she would let him decide his office attire.

Jerry would always be the "Number Two" in their family, allowing Judy to shine. But he was no pushover, not by any means. He would be smart, not as funny as Judy, but would appreciate her humor and always, always support her in whatever she wanted to do. He would know she was truly living her life, and anyone who was with her would be accepted to join in.

"And my wife, Joanne, is tall. Five-foot-seven or so."

"Yup, with long, curly-wavy, medium-brown hair." Judy continued. "Green eyes. And she's a teacher. She wears a lot of peach. Sweater sets in peach."

Neither Judy nor I particularly loved that Joanne wore peach, but it did look good on her. "She wears pearls. One strand of just-a-bit-longer-than-choker-length pearls. And she's musical. She plays a few instruments and sings beautifully." Judy sounded certain of this.

"Joanne is on the quiet side," I stated, "but definitely speaks her mind. Especially with me, whom I thoroughly respect and welcome. No bullshit, no pretense. Straightforward with one another, which allows us both to be our most genuine selves. We'll have a daughter who plays the violin."

For years, whenever Judy and I would talk, Jerry and Joanne would come up, and we'd add more details to their lives, as well as what we needed from them in ours.

One spring, Judy invited me to join her in New York for a fun getaway. She was going to visit her sister, Ellen, who lived in the city, and I was offered the couch, welcome to meet some of Ellen's friends, and learn about Manhattan from a local, rather than from a tourist's perspective. The timing worked well with a break from school, and off I went. Ellen's apartment was small, but large by Manhattan standards. I was told it was centrally located, which meant nothing to me since I had not been to Manhattan before, and I've never had a good sense of direction. I was greeted warmly by Ellen, and lovingly by Judy. The weather was warm, jasmine in bloom and fragrant, throngs of people everywhere, but somehow, as crowded as the streets were, it was as if everyone in the city knew how to navigate through the masses so as not to cause one single physical collision. At first, I moved my head from side to side, taking in each nearby individual to avoid smashing into someone. But it didn't take me long to do as the others around me were doing, to keep walking. Keep moving forward. How fun it was to walk through Central Park, to explore the Guggenheim Museum with its circular staircase and light flooding in from all sides. To eat at tiny bistros that could seat hardly more than a dozen people at any one time, but to feel lost in a sea of people. It struck me that Manhattan was a city I could live in, one where I could be invisible among the multitudes, and maybe live an authentic life without being found out. While Toronto was known as a smaller version of Manhattan, only cleaner and safer, it was my home. There was no way I could be me, *me*, on my home turf. So maybe Manhattan. Or Los Angeles. But not at home. It made me sad to think that in order for me to live the life I wanted to live, to explore sexuality, and to possibly be in a relationship with a man, I would have to sacrifice my family and familiarity. I remember thinking about Israel and how my life changed when my father left and I was the little man of the house. Then, the move to Canada, where I was the English speaker of the house. To move again would mean I would have to forgo some of what I wanted in order to get other parts of what I wanted. Was this how it was for everybody? It didn't seem that way to me, but maybe I just didn't know.

On my last afternoon before returning to Toronto, Judy and I went for a walk, just the two of us. We didn't know when or where we would see each other again, and we needed to solidify these last few hours of my New York City experience with some "us" time. On that walk, I decided that I was going to say the words out loud—*the* words. We walked through the door of a small coffee shop and ordered two teas and a blueberry bran muffin. We took off our jackets and settled into our chairs, and I launched in. It was as if a stream of consciousness took over, and my mouth was no longer receiving signals from my brain.

"I have to share something with you, Jude, something I've been wanting to say out loud for a really long time. To someone who I absolutely trust. But not someone who knows me at home. That's too scary." Words were falling over one another.

"For the longest time now, I think that I know, I know that I am... I am... not who I've been pretending to be. But it scares me. And I don't even know if it's what I want, but I don't think I have any choice. Not really, anyway." Was I breathing at all during this outburst? Was anything making sense?

"You know how we always talk about Jerry and Joanne? Well, I'm not sure that I still want a Joanne in my life. I don't know if I ever did, but now I really think that I don't want her. Not because she isn't a good person or anything, but because I just don't think it would be fair to her. To Joanne. I would be lying to her." I was rambling at this point.

"With all of the girls I've been with and all of the sex I've enjoyed, I know deep inside it's a lie. Not a total lie, because I did, actually, enjoy it all. But it was not complete enjoyment. Each time I was with a girl, rather than feeling the passion and excitement, I wondered if doing these things with a boy would feel better." There. I said it. Sort of. Some of it. And if Judy was still paying attention, then she got it.

"I wanted to like girls more. I really did. And maybe I still do. I guess I could fake it. But I don't want to do that to anyone. And not to myself. But should I? Will I have to do that? Is there a scenario in life that allows me to be me, the *real* me, and still be accepted? Could I be a good son and a good brother and a good friend and a good professional person and a good listener and a good citizen of the world *and* be gay?" And there it was. I said the word 'gay' out loud.

I didn't know anyone gay. Certainly, nobody from my family's immigrant cohort was gay. Gays were not accepted into mainstream society and definitely not into any of the circles I lived in. The 1980s were not portraying openly gay people on television or in the movies. The AIDS crisis was saturating the media, once again marginalizing gays and rendering them as deviants. "Nice Jewish boys" were not gay.

I talked for however long it was until I felt both a relief and a sadness that took over my body. The relief was more of a release, one that had been waiting to be spoken out loud for years. The pressure-cooker feeling inside me finally had its valve turned, allowing the steam to escape, to bolt, from its belly and feel a sense of freedom. And the sadness, really despondency, hopelessness, was palpable.

"What am I going to do? How will I have a family? Children? What about children?" I remember repeating these words through my sobs.

I was having a difficult time catching my breath, trying to talk and cry at the same time, unable to do both. Grunts and groans came out of me, which were completely unfamiliar to my ear. Noises from my mouth and drips from my nose and tears from my eyes all landed on the table between Judy and me. None of it phased her. She let me be. She sat there and, at some point, put her hand on my hand but said nothing. It took me back to that day at Camp Ramah, but this time, I was the one convulsing, not Judy, and she was the one there to be supportive. Where she needed insulin to bring her back to her healthy self, I needed an ear, a body, and acceptance. No judgment, no opinion, no conversation. Just the safety to be *my* healthiest self and show it on the outside, rather than keep it all tucked carefully away deep, deep inside me.

We sat in that coffee shop, at that table, with numerous hot water refills for our tea, nibbling on that one muffin for an indeterminate amount of time. I had no thoughts of anything else, including needing to get to the airport, until Judy said, "It's gonna be okay. You'll make it happen." And with that, as if oxygen had been provided to my gasping lungs, I felt calmer. It wasn't as if any answers were offered, and certainly, no roadmap appeared. But Judy said I will make it happen. She trusted me, and she trusted that I would make my life look like the life I wanted. For what seemed like the first time in my life, I shared my most honest self. And Judy saw me, the me *I* wanted me to be.

5
A PROMISE TO MYSELF

After completing my undergraduate degree in Toronto and having the unique experience of living in England for three years, studying law, I fulfilled my destiny of moving to Los Angeles, permanently. I spent three years in Leeds studying with a myriad of students from all over the world, many of us planning to return to our home countries once our studies were completed. While I never had the experience of living on campus while at the University of Toronto, that opportunity did present itself at Leeds.

My university trajectory was similar to most of my friends from home: we applied to one of the local universities while we were in high school, and once we were accepted, we made our decision. For nearly all of us, it was a choice between the University of Toronto and York University. Both were accessible by public transportation, so we could live at home and travel to and from school whenever we needed to. The odd outlier might venture out of town, but only as far as Hamilton, Ontario, which was less than an hour's drive. If someone was truly adventurous, they headed northeast to Queens University in Kingston, Ontario, about 160 miles away. But that was very much the exception, not the norm. So, to go to graduate school on another continent was, well, curious. Novel. Exciting. Suspicious.

"Why are you going to law school in another country?" Several of my friends asked.

"You didn't get into any of the good schools here?" I remember one of my parents' friends actually saying to me.

"How will it work to get a degree from another country? Will you be able to work here?" That is a fair question.

Unlike the American system, where college and graduate studies are likely to be done far away from home, for the experience of "being launched" and finding one's independence, the Canadian way, at the time, was not so. Just like I was somewhat of an anomaly going to camp in California, I was also different in going to law school abroad.

Once I graduated, a job was waiting for me in Los Angeles, thanks to one of my friends from Camp Ramah. She had her parents ask around, and one of those friends was able to find me a starting position in a law firm in downtown Los Angeles.

"Why Los Angeles? Why not here in Toronto?" my mother asked, with an equal amount of sadness and anger in her voice.

"That's where there is a position for someone with my education," I replied, trying not to sound too defensive.

"But you didn't even try to find anything here!" She amped up her anger.

"That's not completely true. While I was still in England, I went to lots of job fairs, and all of them were looking for people to go to the States. Not Canada."

"I don't believe that. There must be many places in Canada that would want you." That was sweet of her to say. I do think she wanted that more for her than for me, but regardless, I took it as her wanting me to be closer to home, especially after spending three years away.

"I don't know. What I do know is that there were no jobs in Toronto that were looking for anyone with an international law degree. And instead of looking in places in the U.S. where I don't know anyone, Los Angeles made the most sense." To me, this all sounded reasonable.

My father sat at his place at the kitchen table, letting my mother do all the talking. More questions were asked, eyebrows were raised, but I did not care.

As much as I was not fully conscious of why this was so important to me, this was my chance to get away from the inhibited life I would live in Toronto. Bags packed, goodbyes said, I boarded the plane with a round-trip ticket from YYZ to LAX, assuming I would not use the return portion of that ticket for a long, long time.

I settled into a life in Los Angeles, with many of my camp friends still present in my life. I furnished my lovely apartment with 'gently used' furniture. I bought a car that was, looking back, way too small for my six-foot-four frame, but it ran. Slowly, I began to live an "out" life. I met other gay people my age, each with their unique coming out story. We would compare the severity of the declaration and see whose tale bore the harshest response. I was in awe of those who had already come out to their families, thinking time after time, story after story, that I could never do that. "It would kill my parents." For the time being, I needed to see if, and if so, how, this life would work out.

One of my earliest memories of walking into a gay bar alone, anticipating meeting friends there, still lives prominently in my mind's eye. It is so telling of who I was at that time. I walked in, looked around the loud, crowded, smokey room, and recognized nobody. Rather than move into the space, I found a small square of floor directly under the exit sign. Just in case, I could make a fast getaway. When my friends arrived and found me positioned there, that became the running joke: if you're ever looking for Rami in a gay bar, he'll be under the exit sign. I was so uncomfortable in bars, let alone gay bars, that I needed to be prepared to flee at any moment. I am sure my story is not exceptional, but it is the only one I have. Eventually, I became more comfortable in gay venues, met some men, dated a bit, and even had a few relationships. None of them worked out, but that didn't upset me. Thinking back on those relationships, I believe I was practicing dating men, rehearsing for the role that would become *the one*. As much as I had a vision of wanting to be coupled, I also knew I had a lot of catching up to do. I was not ready in the least to be part of a couple when I had not shared this news with my family and close friends in Toronto.

I also found my career in law unsatisfying. While I loved the intellectuality and rigor of law school, I felt constricted in the practice of law. What I did find stimulating was how I spent my Sundays working with special needs children and teaching them to prepare for their Bar and Bat Mitzvah. At first, I volunteered, finding extreme satisfaction in this field, and later, I was offered a paid position. I was around kids. I was needed, I was helpful, and I was happy. In addition, I volunteered my time through the Jewish Federation with Jewish AIDS Services. I, along with others, was part of a Speaker's Bureau, where we would speak to schools, camps, families, and various organizations about the importance of HIV and AIDS education and the need for open communication between children and their families about this topic. Ironic, wasn't it? What I was doing was helping families adapt and accept who their children were, creating realistic expectations, and loving their offspring regardless. Ironically, I shepherded so many others into healthy conversations with their contemporaries, helping them show their truest selves unapologetically. Ironic indeed. It was time. Time for me to reveal the truth.

I visited Toronto once or twice a year, and my parents had come to visit me a few times. Each of their visits was filled with iconic Southern Californian adventures and landmarks. The Hollywood Bowl, Santa Monica Beach and Pier, Griffith Park Observatory, a few fancy dinners, just the three of us, and always at least one meal with some friends. I wanted them to feel assured that their son was happy and ensconced in the city where he chose to make his life. Without fail, on the nights with friends, my mother would attach herself to one of them and not-so-quietly ask if I was dating anyone and why I was not being more proactive in finding a "nice girl" so I could move on with my life. I would run interference and derail that conversation, trying to help the "identified snitch" not have to lie for me and not have to lie to my mother. Every one of those friends was told, well in advance and no uncertain terms, that my sexuality was not to be disclosed or discussed. At least one of them would be ambushed, and the desire to reveal the truth might arise. But, it was not an option. This was my story to tell and my secret to divulge, in my own way and in my own time. Inevitably, by the end of the evening, once my parents and I were headed back to my apartment, where they stayed while in town, I would remind my parents that this was my life, and I was living it in the way I wanted. I tried to convey to them that it was not fair to put my friends on the spot with personal questions about me, but my mother always dismissed that, saying, "We all love you and want the best for you."

I had planned a four-day trip to Toronto. My plan was to find a time during the visit to sit my parents down and actually talk about the history of my feelings, from my earliest recollections to the present. In my head, it was a bit of an "After-school special," where I would gird myself up to the time when the three of us would sit together in our regular chairs around the kitchen table. I would launch into the history of always having felt "different" in some way until I figured out what the "different" was through dating girls and eventually figuring out I was attracted to boys. And now, nearly 30 years old, living on my own, making a life for myself, I wanted to pursue my real identity. In my mental television show, they would be stunned, then sad, then angry, and eventually open their arms wide at me and tell me all they wanted was for me to be happy. We would hug it out, then move on to sharing some strudel or coffee cake. It would be quiet around the table, everyone in their respective heads thinking about the information just revealed, but in the end, I would stand up, take my plate to the sink, give each of my parents a kiss on the cheek, and thank them for understanding. They would stay seated together at the table, nodding, half-smiles on their faces, and I would go upstairs and on with my day. *That* was how this discovery was to be exposed.

But, as is so often the case, the television show is so much different from the real-world version. In the real world, no one is behind the scenes to edit, score, and create a cohesive narrative with an arc. I had shared with my brother and sister-in-law that I would be divulging the news to my parents. I had come out to them almost a year earlier, and to their credit, they were both supportive and loving. When I asked them how and when to tell Mom and Dad, they both said, quite vehemently, "Don't!" None of us could imagine this news would be received well. Forget about well; in no scenario would declaring myself gay to my old-world, immigrant parents be greeted with anything less than hyperbolic devastation. Yet, if this were what I needed to do, they would be there for me in my absence and try to help my parents through it. I was highly appreciative since my brother and I were never particularly close. We loved each other and understood who the other was, but when it came to extreme situations, we were one family.

I arrived early Thursday morning, having taken a redeye from Los Angeles the previous night. I let myself in with my key and looked around the house, wondering if this would be the last time for a long time I would be welcomed there. My mother came downstairs in her nightgown and robe and was thrilled to see me. She looked tired, older, frail. Maybe it was because it was first thing in the morning. Or perhaps I was projecting my feelings onto her. I was aware that my heart was beating faster than usual; I was not only tired from missing a night's sleep on the plane, but I was also emotionally exhausted. I didn't want to lie to my parents anymore, and the burden of carrying around the truth was depressing and demoralizing. The time had come for me to risk the outcome and alleviate at least some of the emotional and mental mass that had been weighing on me. Mom and I hugged and kissed each other and moved into the room where I would be spending most of my time: the kitchen. Mom was always an excellent cook and baker, and she prepared all my favorites when she knew I was coming home. Stuffed bell peppers, chopped liver, meatballs in her special tomato sauce, sour cream coffee cake . . . the list goes on and on. We never had enough mealtimes to eat all of the food she would have liked to serve me. That's why the joke was always that anyone who wanted to see me when I was in Toronto would find me in my seat at the kitchen table.

Thursday came and went, then Friday with some grocery shopping with my mother in preparation for Friday night dinner with my brother and sister-in-law. Saturday was the day my mother and I would visit my aunt and my cousins, and Saturday night was another family dinner with the five of us. I kept talking myself out of any time being the right time to *talk*. I didn't want to do it too early for fear that it would ruin their day. I didn't want to do it at night because that would leave them having a difficult night's sleep, if any at all. I wanted to have enough time for all of us to be able to talk about their feelings, but I suspected they would want, and need, some time away to process and sort out what they were feeling and what they might want to say. Sunday was probably not the best day since I would be leaving for the airport that afternoon. All in all, "never" was perhaps the *best* time to do it, but I had made a promise to myself that this trip was *the* trip.

I decided, in the end, to write them a letter and leave it for them to find after I was gone. The professional diagnosis for someone who acts this way is "chicken shit," but it was either that, or nothing at all. Once both of my parents were asleep Saturday night, I snuck down to the kitchen, paper, pen, and envelope in hand, and took my assigned seat at the kitchen table. Subconsciously, I had been thinking of what I would say and how I would say it countless times. But now to do it . . . that was tricky. How far back should I go? How much detail should I offer? What tone to take? An apologetic one? A strong and affirmative one? Should I acknowledge their probable feelings about this, or should I wait for them to share those with me? Inform them others already knew, or leave that for a follow-up communication? Again, procrastination. And it was getting later than late, now early Sunday morning. I wanted to make sure the letter was complete before anyone woke up.

The letter needed to be coherent. I did not want to cross out words or sentences as I changed my mind for fear that it would devalue the significance and substance of what I was saying. This needed to look mature and thoughtful as opposed to random thoughts in the night that I was flinging onto the page. I decided to make the letter somewhat chronological, sharing with my parents that for years, since I was in middle school, I had felt different. As time progressed, I learned more about what I was trying desperately to reject and deny and that all the years in Toronto, I had not acted on any of those instincts. But, once I was more self-sufficient and living in Los Angeles, I no longer wanted to deny myself the happiness and entirety of what my life could offer. I still wanted to be in a happy and monogamous relationship. I absolutely wanted to have children and a family, and I hoped that in time, they would be part of all the components of my life, only with a son-in-law rather than a daughter-in-law. I was still me, the same good, dedicated person, loving, and compassionate person I had always been. It was still flawed, of course, but not because I was gay. But because I enjoyed too many sweets, and got to bed too late, and often gave too much of myself to my friends at the cost of my own needs. But being gay was not a flaw.

"This is who I am. I tried for such a long time NOT to be this person, but that did not make me happy. One thing you both always told me was that you didn't care what I ended up doing in my life professionally or who I was with as long as I was happy. Well, this will make me happy. I will find someone to love me, and we will make a family. I will use the model you showed me all the years I was growing up, which is that money does not make you happy, and people don't make you happy. YOU make you happy, and then everything else helps along the way. Take all the time you need with this, and know I am only a phone call away when you want to talk. As scared as I am writing you this letter, I would feel even worse if I lied to you one more day. I love you both very, very much, and I know you love me too. I am sorry for hurting you with this news, but please, please know that is not the intention of this letter. I want you to know and see the real me. The son who loves you very, very much."

I reread the letter once and kept it intact. I found many words and sentences I could have changed, but that was more driven by further procrastination than by necessity. I folded all six pages of the 5.5-inch by 8.5-inch lightweight paper in half and placed the bundle into the corresponding envelope. I licked it shut and pressed down on it to flatten it out. On the front, I printed "Mom and Dad," picked it up, and took it with me upstairs to bed. The following day, both my parents decided they would accompany me to the airport.

"Why don't you go outside and sit in the front with Aba, and I will lock the door." My mom was often the one who liked to know that the house was secure when she and my dad left for an outing of any kind.

"Ok," I said. Then, "Wait! I forgot something in the kitchen." I lied.

"What is it?" She asked.

"I'll be right back."

"Hurry up." She said, sounding a bit nervous. Or maybe it was me feeling nervous.

"Ok, I'll be right there."

I left her at the front door, ran toward the back of the house, and removed the letter I had tucked into my back pocket. I placed it on the kitchen table, the one place I knew that they would find it, propped up against the white ceramic bowl with a few bananas in it, the bowl that was always on the table. I looked at the bowl, remembering it from our apartment in Israel so many years before. Part of my life. Part of my history. It was a common link between me and my family ever since I could remember.

6

THE IMMENSE PRICE OF FREEDOM

The entire plane ride back to Los Angeles was excruciating. I have never been prone to high blood pressure, elevated heart rate, or anxiety, but that multi-hour experience from the time I got into the car on the driveway of my parents' house, through them dropping me off curbside at the airport, through customs and security, waiting at the gate, boarding, and finding my window seat, and the five-plus hours on the plane itself, I had a difficult time breathing. Breathing deeply. I was taking short breaths, causing my upper chest to look like it was spasming. I don't know if anyone around me was aware of it, but I felt very conspicuous. Not to mention that I was crying. The person sitting in the middle seat was very kind; she nodded hello when she sat down and then left me alone for the entire flight. She probably didn't want to engage with a stranger who might blubber and whimper for hours.

Sunday night turned to Monday morning, and I was up early, showered and dressed, ready to get into the law office. Not particularly enjoying the work, I soothed myself knowing that I was making some money, saving some money, and putting it toward the purchase of my first home. Owning property was important to me; it symbolized being able to take care of myself in a more adult and responsible way. I left my apartment wondering if I was going to hear from my parents later that day. They had never called me at work, but I thought that once I returned home, the little red light on my answering machine would be blinking, informing me that someone had left a message. Throughout the day, I was both tempted to and deterred from calling in for my messages. Did I really want to hear what they had to say while I was in the middle of crafting a pleading or researching sections of the Code of Civil Procedure? I picked up the phone in my office and began dialing my home number, but once I heard my voice announcing I was not available to take the call, before punching in the code to retrieve any messages, I hung up. It would wait. I would wait.

That evening, consciously or not, I stayed at the office late, "needing" to prepare some documents that one of the senior partners was going to want to examine the next day. Eventually, I rode the elevator down to P-2, the parking level for those of us who were less senior, got in my car and drove home. As I was walking from the parking space to my front door, my short breaths came back. I remember wondering if they were panic attacks. I would definitely talk to my therapist about it the next time he and I meet. Yes, I had become "one of those L.A. people"—I had a therapist.

At the end of my visit with Judy in New York, her farewell words to me were, "You need to get into some therapy. Right away!" Which I did. My doctor referred me to a therapist. He was less than ten years older than me, straight "but very gay-friendly," Jewish, compassionate, and not a pushover. That was how he was described to me, and once I met Robby, that was exactly how and who he was. And still is. I shared with him that I had never attended therapy of any kind, and this was not only new to me, but I didn't understand how talking to a stranger about my life's issues was going to help. I communicated very clearly to him that I had never been one to wallow in self-pity, but this was one of those situations where I had no clue where to turn. And besides, Judy told me I had to go. I confided in Robby more than I had disclosed to anyone else in my life: my repressed feelings for men, my shame about it. I talked about my sadness of letting go of the life I believed I was supposed to live, with a wife and children and in-laws divvying up holiday schedules and celebrating milestone birthdays and anniversaries together. And, of course, my profound sadness and fear of never having children. There was no way I could see integrating being gay and living an out-gay life with having a spouse and children.

Robby's office was an eclectic mixture of furniture. The waiting room was dark, but his office was brimming with light, flowing in from floor-to-ceiling windows. He had a ranch-style, red-and-white checkered couch with a cozy-looking blanket tossed over one corner of it. We never sat there; we opted for the two mid-century brown leather and chrome reclining chairs with a matching ottoman between them. Robby also had a plain wooden desk and an uncomfortable-looking chair next to it up against the wall. Since my chair was the one looking at the desk, I often wondered why he chose to put the desk there as opposed to the opposite side of the room, where he could enjoy the light and the view. His desk always held a few papers strewn here and there, along with a few notebooks, the same ones he used to take notes when he and I would meet. And two images that I noticed and visually grasped every week I was there. One was a framed photograph of three young children, all smiling, tanned, curly-headed, with big blue eyes. And the other was a hand-drawn picture taped onto the wall just above the desk, most likely drawn by one of those adorable children. The picture, drawn in colored pencils, was of a house, some stick-like figures, and the words "I Love Daddy" on it. Every time I was in that office, once I got settled into my chair about to launch into whatever drama was to be shared that week, I noticed those two images. And, I was aware of how disheartened I became and how dispirited I was, looking at the very thing that no amount of therapy was going to provide.

One day, in the middle of sharing my misery of working in the law firm and how ungratified I felt, I stopped mid-sentence and pointed to the photograph on the desk.

"That is what I want."

Robby looked somewhat puzzled, then turned around. "What?"

"That! A family. *My* family." I responded.

Robby turned back to face me. "Why do you think that you can't have that?"

"I just can't see a world where I have my own children. And a partner. And it all makes sense. Like it does for straight people."

Robby looked deep into my eyes. I hoped he would say something, something that would challenge what I had just stated, but nothing came.

"Am I going to have to lie to a woman about who I really am and make a family with her? And deny who I really am? And my true feelings? I can't do that. Or am I going to set off for a life with a man, living as husband and husband, fighting an uphill battle in a country that was still unaccepting of these unions?"

My face was hot. My heart was racing.

"Why does this have to be so hard?!"

Therapy was supposed to help me find the means by which I could make better choices in my life so I could attain the fundamentals of a happier life. A happier life for me included children. So far, not Robby, therapy, or the universe was getting me any closer to that outcome. I vacillated between feeling angry and depressed. Robby would often remind me that anger is not a core emotion but rather a reaction to something deeper. Usually, when one felt angry, it was likely they felt sad, helpless, or hopeless. But, because remaining in that depressed state was intolerable, one would exhibit anger at the unfairness of it, trying to find some power in the sense of powerlessness. All that to say, my feeling angry at not having any options for moving closer to creating a family was really not about anger. I was about sadness and loss.

Walking into my apartment, I immediately looked to the spot where the answering machine was situated. The light was blinking: three quick flickers, then a pause, three quick ones, then another pause. That meant I had three messages. The conflict between my wanting to hear those messages and the fear of hearing what my parents might have said about one (or more) of those messages was palpable. But this was the moment I waited for to stop hiding the truth. The first message was from Sharon, my camp friend who had since moved to Los Angeles herself. She called to welcome me home and see how my trip was. The second message was from another friend, Mark, who was inquiring about the same thing.

That meant that the third message must be the one. This is the one where I hear how sad they are, how angry they are, how disappointed they are, and how disrespectful of me to do this to them and to do it in such a cowardly way. This next message was going to be the end of our relationship, as I knew it to be. I was going to hear the gloom in their voices as it propped up the outrage they were feeling. Their words would be crystal clear in defining their displeasure with me. Would they speak in Hebrew or English? Sometimes, when my parents were pushed to the brink, they would convey their fury in Hebrew, lapsing at times into Romanian. To me, it was a regression to their younger selves, their primary languages coming out in a primal state of being. The computerized female voice on the machine announced that the third message was about to be played. It was Debbie, whom I had just seen in Toronto, welcoming me home, hoping my flight back was uneventful. After that, the lady who lived inside my answering machine informed me I had no more new messages, followed by a decisive click. No one else had called me; no one else was checking in.

As the days passed, I wondered how my parents were feeling and how they were handling the news. There was complete silence from them. I had reached out to my brother and sister-in-law, sharing with them that I had left the letter.

"We know. We heard." My brother said it on one extension, and my sister-in-law listened in on another.

"What did they tell you?" I asked, curious as to how my parents took in all the information.

"They said that you wrote that you are gay, that you've known for a while that you're gay and that you felt you had no choice other than to live a gay life."

"What did *you* say?" I asked.

My sister-in-law spoke up this time. "We told them that we knew, that you told us about this when we visited you a few years ago."

"And...?" I inquired. "How did that go over?"

"Mmmm.... They didn't like that." My sister-in-law responded, sounding like she was trying to be gentle with her words.

"They were pissed." That was my brother, less gentle, more honest. "They told us that we should have told them when we found out."

"But that was not for you to share," I said, somewhat defensively, not meaning to sound angry at my brother.

"I know. But getting into it with them then would not have helped the situation. They told us that they wanted to be alone, so we left."

"Look," my brother said to me, "we're happy that you finally let them know, and hopefully, in time, we'll all come back together again as a family."

"Do you think I should reach out to them?"

"Probably not. Not now. But do what you need to do." Those were their parting words.

I wanted to call them, but didn't. Of course I wanted to talk to them, let them talk to me, but I was afraid. And embarrassed. I was confused as to why I was feeling both of those emotions.

I was still struggling with my own internalized homophobia, not comfortable with being an "out" gay man. Society was neither openly nor happily accepting of openly gay people; there were plenty of incidents of gay bashing and other hate crimes against the gay community. The more visibility there was, the greater the polarization seemed to get. Politics, religion, morals, and ethics were all called upon to offer opinions and judgments on the issue of whether or not it was "normal" to be gay and, if so, "do we need to see it in public?" For every talking head in the media who expressed his or her support, there were more who took the position of opposition to the cause. For every movie and television show that attempted to portray gays and lesbians as "regular folks" trying to make their lives count and matter, there were documentaries and other presentations of the deviancy and aberration of "those" people who were preying on young boys and were sinister and conniving and dangerous.

Add to that the time of AIDS, and entire communities were dying, panicking, and grieving, yet some chose to declare this as the "wrath of God against the sinners." No, being gay in those days was not easy. I had shared with a select cluster of friends, both gay and straight, that I was gay, and this group accepted me for who I was and who I wanted to be. But a larger segment of me was still living a closeted life. Specifically, working in a very junior position in a law firm, I felt no room for expressing my truest self. I rationalized this by telling myself I did not want to be known as a gay lawyer but simply as a lawyer. But that was only a fraction of the truth. What I did not want was to be fired, labeled, marginalized, and black-listed in any way. Nor did I want to be shamed or attacked, verbally or otherwise. Slowly, though, I expanded my comfort zone by disclosing to more people in my life, mostly friends, who I was, hoping each time I did that, it would sound a bit less apologetic.

The later 1980s and beyond truly were years of crisis for the gay community, particularly due to HIV and AIDS. I had been tangentially involved in that world, working clinically with members of the community, both gay and gay-adjacent. In other words, those who were living and struggling with AIDS and those adjacent to their lives. I saw the havoc and the shame and the wreckage and the despair and the suffering and the burials and the tears. So many tears. Families torn apart either because of the physical devastation of the disease or the social devastation caused by it. So many men, as well as women and children, but predominantly men, wasted away from their former selves to hollowed-out shells of flesh and bone. The light gone from inside of them. The life slowly seeping out of them, out of their physical bodies and away from their connections to family.

As a clinician, I wanted to help but felt helpless. Of course, I could sit in a room with a person living with AIDS or a family member affected by it and process their feelings of sadness, anticipatory loss, and anger at the disease and help them come to terms with their feelings of helplessness. As for my personal life, I was scared. I certainly did not want to contract the virus, yet being a newly-out gay man, I wanted to date and explore sex with men. How to reconcile those two seemingly divergent elements of my life was a conundrum. I also knew that if I became HIV-positive, that would be the end not only of my life, potentially, but the end of my chances of becoming a father. The powerlessness of the medical community against this intimidating tyrant did not help either. While drug trials and medical studies were being conducted, these were early days, and nothing particularly hopeful was in sight. The state of the gay world seemed bleak.

Still, rallies, protests, marches, and gatherings occurred in support of the gay brothers and sisters who were shunned by their families and friends. Communities came together to buoy the spirits of those less capable. Gays and allies alike, albeit a relatively small group of allies at the time. The stigma and shame on parents and siblings and spouses were so great in those days that it was no anomaly to hear about someone who had always been integrated into their familial quilt, now cut out and removed from that family system. Out of fear and embarrassment, members of their former community chose not only to excise but to eradicate all memories of those who no longer fit into the mainstream and conventional mold.

The dichotomy for me was that all I wanted to do was live a more mainstream and conventional life but with a twist. I enjoyed the hetero-normative lifestyle of a committed partner and children, living in a home within a community of others, working together to raise our kids to become ethical and proud members of society. Yet, as a gay man, I was not given social permission to do so. Like those who have HIV and AIDS, I was rejected by my parents. I longed for my family to accept me, hold me, and support me in my journey, to no avail. I saw the profound sadness of those around me who were abandoned by their families and empathized, only for different reasons. I found some solace in the gay community, but it was limited. I wanted to pursue what some were calling a "sellout" life, selling out to the straight community by wanting their image of life. And, from the straight community, I was, to some degree, marginalized due to the alternative life I was pursuing. Again, an old familiar feeling: alone. The odd one out.

After three days, I summoned the courage to call my parents. My mother answered the phone.

"Hi, Ima," I said gingerly.

I waited for what seemed like an exceptionally long time, in silence, until she finally spoke.

"I can't talk to you. I am still in shock."

"Ok, I understand," I said. "Can you tell me how you and Aba are doing?" I risked pushing the conversation, wanting to break this days-long silence that was between us.

"We are both still in shock. I need to hang up." Which she did.

The call lasted less than 90 seconds, but the emotional impact on me was colossal. I was supposed to be the "good son," but to be treated this way was not only unfamiliar to me, but was torment. I called again two days later, and again, we had the same brief conversation.

"Can I talk to Aba?" I asked.

"He doesn't want to talk. He needs time." Then, more silence again. I was thinking of something to say, to prolong the dialogue, but she beat me to it.

"Don't call again." She spoke very clearly, saying that she and my dad were "gutted" by my declaration, and they needed time to absorb it.

"I don't know if we can forgive you for this. But it seems like you made up your mind that this is the life you're choosing. Now, you have to let us make our choice if we want to be part of this life of yours or not." And with that, all conversations ended.

Gutted. That was the word she used in Hebrew. The image came to me of her in the kitchen, with an entire carp that she once brought home from the fishmonger, laid out on the center island, on a wooden chopping board. One of her hands held the fish down, and the other clutched a kitchen cleaver, inserting the tip of the blade into the fish's mouth, and, in a very measured way, sliding it all the way down its belly, butterflying it open, revealing its innards. In this state of its being, if there was any chance the fish could have been saved prior to the gutting, now it was dead. Completely extinct. This is how she felt about our relationship; more specifically, this is how she felt about what I had done to her and my father.

I put down the phone receiver and walked over to the couch. I sat. Stunned. What just happened? I didn't feel anything until a burning rose in my eyes. I remember thinking perhaps one of my contact lenses grabbed hold of a fleck of dust or pollen floating in the air, causing me to experience scratchiness on my cornea. I lifted my hand to try and rotate the lens, hoping it would release the culprit when I realized my eye was wet. I was crying.

When I was young, until my early teens, I was extremely sensitive. The slightest negative or uncomfortable comment led me to tear up. This could be at school, at home, with friends, or in any number of circumstances. The fact that people would notice and comment on it became even more of an embarrassment to me than the crying itself. I couldn't help it; it just happened. It was not at all helped by the fact that, as a kid, I was teased and bullied. Tormented for being chubby, laughed at for wearing glasses, mocked for not being good at team sports, and constantly ridiculed for acting like a "sissy" and hanging out with girls. One day, in eighth grade, I decided I would no longer let that sensitivity show. I would bury it. No more crying. Not publicly. What I did to stop it, I don't know, and why it worked, I don't know either. But from that day forward, no matter how self-conscious or humiliated I felt, I internalized it and moved on. No tears.

Inside my head, there was a lot of self-recrimination, rebuke, and scolding about allowing myself to get to the point of the incident. But on the outside, not a glimmer of that scolding would be visible. Until now. This particular conversation about this particular topic opened the tear ducts and unleashed years' worth of pent-up and held back sadness, so much so that I was not in control of it. I sat on that couch, crying. Not sobs, not heaves, but unstoppable streams of salty tears down my cheeks, plopping onto my shirt, my jeans, and the couch, leaving a darker coloration on each surface as they landed with a tiny thud. I remember thinking the darker blue of my jeans and the darker beige of my couch looked like I was feeling inside: the same, but heavier. The same, but not the same. Stained, visible to the eye, yet nothing to do about it. It would leave an invisible scar known only to those who witnessed its creation. In this case, it would be me, a party of one. I would always know that in my home, supposedly my "safe space," the refuge that was supposed to keep me protected from all the dangers and perils of the outside world, was where I suffered one of my greatest sorrows: rejection by my parents. I will never forget sitting on that couch, the one that held me when nobody else could, in a time of desperate sadness.

Days became weeks, and still nothing from my parents. Nor did I reach out to them, respecting their request to be left alone. Sharing this experience in therapy was less cathartic than I hoped it would be. Robby pointed out I was telling him a story and not tapping into the feelings. I told him the memory of shutting down my feelings half a lifetime before this incident and using that strategy as a way to protect myself ever since. He understood but pushed me to feel the feelings. I don't know what he said or how he did it, but once again, there I was, sitting and crying, feeling no control over what was happening.

I heard myself uttering questions of fear: "What if they never accept me?" "How will I live my life without parents?" "Does this mean that if I ever have a family, they won't be part of it?"

Robby sat across from me, looking at me, really seeing me. He said nothing and nodded ever so slightly as if acknowledging there might not be anything to say, but he was with me. He would not abandon me. He, a rare combination of a stranger yet someone who knew cumulatively more about me than any other person in the world, was not going anywhere. No rejection, no abandonment, no ridicule, and no judgment. If no other parent had me, Robby would be there for me. And he was, as were my brother and sister-in-law and the friends I told. Gay and straight, those who knew me accepted me. Some had questions, some said they already suspected, and some just said, "Okay." I tried to be honest with all of them from that point forward, letting those I chose to have in my real life know me for who I was, not some persona or façade. Surprisingly, to me anyway, not one of those I told had any negative comment or disparaging remark. If anything, they were angry with me for holding onto this burden for so long without sharing it with them. As one of my oldest and dearest friends, Debbie said to me,

"Ram, it's not fair for you to be a good friend to others but not let others reciprocate."

"Yeah, but this is different. This is life-changing." I challenged.

"For you, yes, it is. And maybe for some people, you will tell. But it's up to *us* to decide how to deal with this, not for you to decide for us."

She was right. As difficult as it was, and is, for me to let others help me, I have never forgotten what she said. I try, I really do try, but it is so uncomfortable for me to ask for help.

As the weeks became months, calendar events and milestone moments came and went, all without my parents. That time included my thirtieth birthday. Absent from all the well-wishers were my parents. They used to send me a birthday card every year for my birthday, with a sweet note my mother would often write in English, showing me she did, in fact, learn to write the language of the country that took us in. That year: nothing. During that period, I had also saved up money intended to go toward a down payment on the purchase of my first home. I had always enjoyed being one of those "looky-loo" types, going to open houses on Sundays, walking around the house, envisioning which room I would set up as my bedroom, how I would arrange my furniture, what more I would need to buy, and how I would use the outdoor space.

One Sunday, I happened upon a home in the now-trendy, then somewhat transitional area of Silverlake. It was an old Craftsman-style home with a beautiful porch and an enormous tree in the middle of the front lawn, creating shade and some privacy. Three bedrooms and two bathrooms, one being in the primary bedroom. A galley kitchen, a huge living area, and a sectioned-off dining room. Built in 1916, it had been partially updated in a piecemeal way: newer hardwood floors in the public spaces of the house and new carpeting in the bedrooms and hallway. The one original bathroom of the house still had some of its original tiles—white, purple, and green—with a separate bath and shower and a large pedestal sink with hot and cold fixtures that, if not original to 1916, were not much newer. Charm and character this house possessed. Central air and central heat it did not. Two wall heaters were mounted, one in the living room and the other in the hall outside near the bedrooms. In the primary bedroom, there was a window air conditioning unit. The house was on a corner lot, which I liked, and had a fairly sizable yard. It had tandem garage parking for two cars off the alley on the side of the house.

As I considered whether this was something I could afford and see myself living in, I could. I would need to put up a sturdier and more aesthetically pleasing fence, add a newer garage door, spruce up the main bedroom bathroom, add a window here, and paint a wall there, but overall, this could be the house. My house. The one in a neighborhood. The one where I could set up one bedroom for me, one for the baby, and one as a guestroom/nanny's room when the time came. The streets in the area were flat, so I could easily push a stroller around. Hopefully, I would see other families with young children, and we could create community playdate areas and support for each other. Yes, this house met my needs, and after a short back-and-forth negotiation, it was mine.

I desperately wanted my first phone call to be to my parents, informing them of my happy news. I remembered something Robby had said to me over the years and decided to follow his suggestion: "If you want to do something, do it." Basically, if I did it, and it worked out, then success. If I did it and it didn't work out, at least I would know I pursued what was important to me. Gratification comes more from the determination than from the outcome. The outcome is the prize for the *effort* put forth. If I wanted to do something but were afraid to do it, I would always live with the "what if" questions that would ensue. What would have happened if I had called? With that in mind, I took an emotional gulp, picked up the phone, and dialed their number.

My mother's voice, sounding very depressed, said, "Hello?"

"Hi, Ima." When I announced it was me, she said nothing. I waited for what seemed like minutes but was likely just a few seconds.

"How are you?" I asked, hoping that she would brighten a bit.

"Why are you calling?" She asked.

"I wanted to know how you and Aba are," I replied.

"How do you think we are?" Now, there was bitterness in her voice.

"I can imagine that you are still upset." I hoped that the next part of my conversation would cheer her up.

"I have some very exciting news that I wanted to share with you and Aba."

"I told you that I don't want you to call us. We need more time." She didn't question me about my news at all. "Everything you told us is still very painful. Don't call again."

There was quiet from the other end. I wasn't sure if she was still there or not until I heard an unfamiliar voice say, "If you'd like to make a call, please hang up and try your call again." My mother had hung up.

7

EXPLORING UNKNOWN
TERRAIN

————∽∾∿∿∾∽————

D riving over to the Center, my thoughts were racing with all the possible prospects and options that might be offered. While I did whatever research I could, it was minimal. This was one of those situations where I had to be there to talk to people, listen to people, be among the people, and see if, in fact, this was a viable potential for me. This particular agency had been around since 1908, originally founded as The Jewish Orphan's Home of Southern California. From what I was able to ascertain, in the early 1900s, huge numbers of Jewish families fled Eastern Europe to escape oppression, torment, and discrimination. Many of them arrived on the already crowded eastern shores of the United States. Because these cities were not only congested but also ripe with diseases, many of the newer immigrants were encouraged to move west, where the population was more scant. In addition, the warmer weather of the West was thought to help with illness, but sadly, many of the migrants died along the way, leaving behind homeless and destitute families to fend for themselves. In Los Angeles, the Jewish community was aware of these unfortunates and established a Jewish orphanage to care for the growing numbers of Jewish children living on the streets. As the years progressed and the Center grew, it added to its services education, psychiatric and mental health care, assistance to single mothers, and adoption and foster care, among other social services. It no longer served only Jews; it was now a widely recognized and lauded center helping all races and religions of all socioeconomic abilities. In short, it was, and is, one of the country's most acclaimed full-service facilities helping those in need.

Given its genesis and history, it felt right that I look into a facility that once addressed the needs with which my very ancestors had struggled. Fleeing Eastern Europe, immigrants, Jews looking for a better life. My parents were lucky enough to escape Europe after World War II, settle in Israel, and make a new life. Then, again, leave the uncertain life of Israel and start anew in Canada. Now, it was my turn. I ran away from a life I knew would feel oppressive, one where I could not be the me that I wanted to be in the world. I found a new home out west and was ready to establish the next generation, one which would hopefully benefit from the history of its predecessors and find a peaceful home, physically and mentally, in the environment I would create for them.

The truth is, I had not really considered adoption as a way to have a child, mostly because I had always thought I would have my biological child. I never had any objection to adopting; it was just not on my radar. I grew up around many types of families, including natural and adopted kids. It didn't matter. All the parents were the adults in the neighborhood who opened the door for us when we knocked, needing to use their bathroom in the midst of a long bike ride, or invited us in for cold lemonade in the summer and hot chocolate in the winter. We didn't think about who looked like their mother more than their father or whose genes made up the person we were spending time with. What mattered to us kids was if those other kids shared their toy treasures. Or if the few who had color television would let us see that Wilma Flintstone had red hair, not gray. Or, when one neighbor boy was gifted with Pong, the first video game. Then, it was a fascination; by today's standards, it would be a total bore. And, of course, when needed, the parents who drove us to and from an event so we would not have to wait for buses and subways. *Those* were the parents of the kids I grew up with.

It seems to be somewhat different today, where the current common convention advises that children should be told they are adopted. The adoptive parents specially chose them to be a part of this new family since the children did not have a family of their own. It is suggested the conversation start when the kids are young, and as they get older and start asking questions, give them honest and age-appropriate responses. Plenty of therapists specialize in adoptive families, where new parents can go and gather tools and language to help them with the gentle integration of their adopted children into the fabric of their new family.

I walked into the building, following the signs to the adoption seminar. At the door to the medium-sized auditorium, I looked inside, seeing various couples, some older, some mixed-race, one particularly tall man with a disproportionately tiny woman standing to his left, and a couple of women who looked as if they were there on their own. I wondered if I should walk in at all. Nobody there was a single male, and nobody there appeared to be gay, not that I would necessarily know what "gay" looked like at an adoption seminar. Certainly, no male couples were standing together, looking anxious and excited about starting or expanding their families. If I turned around, I would have spent 45 minutes driving to this part of town and ensured it would not be the night I would learn about how I might be able to bring a child into my life. And, if I entered this room, the one that felt like a foreign country to me, then . . . who knew? It might be a waste of time, or it might prove fruitful in some way. What the hell! I was there, and nobody knew me. Driving home at that hour would only frustrate me, both for sitting in traffic and for not having at least listened to what the speakers had to offer. Onward.

The room was set up lecture-style, with a long rectangular table at one end with a few chairs behind it, and opposite that table, several rows of well-used folding chairs, configured in rows of eight across and six back. Were they really expecting that many people? Only a small fraction of that was in the room, and the meeting was scheduled to begin. Regardless, with memories of walking into the high school cafeteria and wondering where I should sit, I approached an aisle seat midway through the arrangement. For a quick getaway, I half-joked to myself.

Three individuals approached the front of the room, and each one took a seat behind the table, calling out that they would like to start the evening's program. One woman, somewhat heavy-set and nearing the end of middle age, introduced herself as the Director of the Adoption and Fost-Adopt Program at the agency. A younger woman, strikingly thin with messy long hair, introduced herself as the primary social worker who would be working with all the families who ended up in the adoption program. And a Hispanic man in his mid-thirties, casually dressed in jeans and a button-down shirt, announced that he, too, was one of the social workers. Each, in turn, imparted some information about the agency and its specific roles, offering glimpses into the adoption process. We, the prospective parents, learned that this process was usually a two-year course of action, which would include personal interviews with each one of us, individually and as couples, a home study where social workers would come by a few times during the 24 months, sometimes announced and sometimes spontaneously, to ensure the premises were suitable for a child. We would have seemingly endless amounts of paperwork to fill out, as well as references to provide so others could share their impressions of us. Other family members, friends, clergy, employers, and fellow employees were all fair game in this undertaking because the primary importance was the mental and physical well-being of the children who would be coming to live with us.

The speakers began.

"Now, don't be overly frightened by all this information. It's not meant to scare you, but we do want you to know what you will be getting yourselves into." It was the man who tried to reassure us. I found it comforting that of the three of them, the man, or the "dad" in the group, took the lead, as opposed to one of the "moms."

The younger woman then added, "We're sure you're going to have questions. Try and save them for the end. We hope to cover most of what you might want to know."

"Those of you who proceed with us will be assigned individual counselors." Continued the man.

"And then you will also have opportunities to ask more specific questions." The younger woman again.

It was as if they were playing verbal ping-pong.

After some more talking by all three of the moderators, the older of the two women wrapped up the evening.

"Thank you all for coming. We hope that this will be a journey that provides you with an infinite amount of excitement, ending in what is best for each one of you."

She invited us to partake in the cookies and cake on the back table.

"Feel free to introduce yourselves to one another. Have a lovely evening."

I cannot say the presentation was encouraging, but neither was it off-putting. It seemed to me that the information was to provide facts; it was up to those in attendance to deliver the emotions. Personally, I was not daunted, nor was I excited. I gave myself permission to go to the next step.

Paul was assigned to me, or me to him, and we met twice. The first time, at the center, he had reams of papers, some of them looking like they were mimeographed from decades in the past. These were the innumerable questions that needed to be asked, answered, considered, some asked again, and filed in a manila folder with my name printed on the front.

"Let me go over some of these questions with you to start the initial file for you," Paul announced, picking up a pen and looking down at one of the many sheets in his possession.

"Full name?"

"Rami Aizic."

"No middle name?"

"No."

"Hmm… ok."

Was that bad?

"Where were you born, Rami?" Paul continued.

"I was born in Israel. I can spell the name of the town for you if you want."

Paul briefly looked up. "Sure. Spell it for me."

"The town is called Petach Tikvah." And I proceeded to spell it.

Paul wanted to know my date of birth, address, place of employment, and a myriad of questions that, to me, seemed, if not insignificant, very superficial. There were questions about my friendships as I was growing up, the foods I liked, and what subjects I enjoyed in school.

"If you could only save one, which would it be, a dog or a cat?" What? Why was he asking me this?

"That seems like an odd question to ask me. What's its purpose?" I couldn't hold back.

"These are questions that help us understand a bit about your values and your ethics."

Really?!

"I can't answer that since I don't have either." I retorted.

"I didn't ask if you had a dog or a cat. Which would you save if you saw both about to be hit by oncoming traffic but could only save one." Paul was not letting this one go.

"I would have to make that decision at the moment. How close to either of these animals was I? What was my potential injury in attempting to save them?" I said.

"I can tell you were a lawyer at some point." Said Paul, smiling.

"OK, moving on, tell me about your formal education."

The interrogation resumed, Paul adding to the paperwork that was balanced in his lap. Did I enjoy music? Why? Why not? Did I play any musical instrument? If so, would I insist that my child do the same? If not, why not? Inquiries about my employment and my feelings about employment. Sweet or savory? Beer or wine? Hot or cold? It was an endless parade of queries, all leading somewhere, I'm sure, but I could no longer see the questions for the trees. As long as Paul had some idea where this was going, I trusted him and the process.

About two weeks later, Paul and I had arranged for our second meeting, the one where we would review not only my responses to the questions but their meaning as they related to adoption. Walking into his small office at the center this time, I was much more aware of my surroundings than the first time. Maybe I was too nervous at the previous meeting to appreciate what was around me, and all I could do was focus on being present and satisfying Paul with the right answers to his questions. This time, I was keenly aware of the mismatched and dated furniture along with the aluminum-framed posters on the wall of landscapes. The bargain-basement desk, made of cheap wood with gouges in it, stared back at me sadly as I looked in its direction, seeing my file sitting on top. Slight discoloration in the threadbare carpeting made itself known to me, too, with a short but distinct path from the door to the visitor's chair. Also, an odor, a hint of something, permeated throughout the center, but somehow was more prevalent here. The only word that came to mind in trying to identify the odor was "sadness."

Paul motioned for me to take the seat that undoubtedly countless others had sat in, which I did. He reached for my file and put it on his lap, but he did not open it.

"You are certainly not one of our mainstream candidates, but you *are* a good and qualified candidate for us to consider."

The words were positive and promising, but they, like the furnishings and the scent, seemed sad to me.

"Why do you sound so sad?" I had to ask.

"My apologies. I don't mean to imply anything negative."

"Is there a 'but' coming?"

Paul looked confused. He quickly rallied and continued.

Paul wanted me to know that pursuing adoption, for anyone, be it a couple, a single person, gay or straight, takes a lot of internal assessment and soul-searching. He wanted me to think about what type of child I would be willing to adopt. Newborns only? If older, how much older, and up to what age? What about ethnicity? Was I willing to adopt and raise a Black or brown baby? Asian? Native American? What about special needs, and if so, what would I agree to, and where would I draw the line? What about a baby born to a drug-addicted mother? Physical and mental issues were likely and might not appear until the child was older. How would I feel about that? A child with physical disabilities? Open adoption or closed?

Paul continued, not expecting me to respond to any of this on the spot but to think about it, consider it, talk to friends and family about it, and make as informed a decision as was realistic to make in these types of uncertain situations.

"The truth is, this is not a time to be 'politically correct' or overly sensitive. This is where you have to confront your deepest self and make the hard decisions. We here at the center have seen way too many kids who have already gone through trauma and heartbreak. They don't need to experience anymore. As for the adoptive parent, if you know that certain ethnicities or disabilities will be too difficult for you to live with, *don't* adopt that child. It does not say anything bad about you if you are being honest with yourself and with us."

We talked for a while longer, and I concluded my time with Paul by telling him that I had a lot to think about. We shook hands, and I turned around and left. On my drive home and for the next many days, I churned the details of that last meeting with Paul over and over in my head. I took to heart in a very serious way the admonition he presented, the one with my needing to be wholly honest with myself. I wanted to be a dad. I also always envisioned myself starting with a newborn. I always assumed my child would look somewhat like me, that is, be a white baby. Boy or girl did not matter, and special needs . . . well, I would like to avoid those if possible. Of course, in traditional situations, there was no way to guarantee what fate would provide in the birth of any child. Choose a child with special needs, especially where there might already be a unique circumstance of having a gay father, that might be too much for a child. And maybe for me.

After more than a week, I became aware that every time my mental deliberations on this subject resumed, my head felt like the inside of a snow globe just after it had been vigorously shaken. Endless permutations to these hypothetical outcomes existed, none of which could be known until they were, in fact, known. And, when the thoughts settled and the entirety of the landscape came back into focus, one conclusion was always the same. I wanted my child. A biological child. I could come up with reasons and justifications and rationales and excuses, but my most honest self said, "You want your child to come from you." One thing I knew: I never wanted to risk feeling resentful or emotionally disconnected from a child for any reason. No child I would adopt would deserve anything less than complete love, attention, and acceptance. If the truth of truths be told, I might, from time to time, wonder if I made the right decision in adopting instead of pursuing a genetically connected child. That would not be fair to a child. Nor to me.

I sat with that finale to my mental and emotional production, and it did not waver. I knew what I knew. I believed what I believed, and this was my decision. I did not know how it would happen or if it would ultimately happen at all. But for the moment, I was putting adoption on hold. I called Paul and told him to close my file.

8
SOME ENCHANTED EVENING

———⁓———

Mason Sommers was born on April 18, 1956, the youngest of two children and the newest resident of Beverly Hills. At the age of sixteen, while running on the track at Beverly High, with no warning and no lead-up, Mason collapsed. The newly established Beverly Hills Paramedic Team was called, and Mason was their first "save." When examined at UCLA Hospital, he was diagnosed with *hypertrophic cardiomyopathy*, or, in layman's terms, an overly muscular heart. This results in an obstruction of the outflow of blood from the left ventricle, slowing down the flow of blood to other organs. He was prescribed medications and some dietary changes, and within a few weeks, he was back on the track, running laps. Fast-forward approximately four years, Mason, this time dancing with his sister and her friends in their home, collapsed again. One event like this was a fluke, an anomaly. But two made it more of a pattern. Exhaustive examination and investigation proved that Mason's particular syndrome was a genetically linked one, which would ultimately likely lead to a deterioration of Mason's heart function. There was no way to tell when, but the doctors did believe it would, in fact, occur. While the collection of relatives around him was wringing their hands with worry, nervous about Mason's future,

Mason, the patient, took matters into his own hands. The first thing he did was kick everyone out of his hospital room. Secondly, he asked questions and researched his medical condition. And third, he decided to *live* his life. He was not prepared to become an invalid or live in any compromised way.

He was released from the hospital, and life began anew for him. Mason was openly gay, which, in the 1970s, was unique. He graduated with a PhD in psychology and worked in private practice as a clinical psychologist in Beverly Hills. He volunteered and participated in many social justice causes, specifically ones that involved discrimination of gay and lesbian individuals; he fought for the rights of the marginalized; he raised money for AIDS research and treatment; he was the co-president of the Los Angeles Gay and Lesbian Center; and he dated a lot. One reputation that preceded him was that he was grandiose, which, to me, was in direct conflict with the charitable standing he had in the community. Most intriguing to me was that Mason, in his 30s, was a gay man living a gay life who had a biological son with a lesbian couple, and the three of them were raising this boy as a family.

Mason and I met seven separate times over several years. Once, I was at Rosh Hashanah services, where he was seated behind me, and when he sang, he had the most resonant voice. I remember turning around and complimenting him.

"I wanted to let you know that I think you have a beautiful voice," I said.

"Thank you!" Mason replied, smiling.

"I am really enjoying sitting in front of you, listening to you sing." I continued.

"Thank you," Mason repeated.

We introduced ourselves, and that was that. Another time we met at a charity event, a movie release raising money for the Jewish AIDS Services, where I was volunteering my time. I thought how nice it was to see him again, and we might reminisce a bit, recounting what we had both been doing since we met at the temple. Extending my hand, I was about to say, "Nice to see you again," Mason beat me to it, presented his outstretched right hand, and said, "Hi, I'm Dr. Mason Sommers. Nice to meet you." Oh well. I reintroduced myself, we chatted a bit, and then we each retreated to our seats to enjoy the film. This occurred another few times until the seventh occasion.

In November of 1996, I was working at Jewish Family Service, having left my unsatisfying career in law, returning to school, and enrolling in a master's program in psychology. After years of frustration and discontent with the law, I realized that working with children and families was where I was better suited. Robby was an excellent role model for me, showing me how a therapist could play the role of a healthy parent, firm but not strict or punitive, helpful but not pompous or vain, and be present with me on my journey rather than judging it. I appreciated the time I spent with the families whose children I helped, both from the perspective of the parents and of the kids themselves. I knew, intuitively, that I had an aptitude for working in the field of helping others; what I realized after years in a law firm was that I needed to find a different way of helping. One that was more one-on-one, more direct, with less paperwork and bureaucracy, and more immediate results. Finding a master's program in marriage and family therapy was my answer. I applied, and was accepted. I would have to make it work, somehow, because this was what I truly believed was going to be the next chapter of my life. This program was designed for working adults, with classes during the day and in the evenings. I decided to leave the law altogether, use some of my savings to pay for school and my living expenses, and hopefully find some part-time job or jobs to help along the way. The program was a two-year course with an accelerated 18-month option, which I resolved I would do. The school was going to teach me how to be a therapist, as well as find me some internships where I could practice doing that work first-hand. I would be supervised, I would be trained, and eventually, I would become licensed in a field I was working in unknowingly all my life.

During the period of time I was driving back and forth to classes, I had also taken on four part-time jobs. Three of them involved working with families and children, and one was working in the Jewish community. They all paid very little, but I cobbled together the salaries each week to assist in paying my bills so I would not have to drain my savings too rapidly. I had no time for friends, really, other than the occasional Saturday night outing to a cheap restaurant. Several of my friends did offer to pay for me, but that was not something I was comfortable with. I was always appreciative of the offers, but somewhere deep, deep down in me, I worried that if I did not live up to being who that person wanted me to be, there would be a price to pay. Better for me to take care of myself, rely on myself, and not be beholden to anyone. Between reading for school, homework, driving from job to job and trying to fit in some sleep, my social life was less than lackluster; it was pretty much nonexistent. I reminded myself over and over again that this was an interim glitch, that life would resume again. I did make some friends at school, other adults who were venturing out into the world of psychotherapy after having had practically productive but emotionally hollow careers. A fellow lawyer was leaving his depressing practice of law. An AIDS activist and artist wanted to make a greater difference in the world. A woman who raised two great kids found herself wanting to "raise" more. There are so many stories in each of my classes, each one of them worthy of telling, including mine. While I was not quite openly gay everywhere, I did feel more comfortable opening up about this aspect of my life at school, wanting to integrate as many parts of myself into who I was becoming. I had been the "closeted lawyer"; I did not want to start my voyage into a new career, holding onto a secret.

While pursuing my new designation and new vocation, money was becoming more and more of a concern. My savings were diminishing, and my current income was not totaling what I needed to cover, so I decided I would sell my house. The house I had bought with my own money was the one I was so proud of, the one that my parents had never seen in more than five years I had owned. As much as it was a symbol of accomplishment, it now needed to be what helped me move forward. I needed to change my mindset: the house was a conduit rather than a destination. As much as I had envisioned my child in the back bedroom, down the hall from my bedroom, with a room in between us, which would be the nanny's room and playroom, I would find another house, at some point, with a configuration that allowed for all that I wanted and needed for my family. At some and place in my life. But now, I needed the money from this house to situate me professionally. Unfortunately, I had to take a loss on the house since the real estate market had dipped between the time I purchased and the time I sold, but I was still able to get some cash to help as a financial cushion. I moved into a single apartment, which was somewhat depressing, where all the living space was immediately visible upon opening the door. My apartment, and my life, were now small, but felt whole.

That November, while working at one of my jobs, I was put in charge of the silent auction at the Jewish AIDS Services charity event, raising money and awareness for HIV and AIDS in the Jewish and secular communities. Mason was in attendance, and I was going to say how nice it was to see him again. But once again, Mason extended his hand and announced, as if for the first time, "Hi, I'm Dr. Mason Sommers."

The evening was a success; we raised both money and awareness and while I took away many memories of that night, Mason was not one of them. But that following week, I received a call from Mason while I was at work.

"I wanted to let you know that I had a really good time at the event," Mason said.

"Thanks. I have to admit that, although I was working, I really enjoyed it too." I replied.

"Thanks again for putting aside the small cars that were on the tables. My son is going to love them!"

"Happy to do it," I said. "After all, you offered to make a donation to a very good cause, so it was a win-win."

We chatted for only a minute or so more when Mason boldly declared, "As much as I enjoyed the event, the most intriguing part of the evening for me was meeting you."

I had to smile to myself at his use of the word "meeting," but I said nothing.

"I was wondering if you would like to have dinner with me some time."

"That sounds nice. Sure." And just like that, a date was set.

I was a stranger to Mason, but he was not to me. At least not by reputation. While our evening out would be a date, to me, it would also be an informational interview of sorts. After all, he was living the life I wanted: an openly gay psychologist raising his biological child. I contemplated telling him that we had met six times before this most recent event, but I didn't want to embarrass him. And I certainly didn't want to put him off before I could gather whatever intel I could about how to proceed with having a child. Truth be told, I was flattered that Mason asked me out. To me, he was a "somebody," and I was a "nobody." Standing at about six feet in height, barrel-chested, muscly but not grotesquely so, with red hair more rust in color than orange, he was not my "usual" type, but I did find him attractive. At the very least, I would (hopefully) finally make an impression on this man, allowing my slightly bruised ego at having been forgotten six times to heal.

November 15, 1996, I drove up the hill to Mason's house, meeting there, followed by Mason driving us to a nearby Italian restaurant. There, we sat for hours, talking effortlessly and getting to know one another. We found out that his sister Laurie lived with her family less than two miles from my parents' house, the house where I grew up, in Toronto. We both had a strong interest in music, having studied it growing up. He was an established clinical psychologist, and I was back in school en route to my master's degree in psychology. And we both love children.

"I have to admit, Mason," I said, "that for me, *the* most compelling attribute of yours is that you are an out gay man who has a biological child, and you've been able to establish a family in a society that is not particularly receptive to gay women and men having and rearing their children."

I probably prattled on and on for way too long. I told him how important this was for me and that I would love to "pick his brain" about it.

The restaurant was a charming, authentic Italian trattoria. Less than two dozen tables, mostly two-tops and four-tops, were spaced evenly in the space that housed murals of the Italian countryside on the walls. The smell of garlic wafted through the air. Our waiter spoke English with a very pronounced Northern Italian accent, which he was very honored to announce to us. We ordered, and he paced our appetizers, main course, and our shared dessert evenly. As I looked across the table, I became more aware of how handsome I found Mason. I always appreciated his good looks, but sitting eye to eye with him, only a few feet between us, I found him striking. His eyes were the same golden-orange color as his hair, and his complexion and coloring complemented it all perfectly. His strong nose and shapely lips were rounded out by a strong chin and cheekbones that were not shy to show themselves proudly.

Along with the small world stories we exchanged, sharing the names of the people we had in common, I also wanted to know what it was like for Mason to be a gay dad. I was both inquisitive and inspired to think about one of my dreams being lived out by someone I knew. This was no longer a dream in the sense that it only appeared in my head. Here was a real-life, flesh-and-blood gay man who was living the life I had been pursuing. Mason shared with me the process, the struggles, and the profound joy that were all part of this journey, none of which he would change.

"The moms and I spent years getting to know each other. It was only then that they asked me if I would consider being a donor but also an active dad."

"I can barely imagine what that conversation was like for any of you." I wondered aloud.

"After years of traveling in the same gay social circles and deciding that we had quite a bit in common, we went ahead with artificial insemination." Mason continued, "It was not always easy, and believe me, it is definitely not a fun position to be in when you are the third parent."

"What do you mean? If I'm not being too nosey." I was so curious about what he was alluding to.

"Ben has two primary parents, his moms, and he lives with them. I'm the only dad, and I see him a few times a week. We do a lot of father-son things together, which is great. Overall, we are figuring this out, and it's working."

Mason liked being a trailblazer, admitting to me that he knew he was gay from a young age, came out at a young age, and did not ever have shame or discomfort about it. Whether it was pride or not, he presented it as such because it was his goal to feel proud of *all* of his accomplishments: being a psychologist, being a fundraiser for those less fortunate, being an openly gay Jew, and being a dad.

The more Mason shared, the more I was attracted to him. Despite his being six years older than me, it seemed as if he was so much more evolved. So mature. I was impressed by his openness related to his vulnerabilities, especially in being a heart patient, and his overall strength in coming back from adversity to pursue and create the life he wanted. As he spoke, I could not ignore his barrel chest and muscular arms moving in harmony with his words. But it was more of the tenderness he was not declaring outwardly that I was noticing. The losses he endured due to the AIDS crisis. The dyslexia he suffered as a younger student made academics much more challenging for him than for his peers. He did not speak of these issues with any self-pity.

"I guess I am a survivor." He said. "Life threw some curve balls at me, and I was not going to let them derail me. I had, and still have, goals. And long-term objectives."

There was no defeatism in tone or words.

We sat for more than two hours, enjoying all three courses of food, and each other's company. In those hours, I believed I saw in Mason so much more than so many others knew about him. The reputation that preceded him was mixed, but the man with whom I had just dined was in many ways similar to me on the inside. Here was a child who grew up wanting to feel seen. Overall, he was a good person by society's standards. We were both willing to put in the hard work to produce the desired outcome. What we longed for was acknowledgment. Respect. Only Mason was ahead of me both in years and practice.

When we said our goodbyes back at his house, Mason said, "I had a really good time."

"Me too." I mirrored. It's been nice getting to know more about you."

As I was getting back into my car and moved closer to shake his hand, Mason spread both of his arms open and embraced me. Not superficially, but a real hug. We held that hug just long enough to say, without words, that there was very likely at least a second date to come. And there was.

9

SO NEAR...AND YET SO FAR

Going back to school at the age of nearly thirty was no easy feat. Giving up the stability of a workplace, a paycheck, a professional trajectory, and something "known" was scary as hell. But, when I checked in with myself, deep down in my gut, I knew I had to leave the practice of law. As had always been my way, I found a way to make it work. I sold my house and rented a single apartment while I explored the path of a new career.

Mason and I had begun dating, and we were enjoying the time we spent together. He was integrating me into his life and friends, and I was doing the same. Truthfully, I was a bit apprehensive about introducing Mason to some of my people because I worried about them not "getting" him. As I had seen in prior situations, Mason could feel vulnerable, leading him to appear competitive or boastful. I was quickly learning to call it out, respectfully, and reflect to him that his actions were coming from a place of insecurity, not desire. Mason was more about appearances than I was, which was sometimes uncomfortable for me. I avoided particular friends of mine at the start of our relationship so as to prepare them, and Mason, for the inevitable meeting. Both were important to me, and I didn't want to feel caught or trapped between them. It did not take long for all to even out, but those early days were, at times, less than easy.

My academics were advancing well. I appreciated the substance of what would ultimately become the foundation of my new career. Once I completed a certain number of courses, part of my academic requirement was to find a trainee position where I could put into practice what I was learning theoretically. The school assisted me with finding a suitable facility, and I decided to continue my work with the HIV and AIDS community—this time, from a clinical perspective rather than through a Jewish context. I already had some familiarity with those living with this disease, and I idealistically wanted to be part of the solution.

Day after day, I continued to drive all over the city. Regarding school and schoolwork, I kept up with it, but I also knew, at this point in my life, that I did not also need to learn how to be a student. I was able to differentiate between a good student and a student with a mission to move on to the next chapter of his life. I did the readings, I wrote the papers, and I showed up to classes, but I was counting down the days to be able to start seeing clients on my own. I was very appreciative of the supervision I was receiving, but I was thirsting for practical, in-the-room experience with clients. To do that, I first had to complete a certain number of classroom hours and specified courses. After the second semester of my master's program, I ticked that box. Now, I needed to find a place to take me on. At this point, I would be a trainee as opposed to an intern. Trainees were still in school, while interns were already in possession of their master's degree, and between both designations, 3,000 therapeutic hours were required prior to sitting for the written exam, followed by the oral exam. Several steps still to go.

At school, many of the students in my program were agonizing over where to apply, whether they would be accepted, whether they were ready, how they would fit into school and traineeship, and the rest of their lives. I had little patience for that talk. Maybe because I was older, already having had a career, and eager to head into my next one. Or perhaps because I knew it could all be done. Regardless, I listened more than I complained, heard about a few facilities taking on trainees, and began to make phone calls. A number of the places vetted by the school were already at their capacity with trainees, so they were out. I didn't want to work with certain psychological populations, so they were out, at least to begin with. I could always come back to them if I did not find what was better suited for me. An acquaintance, who was ahead of me in the program, called me one day to tell me the place where he was amassing hours and experience was taking on new clinicians. This was an AIDS center associated with a local church, offering help to those in the community dealing with all aspects of HIV and the illnesses related to AIDS. My friend said he was seeing mostly adult men, but the center also had women clients, as well as various groups, all supervised by competent therapists. The center had designed a comprehensive program accredited by our school, and former students who had been there had spoken well of the setting and the instruction. I made an appointment to meet with the director the following afternoon, a Friday. At the end of the 90-minute interview, I felt good about being there, should I be offered a position. The director told me that he was interviewing all of the following week and would reach out to me once he knew how many candidates he had for the number of open spaces. It would likely be a couple of weeks, so if I didn't hear anything sooner, I shouldn't take it as a sign of anything. Other than bureaucracy. The following day, I came home from a hike and found a message on my answering machine, offering me a trainee position, beginning the following month.

It was 1995, and AIDS was very much in the news, especially in the gay community. This center was dedicated to helping lower-income families and individuals attend to their needs as they, or their family members, became infected. I was the new kid at the center, and the other employees and interns wanted to know my story. As I was becoming acquainted with my colleagues there, I described myself as a former lawyer, Jewish, newly dating, and revealed my desire to be a dad. That last element often had whoever I was speaking to either do a double take or smile, as if I had made a joke. More times than not, I had to reiterate that last detail, reinforcing the veracity of my pursuit of fatherhood. I figured that if people were asking about me, I would tell them about me.

The majority of the other clinicians at the center were gay men. Most, if not all, had no interest in "recreating the hetero-majority" of society. I often heard from them that the straight population was meant to procreate while the gay population was not.

"Why would we want to have children?" One colleague asked somewhat caustically.

"Why not?" I retorted.

"Aren't there plenty of kids in the world already?"

"Sure, but should that mean that a pre-selected part of the population should be excluded from participating in procreating or raising children?" I shot back.

"No, that's not at all what I'm saying. My point is that there are those of us who really don't want to have children, gay and straight, yet mainstream society looks at us as outliers."

He had a point, which I acknowledged and then continued. "Just like you don't want to be labeled an outsider for not wanting children, I don't want to be labeled that way for being a gay man who *does* want them."

I noticed that the preponderance of the gay men there had been ill-treated in their youth, possibly up to that very time, and did not wish to validate that part of society that harmed them. Creating families and bringing more children into the world who might become tormentors was certainly not the goal any of these survivors wished to achieve. Once again, as a minority figure in my surroundings, I stood my ground. I did not flaunt my desire, nor did I shy away from truth-telling if the conversation steered itself in that direction. I was also working in an environment where many of the other therapists and administrators were affected by the ravages of HIV and AIDS. Infected partners, family members, friends, or themselves, these were people who were already living with the shame that the disease brought with it, along with loss and sadness. I had compassion for them, and allowed them leeway when they asserted their wishes for fun and responsibility-free lives. They understood that time was a precious and limited commodity, so taking on the rearing of a child was likely seen to them as a failed mission. They would not live long enough to do the job.

Ian, my supervisor, was not known to be warm or fuzzy, but he was known for being a skilled clinician and a tough supervisor. Everything I had heard about him prior to meeting him was true. He provided me with clients, and once each week, he and I would discuss, assess, and process how it was all going, specifically, how I was interacting with the clients so they would walk away from a session with me and the center, feeling better in some way about their lives. We also discussed how I was growing as a clinician. Ian challenged me to be more present with the clients' feelings rather than their stories. He helped me look for the underlying subtext rather than what was being discussed on the surface. He pushed me to look at my historical triggers that might become activated and compartmentalize them. What was most important was that we, as a team and individually, provided clinical mental health care to those who were taking the risk to come in and ask for it. I learned a lot at the center.

I was quickly identified as a highly-skilled intern, an oxymoron to some degree, but I gladly accepted the moniker and made use of it. Not in an arrogant way, but as a tool to garner more clients and more opportunities to grow as a therapist. In addition to seeing individual clients, I was also offered a co-teaching position for a parenting class, as well as to update the manual that went along with it. Once each week, for eight weeks, I met with mostly single mothers, mostly of lower socioeconomic status, and imparted information and answered questions about their toddlers, tweens, and teenagers. Somehow, it all came intuitively to me. It was natural, and it showed. I received high praise and compliments from the participants at the end of the course, which led to near-praise from Ian. It all felt good, regardless.

Christine was one of the several new friends I made at the center. She seemed young to me, but she was in her late twenties. She stood about five feet five and had medium-brown wavy hair, blue-green eyes, and a melodious voice. And happy. I don't remember a day that Christine was not smiling. She shared with me that she came from a devout Catholic family, and her parents' plan for her was that she finish high school and go straight into doing God's work. In a convent. Christine had other thoughts, which caused a rift in her family. She wanted to work with the less-privileged population in Los Angeles from more of a social work perspective. She was attending community college part-time while working at the center as a receptionist/babysitter/hall monitor/social work assistant. As Christine (never Chris, as I found out) and I became friendlier, she shared with me that one thing that would likely make her parents happy was that she never wanted to get married or have children.

"Really?" I was truly surprised. "That seems odd to me. Don't most parents, especially in Catholic families, want their children to grow up, get married, have children of their own, and continue to live a Catholic life?"

"Really. For them, if I got married and had babies, then I would probably never pursue a life of service to God."

The interior of the center was arranged with cubicles in the heart of the building, all fairly open to one another. Along the outside walls on the perimeter were small, enclosed offices, each approximately six feet by six feet, most windowless. Inside each was one chair for the therapist, either two cushioned chairs or a small loveseat for the clients, and a small table or ottoman in between, upon which rested a box of tissues. The cinderblock walls were painted a pale gray, with posters attempting to liven up the room. The flooring reminded me of the adoption center I had been to, with stained, threadbare carpeting. To be fair, the center was a non-profit organization, one that relied heavily on government funding and private donations, neither of which was in abundance. It was not uncommon for the staff to donate small pieces of furniture and art from their own homes. This was grassroots at its finest, an amalgamation of individuals joining together to create a common setting, brightened up by mismatched knickknacks, all blended, where important work would be done.

Christine and I were standing in one of the maze-like hallways, far enough away from anyone working at their desk. Christine had her back to the front doors and windows, which were flooding the room with sunlight. The light halo around her gave her a beatific aura, causing her hair to glisten and her aqua eyes to appear almost transparent. She looked beautiful at that moment. Facing her, standing two feet away, I was struck by her radiant skin and her faint aroma of lavender. The kindness on her face was so present, making me think this was an exceptional woman. Caring, smart, good-hearted, non-pretentious, pretty, charitable - these are traits of someone I admire and respect. Could she be the one? Could Christine be the woman I've been fantasizing about, the woman who might want to bear a child, *my* child, and let me raise him or her?

We stood there talking, but I was having a much bigger and more important dialogue inside my head, romanticizing the life I wanted, hardly paying attention to the outside world. Was this a sign? Was I meant to leave the practice of law, a life I thought I had wanted, perhaps more for my parents or social worthiness than anything else, and find my way to a place that respected and helped to heal the underdog? Like me? While I was not a casualty of the AIDS epidemic in a primary way, being a part of the gay community made me, de facto, affiliated with that very community being maligned, ostracized, and ravaged. Finding my way to fatherhood through working with the gay community could be the biggest irony, yet a wonderful "fuck you" to those who said it could not and should not be done. Perhaps it was arrogant of me to think Christine might be willing to experience pregnancy without the long-term obligation and pleasure of raising a child, but that is where my mind went. She had told me that she didn't want to be married or have children, yet maybe some part of her would be willing to be benevolent enough, giving enough, to help me create the family that I wanted. It could be in keeping with her desire to do good in the world and to work with those less fortunate than herself; as a man, I could not do this alone. She could help. Of course, it would not be without significant effects on her body, her time, and her finances, but I would help in all the ways that I could. This could be a real possibility. I quickly remembered we were still in the midst of a conversation, so I mentally pressed the pause button on my daydream and returned to the center. I was leaning against a filing cabinet, nodding to Christine's request that I provide her with the data she needed for the month's-end client statistics, promising to gather it all for her by the end of the day. She reached out her hand and gently placed it on my forearm, thanked me, and turned.

Throughout the months of my internship, Christine and I strengthened our friendship. Over time, I revealed to her my desire to be a bio-dad and my plight in pursuing that goal. We talked about my love of family, and the work I was doing with the single parents at the center was proving to garner positive results. Some of my kid clients would tell Christine, when she watched over them while their parents were in therapy, that I was really "cool." They said that the games we played and the walks we took to the park were fun, so much better than the past therapists they had, who were really boring. On Monday afternoons, I would share with Christine my explorations and activities of the previous weekend, be they about dating, my work with the synagogue children and their families, or anything else. She did the same, reciprocating with stories of her church work the previous day and her satisfaction at being able to give back to her community. Both of us knew we shared a bond, a connection of sorts that we didn't talk about. Different from the others at the center.

After my experience at the adoption seminar, I shared my experience with Christine all the way through to the result I had reached, where adoption was a wonderful option, only not for me. She was so kind and generous with her sensitivity to my story that she became teary-eyed.

"I know how much you were hoping this would be the right answer for you." She moved forward, extending both arms and wrapped them around me. It felt as if she were more in need of that hug than I was.

"It's not fair, is it?" she asked.

"What?" I replied.

"That you can't have your own child like a woman can."

Christine expounded on the unfairness of life, yet believed there was a reason for everything. She continued, saying that sometimes we cannot figure out what God's plan is, but there is always a plan. We have to trust that. And, once it is revealed, not only do things make sense, but the outcome feels so much sweeter and more relevant than if it came to us through the usual means.

Was Christine telling me what I wanted to hear? Was she offering herself to help make my desired conclusion a reality? I needed to ask her. This might be *the* opportunity I was waiting for. Maybe this was, in her words, God's plan. I wanted to believe that so badly, but . . . how does one come out and ask a friend to have a child for him? This was insane! I could feel my face flush. The thumping of my heart was so loud in my ears that it felt as if my temples were pulsating. Could she see that? I ran a few lines in my head, the ones that could be the way to start that conversation in a direct way. None of them seemed logical, yet I had to do it. What if this topic didn't come up again between us? And if it did, what if Christine was not in the same frame of mind that she was in right then? She just admitted it was not fair that men cannot have a biological child alone, yet women can. Christine was aware of the biological inequality and social injustice. But was asking her too extreme? Too radical? Too inappropriate? By not asking her, was this a missed opportunity, a rejection of a sign of some sort? Time was running out. This was the moment. Should I do it seriously? In a funny way? Should I blurt it out or preface it with something?

"Hey, I have an idea! You and I could have a child together!"

Her blue-green eyes opened wider than I thought was humanly possible, her lips unsealed as if she were going to say something, and then . . . nothing. It was as if Christine stopped breathing, stopped blinking, stopped . . . everything. She just stood there. Was she staring at me? Was she thinking? She just stood there. While all this was happening in front of me, I was having my reaction. It felt like I had just fallen into a crater. The "whooshing" noise in my head was quieted only by the high-decibel drilling noise happening at my temples. I felt my face go redder than before. Edgar Allan Poe would have been proud of the volume of my thumping heartbeat. I had finally said the words I'd been thinking out loud. To a real person. Not as a joke.

I have no idea at all how long we stood there. Finally, her parted lips curled up at the ends, and a smile appeared on her face. She blinked. I remember thinking it was, if not the longest, certainly one of the longest blinks I had ever seen. Her head tilted back, and she shook it from side to side slowly, like in a L'Oréal commercial, and she said two little words: "Yeah. Right."

I'm not sure what I expected or wanted from that exchange, but I felt deflated. Did I really think she would say, "Oh, okay, sure!" And say it with enthusiasm? Again, "fantasy me" would have loved that. But "reality me" was nowhere to be found. I had nothing to compare this event to, to know what might have been realistic and reasonable. Other than coming out to people, I had never expressed a string of words that alone seemed benign, but, in that particular order, had such profound meaning. I had just asked someone I had known for less than a year, a near stranger, to have my child for me! Not that there was any real risk in asking the question other than humiliating myself and gaining a reputation at the center as a crazy person. This request would bypass eccentric, zany, and even outrageous. More than likely, it would go straight to crackpot or lunatic, perhaps with a "scary" chaser. But it was done. No taking back that particular declaration. Yet, she didn't say no, now did she? Or did she, in fact, say yes in a satirical way that, in truth, was a no? Or, more likely, "You've got to be out of your fucking mind if you think that is something I would ever consider for anyone, let alone someone I barely know!" This latter phrase is most likely what she meant.

In the days and weeks that followed, Christine and I continued to talk, and we spoke more openly. I explained how badly I wanted to be a biological dad, and I decided I was going to put the word out there to the women I knew. I apologized if I caught her off guard the other day, clarifying that if I came across glib or flippant, that was not my intention. One of our conversations led us to an intimate exchange about Christine's longings and internal conflict. We were both at the center quite late one night. My last client of the day had not shown up and had not left a message that he was not planning on coming in. It was the center's policy that the hour was booked for the client, so it was our responsibility to wait for them. Even if they arrived for the last five or ten minutes, that time was theirs. Therefore, even the last scheduled hour of the day meant we had to wait until 9 p.m. before packing up our things and heading out. Christine had shared that going home was more depressing for her than staying at the center. At home, she was alone in her apartment, and sometimes her thoughts were louder than she liked. At the center, she could be around others and remain happily distracted, as well as get more work done. I was seated in the therapy room allocated to me for that time, in the therapist's chair, reading a book. I always carried a book around, one that I would read for pleasure, as a diversion from all the psychology texts that I was expected to consume.

The door was open when Christine walked by and saw me there. She came in and sat on the couch opposite me, jokingly asking me if I wanted to practice being her therapist.

"How can I help?" I offered.

Christine put down her light brown manilla file folders onto the couch, leaned back, and began sharing. Throughout the years she was growing up, Christine was led to believe she wanted to become or was supposed to become, a nun. Religion and faith were prevalent in her household, and from the time of her earliest memory, she heard her parents say she was named after the Lord and Savior, and she would do his work on Earth. When little kids were asked what they wanted to be when they grew up, she remembered some of those around her saying things like ballerina, fireman, Power Ranger, but she said, "a nun." She admitted that she didn't know what that meant, but whenever she would look over at her parents after saying that, they both wore huge smiles, which made her happy.

As she matured and thought more about the life she was ostensibly pursuing, having a child was in no way part of that tableau. Yet, as she was getting older and living amongst other young women who were finding boyfriends and talking about marriage, her thoughts of her own life became more important. The path she was on didn't seem as fulfilling as theirs. This was her struggle. While Christine never wanted to raise a child, she was thinking more and more about being pregnant.

"I don't know why I've been thinking about it, but being pregnant is so curious to me."

I was a bit taken aback. "Curious? Why curious?"

"The whole idea of my body feeding and nurturing another life until it is ready to come into the world seems, I don't know, weird and intriguing at the same time." She looked away as she said this as if going into an imaginary land where this was happening.

"I have to admit," I chimed in, "that to think of being pregnant, from a biological perspective, is fascinating to me too."

"Besides, women talk about feeling some sense of loss if they have never been pregnant. I don't want to live with regret."

Being pregnant frightened her, but not ever being pregnant frightened her just as much. She knew absolutely that she did not want to raise a child. But would God look badly upon her for having a child and then giving it away? Christine admitted that ever since that day when I proclaimed she and I could have a child together, she thought more and more about it. She confessed it still seemed like more of a fairy tale to her, but in between those thoughts were actual considerations of how this could materialize. She didn't want me to get my hopes up, but she wanted me to know she was genuinely considering it.

A few days later, when Christine and I had the opportunity to be alone in the kitchen at the center, she asked me questions about Judaism.

"How strong a Jew are you?" She asked.

"I'm not sure I understand your question, but if you're asking me how religious I am, then not much. But if you want to know if I identify with the customs and culture, then yes, a lot."

"Yeah, that's more of what I meant. You don't look like some of the very Jewish people I see sometimes, the men who wear black and have long bushy beards."

It was sweet that Christine was trying to make sense of the various elements or factions of Judaism that she knew. Obviously, none of this was familiar to her. I tried to help.

"I like celebrating the holidays with customs, songs, and traditional foods. I like the history of knowing that for generations and generations, Jews were singing some of the same songs, eating some of the same foods, and telling the same stories, year after year."

"I like that!" She interrupted. "Sorry, go on."

"But the prayers themselves, or going to a synagogue, or following the strict laws of the Torah, doesn't make me feel more Jewish."

I shared with her that I was a knowledgeable Jew, although not a practicing orthodox one. We compared the Old Testament with the New, interpreting scripture as we understood it, trying to make sense of the prohibition in Leviticus on being gay and various other tenets of religion we both saw as hypocritical. Neither one of us believed that God, the Jewish God or the Catholic God, would create gay people only to have them be the scapegoats and victims of hatred and persecution. I painted the picture for Christine of a child being raised in a Jewish home. Jewish holidays such as Rosh Hashanah, Hanukkah, and Passover all have meaning and cultural ceremonies that go along with them. I described the meaning of *latkes* and the symbolism of the oil lasting for eight days when there was only enough to last for one. A miracle! I orated a short, very short Passover *Haggadah*, the story of the exodus of the Jewish people from Egypt and, along the way, receiving the *Torah*, the holy scriptures that guide us Jews.

The foods, the preparation for the holidays, the coming together of family and friends, lots of eating and conversations around the tables, all of it somewhat frenetic but always spirited and high energy. After all, we've been doing this for more than 5,000 years, whereas the Catholics have had less than half of that time to create their rituals.

"I am sad to say," I joked with Christine, "that none of the Jewish holidays, not even all of them joined together, compete with Christmas. At least not the Christmas depicted and idealized on television and in the movies."

She smiled.

"Still, we Jews always seem to find at least one or two friends who *do* celebrate the birth of Jesus and join in on tree-trimming parties, hanging stockings and sharing in the delight of the Christmas tree."

I explained the meaning behind the rite of a *bris* for a boy, a *Bar* or *Bat Mitzvah*, the *chuppah*, or ceremonial canopy for the bride and groom, and the burial and grieving conventions at the time of death. Christine wanted to know it all. She asked good questions, and I was able to provide smart and educated answers. Never having had these conversations with anyone before, Christine seemed sincerely inquisitive and interested. I, of course, was glad I could give her the information she was seeking. Anything to keep her thinking positively about what it would be like to be raised Jewish. I was equally interested in her religion's customs, which she was happy to explain. More intimacy shared between us made me quietly hope that these were the building blocks of our destiny.

More conversations led to more revelations between us. I was planning on raising my child as a Jew.

Christine responded. "If I ever *did* have a child, I would want that child to know my background, including my religion."

"I don't have a problem with that. Not at all."

I assured her that I intended to let my child learn about and experience all religions. We considered the costs involved with artificial insemination and medical expenses, all of which I pledged to take care of. Christine had no intention of not working but was concerned that because she was overweight, she might be at higher risk. I assured her that if we were to move forward, we would consult with all the appropriate doctors so both she and the baby would be in optimal health.

Another apprehension Christine shared with me.

"How and what would I tell people?" Her voice was louder than she intended and at a higher pitch than normal.

Having a child and giving it away was not something she could envision herself doing, but in fact, that was precisely what she would be signing up for.

"Would I be a surrogate? A surrogate with some involvement in the child's life later on?" Neither of us could imagine what that would look like. We agreed that we would seek out the wisdom and knowledge of a counselor who could help us identify blind spots we weren't seeing. Or ones we were both choosing not to look at.

I was feeling afraid there were issues I was not addressing because of my fear of rocking the boat. I wanted a child, and here was a woman who was offering to have one for me. The conditions seemed not only reasonable, but doable. Why would a single, young, mentally healthy woman do this? Was Christine this altruistic? Was she deluding herself? The more we fleshed out this scenario, the more reserved I became. And the more reserved I became, the more conflicted I felt, wondering if there was something wrong with Christine or if I was the one who feared that this would become a reality.

"How would you choose a doctor for the baby?" Christine asked.

"Hmm. Good question. I would ask around, see if anyone in my circle of friends with babies liked theirs." I replied.

"And what about food? Are you ok with the baby eating formula right from birth, as opposed to breastmilk?" Christine wanted to know.

"I believe that breastmilk is best, but so many babies don't have that option, so I'm sure formula would be fine." I guessed out loud.

We kept talking about it, digging deeper and deeper into the minutia of what this would look like, and the more this progressed, the more Christine seemed to enjoy talking about it. It was as if we were doing research for a screenplay we intended to write.

Was this really happening? Is Christine the woman I have chosen to do this with?

We talked about names and travel plans I had for my little family of two, and I said that I would document it all with pictures and send them to Christine. We described in painstaking detail the experiences this baby would have being pushed on a swing in the park, and me calling out how brave this little one was being, flying up, up, up into the sky. I, holding my child in the cradle of my lap as we both ventured down a slide, with me shouting "whoooooo" as we descended. Driving out to the beach and learning how to gently step into the crashing waves, knowing we had to hold hands to be safe, but not being afraid of it. And when the salty spray hit our faces and maybe even our eyes, we could both commiserate with the stinging but know this was a small price to pay for the pleasure of standing where the tip of the land met the start of the miles-broad ocean.

My time at the center was coming to an end. All interns had a one-year commitment, after which they moved on to another facility to gain additional and different experiences with other populations. I had acquired many hours toward my needed 3000, but I was still short on "couples" hours. The total number of hours required by the Board of Behavioral Sciences, the governing body of Marriage and Family therapists, was a required number for individual clients, children, families, and couples. The center provided me with many of the first three, but I was low on couples. I also wanted to experience issues other than HIV and AIDS. I would be moving on by the end of August. I shared this news only with my supervisor and with my counterparts, including Christine. She was not surprised but was also somewhat sad that she and I were not going to be seeing each other on a regular basis.

"Who will I share all this 'gushing over a baby' with?" was her question to me. A red flag. Perhaps one of many that had been present, but the first one I chose to see or could no longer pretend was not there.

"Well, uh, I guess you can share it with anyone you want," I replied.

Was this more of a game to Christine? An exercise in passing the time while at work? Was this Christine's way of living out a dream without having to take any risks or steps toward making it a reality? All this 'gushing' that we were doing, or at least that I was doing, was to show her how seriously I was taking this, considering not only having a child but looking forward to raising that child with the most attention to provide that child with a happy and stimulating life. What was her motivation?

The weather that particular summer was sweltering; thankfully, the center had central air conditioning. Almost every time someone walked in the door, client, employee, or intern, they gave a thankful sigh of relief that it was cool inside when it was so hot outside. My clients continued to show up regularly, and a month prior to my leaving, I had to begin my termination process with them. That consisted of telling them I would be moving on and would no longer be their counselor. We explored the work we had done together, the issues covered, and the importance of their ability to overcome certain issues. I encouraged them to continue with another intern who would be assigned to their case. I assured them that because I knew them quite well, I would have a say in who might be next for them, hoping I could facilitate a good fit in terms of rapport between therapist and client. Bar none, all the clients were sad that I was leaving and that we were not going to be seeing each other anymore. It was so validating for me to know that although I was still in my professional infancy. I was making a difference, and I was good at it. It boded well for my future. Hopefully, wherever I go and whatever type of therapy I am practicing, intuitively, I am able to connect with clients in their vulnerability, showing compassion but not lapsing into commiseration. Truth be told, I was also looking forward to working with clients who had other presenting problems. I wanted to know what it would be like to address issues that were not HIV-driven. Yet, in my heart, I knew this work, the AIDS work, would always stay with me. It was too significant not to.

Christine, on the other hand, reacted differently. There was an apparent change in her demeanor toward me and in our dynamic. She was still always friendly, smiling, jubilant, and ebullient, but she was no longer as engaged with me. We would always say hello to each other and exchange a few pleasantries, but gone were the conversations of pregnancies, inseminations, and babies. I tried to engineer our chats in the direction of my wanting a child, but she no longer latched onto them as she had in the past. Straddling between wanting to confirm if we were, or were not, still considering this endeavor and not wanting to create an uncomfortable work environment, I felt torn. Torn on the outside as to what to do and also torn on the inside, what seemed to be a possibility was now gone. Christine had been my first tangible option for becoming a father, but for some reason, that option faded quickly and somewhat mysteriously. Not for a minute did I forget that this was a fantastical folly, but it seemed so real. For both of us. What happened? Was it something I said or did? Did it become too real for Christine? She'd obviously changed her mind, but why? Why was she not sharing with me the process she was going through? And why was

I not asking her? What did I have to lose? I knew the answers to both of those questions. She was likely not talking about having a child for me because she realized she did not want to. I don't know why, but she obviously made that choice. I was not asking her why because, deep down, I did not want to completely shatter the fantasy that I could become a father. As long as I didn't know why, there was still hope of it coming true.

When my final day at the center arrived, I said my goodbyes to the staff and my colleagues. I saw my scheduled clients and reminded them that I could be reached if necessary, but I was sure they would quickly engage well with the new therapist assigned to them. I had a lovely conversation with Ian, the supervisor who was sometimes from hell and other times from heaven.

"You've been a real asset to our group of interns, Rami." He said.

"Thank you, Ian. It really has been a pleasure to work here and to learn so much, both from you and the others." I said in response.

"I hope that our paths will cross again in the future."

When Ian said this, I was somewhat surprised.

He taught me so much but made it so hard to like him for doing so.

Lunch was brought in for us interns: sandwiches, potato chips, and soda. A few of the staff baked cookies and brownies, which were also added to the buffet table. Ian spoke, along with a few of the other senior staff, praising us for the work we did and for the positive energy we brought into the center on a regular basis. That was nice to hear. As the afternoon wore on, once I was done with my last client, I decided to go around and say some personal goodbyes to some of the staff with whom I had become friendlier than just a passing hello. Hugs and handshakes and statements of "let's keep in touch" were all around, knowing this would likely be the last time we saw each other. As we interns began to leave, we, too, shared our farewells, wishing one another the best of luck in our next intern endeavor.

I had seen Christine earlier in the day, and we exchanged sweet and smiling glances at each other, but neither of us approached the other with any conversation. At lunch, Christine was among the attendees, wishing us all well at our sandwich sendoff. But we didn't have the opportunity to chat other than a quick nod between us. When I was ready to leave, having said what I wanted to say to all who were there, I packed up my book and my file folder and put them into my satchel. I headed in the direction of Christine's cubicle, hoping to steal a few moments in private with her. When I reached her desk, her mug had been washed out for the day. Her desk lamp was turned off, and her chair was pushed in under her desk. She was gone.

10
ANOTHER ONE BITES THE DUST

———⟡———

Growing up, I always had more friends who were girls than friends who were boys. Maybe I felt more emotionally aligned with them, maybe less intimidated by them, but that was my history. Once I got to Camp Ramah, that changed. While I was still friendly with girls, many boys seemed nice to me, accepting of me, wanting to be my friend. At first, I didn't know how to feel about this—not that I was conflicted about them sexually, it was just unfamiliar to me. Truth be told, I really liked feeling like "one of the guys." Then, again, in law school, I was friendly with girls, but I lived with guys and had friends who were guys, which felt nice. To me, again, it seemed familiar to present one way on the outside but not feel on the inside. The secret I was guarding always existed, sometimes stronger, other times less so, but the current of "you're different" hummed along continuously in the background. I made it my mission to integrate it rather than let it consume me, which worked for the majority of my life. Family and friends from my past saw me progressing academically, dating girls, being social, and living a seemingly typical, ordinary, happy life. And I enjoyed it all, even the dating. It's not that I didn't like or appreciate the female body; on the contrary, I was always a "breast man." Physically and sexually, I had my share of experiences with girls and women, and like most people, some were more exciting than others. As a man, I have to admit that sexual gratification was sexual gratification. Sometimes, it mattered less who the person was or what gender that person was as long as I could reach the finish line. I'm not proud of this, but this was the truth and my reality when I was younger.

When I finally did venture out of my comfort zone and experimented with men, I became aware of the added dimension of emotions. More feelings were connected to the sensuality and the intimacy with men I cared about than I had felt when I was being physical and sensual with women. I couldn't then, and still to this day, cannot adequately express what the difference is, but there is one for me. After the initial experiments with random and anonymous men, once I was in my first relationship with a man, I had a feeling that *that* was what I wanted. Not the trappings of societal rejection and parental rejection, ridicule and harassment, and risk of dying from AIDS and images of lonely old gay men living their golden years in dilapidated apartments somewhere, discarded by their families and marginalized by their communities. But the amalgamation of the physicality and sexuality and intimacy and fun of these feelings, all in one person, that person's gender being male rather than female. Of course, like the majority of first loves, that relationship didn't last. But I took away an abundance of personal growth and knowledge for my future pursuits.

Prior to that first man, I had been in relationships with women: in Toronto, at camp, while in law school, and even upon my arrival in Los Angeles. Interestingly, all of those relationships involved some discussion of the family we would have. One of these girls came out to me when I came out to her, admitting that while she and I were dating, she was intimately involved with a female friend of hers. She had chosen to compartmentalize that part of her life, creating a mental narrative that she could be with this girl until she found the right man, at which time she would give up women and live a straight life. While a very nice fantasy, we soon learned that that was not feasible. She and I both came from traditional Jewish families and wanted similar futures, so we created the construct of the "Big House."

"We could get a big enough house for you and your partner, me and my partner, and our kids." This was my suggestion.

"How would we explain this to people?" She asked.

"I don't know," I replied. "But at least it would give us what we want. We could figure out the rest later.

She and I would be a couple, of sorts. She could date whomever she wanted, as could I, and we would all live in the same house. She and I would have children together and raise them together, along with our partners. The more people in the house, the more hands to help out and the more love to spread around, especially to the children. The concept was doable, but reality seemed to get in the way.

She and I stopped dating, she became involved with a woman, and all the while, we remained friends. I was genuinely happy for her, seeing her more relaxed and comfortable in her skin. We continued to talk about the Big House and having children, which she and her girlfriend very much wanted. Many exchanges took place, sometimes the three of us, sometimes just us two, but they began talking in earnest about starting a family. And they discussed it with me. I understood this was with the view of me being the sperm donor as well as the involved father, while they would be the moms. The more time passed, the more excited I became, thinking that, finally, this could come true. I knew both of them, one for decades. We had similar values, political views, and dreams for our futures. I backed off from too many exchanges about this, letting them set the pace and take the lead. After all, they would need me at some point, and whenever that time came, I would be happily ready and willing to move forward with the arrangement. One day, when I was away for New Year's with friends in the San Francisco area, I dialed in to get my phone messages. One message was from them.

"Hi Ram, it's me. I wanted to wish you and Mason a very happy new year. We would like to let you know that we have some very exciting news. We're pregnant! I can tell you all about it when we talk, but I just wanted to share the great news. Happy New Year! Bye."

Brokenhearted. That's how I felt. Leaving me a message on my answering machine that they were moving ahead with having a baby was not how I thought that would turn out. And that they were now telling people since the dangers of the first trimester were over made it all the more real, and hurtful. It was as if a slow-motion montage were happening in my head, crash after crash after crash of each of the images I had about this dream. The collapse of the baby's room, each toy falling slowly in my mind onto the hard surface of the floor. The crash of the playset in the yard, wood splintering and falling into a heap. The image of a baby being snatched out of my arms left me stunned, looking at a door being slammed in my face. I was outside of the Big House, with rubble all around me. As melodramatic as this might sound, that is exactly how I experienced this. All the emotional investment I made over the years, not without their participation, was snatched away in the span of a 20-second voice message. I felt gutted. My dream had been stolen from me, yet they were moving forward with theirs. *They* would have a big house with the child and the extended family celebrating holidays and birthdays, and if I were lucky enough to be invited, I could come and be one of the *guests*.

Another friend of mine, a lesbian, often talked about wanting a child but wasn't sure how she would become a mother. Of course, she knew of my desire, and while she and I often talked of the visions and dreams of parenthood, she made it quite clear she did not want to co-parent with me or any other man. She was waiting to partner with a woman and create their family together. While I was not happy that she was not interested in my version of the family plan, I respected her for her honesty and directness. She was hoping to find a male friend who would be willing to be the sperm donor and maybe be involved to some degree in the life of the child, but not to be the father. If that did not come to pass, she would be comfortable seeking out an anonymous donor from a clinic.

I was so envious of her ability to feel so confident that she could create the family she wanted. As a woman, she could conceive and carry a child. After all, plenty of families had a single mother, whereas a single dad with a full-time child was uncommon, sometimes even considered odd. Also, to have a lesbian mom was, in those days, and in many parts of the world still today, an aberration, but a gay dad was seen as far worse. Deviant, abnormal, and sometimes literally criminal.

While Los Angeles was always known for its forward-thinking and liberal way of life, when it came to children, that was not the case. Children have to be protected since they are vulnerable and unable to care for themselves. An openly gay dad strutting around broadcasting to those around him that he is the biological single father of a child was such an anomaly that neighbors, teachers, clergy, and even family members could, and did, look askance and suspiciously at that family unit. Was the child safe? Would that child get the warmth, nurturing, and love needed if there were no females in the household? Some friends would ask me, "What if you wanted to go out on a Saturday night? What would you do with the child?" I was sure a woman would not be asked that question. But somehow, a gay man was still thought of as irresponsible and possibly reckless. "What if you wanted to bring a guy back to your house?" The answer was that "I could *want* to do that, but I just wouldn't. Period." This was not a whim for me. Not some capricious, flighty craving that would pass once I had the child for a couple of weeks or months. I wanted a family. I wanted the trappings of carpooling and making breakfast, lunch, and dinner, leaving funny notes in my kid's lunch bag. I wanted to juggle my work and the extracurricular activities of my son or daughter, figuring out how to make sure I was there to see my kid run up and down the basketball court, spike the volleyball over the net, or pirouette on the floor while the mirrors that surrounded the dance room showed them from every angle. I wanted to have neighbors with whom I could leave my son to play with theirs and to be able to host playdates where my daughter could bring home a friend for a sleepover. I wanted to feel beyond tired at the end of the day, ensuring we were fed, dishes were washed, homework completed, bath time enjoyed, teeth brushed, books read, and we both fell into our respective beds. I wanted my offspring to complain it was too early for bed while I thought and felt exhausted, longing for bed. When friends would tell me this was more of a pipedream than a potential reality, I felt both angry and deflated.

One Saturday night, Mason and I were invited to a party at a friend's house. Amy worked in the entertainment industry, behind the scenes, and had not only many friends but also eclectic and interesting ones. She and her girlfriend lived in a multilevel townhouse that they rented, decorated magnificently with mid-century modern furniture and art, and we always had fun with them. On our way there, Mason and I discussed whether this might be a gathering where there might be a woman, gay or straight, or a female couple, who might entertain the idea of me and her partnering in creating a child. "You know those Hollywood types!" Mason said to me. We admitted we had nothing to lose as long as we did not embarrass ourselves or our host. Yet, it was going to be a full-on aggressive pursuit of finding a womb.

Once we finally found a place to park, which was no easy task, we speculated that with so many invitees there that night, maybe one of them really might be *the* one. We were on a mission. We saw a few women outside, chatting amongst themselves.

"Good omen," Mason said.

One of them was smoking. "Not her," I said back to him.

We nodded hello to them and maneuvered through the maze they had created to get to and through the front door. Music played, the aroma of indiscernible foods was wafting, and crowds of people were everywhere. I looked around but couldn't spot Amy. Mason and I made our way inside, pressing up against many people, at times more intimately than was comfortable. Noticing Amy to our left, we walked over to say hello. Understandably, many of her other guests wanted her attention, too, and she told us we could catch up with her later. We meandered through the throngs in the direction of the drinks and food.

We saw a few familiar faces, more familiar to me than to Mason since I had known Amy long before Mason and I met. I greeted them as the night went on, introducing Mason to them, finding out what television shows and films they were working on, hearing about new loves and lost loves, and looking for love. Mason shared about his work in the field of psychology, which seemed novel to the majority of those around us. Even though not all of Amy's friends were in the film business, very few were in the world of psychology. It was as if I brought someone quite fresh and different to a group that seemed to know each other quite well.

At one point, Mason wandered off somewhere, and I went for a Diet Coke refill. In front of the drinks table stood a woman I didn't know. I introduced myself to her. She was of average height, maybe five feet four or five, approximately my age, thirty or so, with brown curly hair that just hit her shoulders, green eyes, and a pretty smile. She and Amy knew each other from a show they had both worked on, and I asked her how she liked being in her industry. The more she disclosed, the more I realized she was well-educated, was interesting, had a wicked sense of humor, and had traveled quite a bit, mostly for her work. She was currently single, although I didn't know, or ask, if she had been partnered with a man or a woman because it didn't matter. It was evident to me that she was financially comfortable, given how she described her lifestyle, and that she was close with her family. We shared academic stories, including my journey out of the law and into psychology. I was in the midst of completing my necessary hours prior to sitting for the licensing exams, then hoping to go into private practice.

Mason found his way back to me, at which time I introduced him to my new friend. I put my right arm through Mason's left one, showing her that we were a happy couple, and stated unequivocally, "I hope to get my license, set up an office, and start a family." I was trying to find somewhere between subtle and direct. She looked at me curiously, asking what I meant, which allowed me to go into my spiel. As I was winding my way through my story, she interrupted me by saying that she'd had a child for a couple in the past, "which was one of the most gratifying experiences" she had ever had. My ears perked up, and I felt a surge of adrenaline go through me.

"I believe that gay people deserve the same rights as straight people when it comes to having children." She was emphatic and passionate about this.

"This is so refreshing to hear since our society seems to be way behind the curve on this one, in my opinion," I responded.

"I know it's not the norm, but if I can help those who can't do this for themselves, then that's what I want to do."

I didn't have to sell the rest of my story; she took the reins from me and was selling hers. This was, in its truest sense, unbelievable. Is this how it would happen? I would be at a party, and in some random, arbitrary way, I would meet a woman. She and I would trade tales, and then, in the not-too-distant future, I would be home with a baby that she had carried for me? The more we talked, the more excited I became. Piece by piece, the puzzle of my elusive future was being filled in.

She told me that the union she was a part of offered exceptional health benefits, which covered all the prenatal and postnatal expenses, as well as nearly all of the hospital costs of the labor and delivery itself. They allowed for generous time off for medical appointments along with several months off for maternity leave. Her last pregnancy was unremarkable and easy. She said that her work was not taxing on her body, and she worked all through her nine months. Her family lived nearby, which gave her support in case she needed anything, and she had wonderful friends who were there for her whenever and for whatever she needed.

"I do still hope to meet someone, a man to spend the rest of my life with, but until that happens, I know I won't take on the responsibility of raising a child on my own." She stated confidently.

"I know I am a 'whole person' with or without a man."

The decisions she made in her life were based on her values, her morals, and her interpretation of justice.

"I love children." She stated.

"We do, too," I said in return.

"They bring so much joy to the lives of those who want them." She leaned forward, closer to me and Mason, as if she were disclosing a secret. "Why shouldn't *everyone* who wants them have them?"

I thought about this for a moment. "Well, just because someone wants a child does not necessarily mean that they would be a good parent."

"True. But still, if you and a significant other decide that you want to have a family, what's the difference between adopting a child and having a natural one?" This was her comeback, which did make sense to me.

"We are all preaching to the same choir," I said.

Having children for others was part of what she could do, and she was committed to it. After a while, she gave me her phone number and told me to think about all of this "and be in touch if you really want to move forward." We hugged goodbye. She went one way, and Mason and I went another.

I looked over at Mason, wondering if this woman was an angel sent from above. Was this the actual materializing of the dream I'd had for so many years, coming to life in Los Angeles on a Saturday night in the fall of 1997? Would I be one of those people who ended up on a morning talk show, sharing my experience in the segment they liked to call "Never Give Up!"? I was lightheaded from this. I began thinking of boys' names and girls' names more fervently than in the past many years when I was doing this, thinking that in the next year, I might actually need to pick one for the birth certificate. In those few seconds, as Mason and I were walking through the crowd further into the house, I continued to think. I might have to cancel my clients at the last minute, clients I did not have yet, if my baby, who did not exist yet, became ill during the night, and I had to take him to the doctor, whom

I did not know yet. Did I want to live in the valley, which seemed more kid-friendly, or the city, which seemed more progressive? How would I explain to the preschool that I had not yet found, that I was a gay man with a child, and that if there were any issues with it, it was not the right fit for me and my family? For that matter, how would I find a preschool? Would I join any of the fledgling gay parent groups starting up in Los Angeles? If so, what would I want to get out of them? If not, why not? Did I want my child to call me Daddy or stay with my roots and be called Aba?

While I was looking around for Amy to say goodbye and thank you, my head was not spinning, but the thoughts, options, and considerations inside it were certainly swirling around with gusto. I gently nudged Mason to the side, nodding in the direction where Amy stood, near the open sliding glass door leading out to the patio.

"We probably shouldn't say too much to Amy, right?" I posed to Mason.

"Why not? Maybe she could tell us more about her friend."

"Yeah, but this could turn out to be nothing at all." I felt the inner conflict between not wanting to get my hopes up and wanting to move on this *now*!

"Look," Mason said, stopping in his tracks, looking at me squarely in the eyes, "I will follow your lead. I know how much this means to you, and I am here to support you."

I nodded slightly, smiled at Mason, and we continued to walk toward Amy.

I placed my left hand gently on Amy's left shoulder as we reached her; she was standing with her back to us, talking with others. She turned, donning a big broad smile on her face, still from the conversation I had just interrupted. I apologized for the intrusion but told her we had to head out. "Thank you so much for inviting us."

"Before you go, did you see my new table and chairs on the patio?" She had just completed work on a movie set in the 1950s and had told me she fell in love with a patio set she had found for the film. Once shooting wrapped, she was able to purchase the set, and since she had the outdoor space to use it, she was proudly showing it off all night long. We confessed that we never made it outside; soon after we walked in, we met one of her friends and ended up talking with her most of the night.

I could feel my words wanting to escape, craving to share everything we had discussed. But I held back. "I hope you had a good time," Amy said.

"We did," Mason replied.

I could no longer hold back. I blurted everything out, from the moment we had met Her, the details of our conversation, and all my hesitation and reluctance to believe this could be the answer to my prayers. I told Amy that I hoped, at some point soon, she and Mason and I could talk so she could fill me in on everything she knew about this woman who might possibly be tied to me for the rest of my life, the mother of my possible child. What a fluke it was that this woman had brown curly hair and light eyes, two physical traits I always believed my child would have. How sweet and compassionate she seemed, wanting to help those who couldn't do this alone. How fantastic that, as a friend of a friend, this woman was somewhat vetted; after all, Amy would not have invited her to the party had she not been at least somewhat friendly with her. This could end up being one of the happiest nights of my life!

As I was winding down my monologue, and the air was coming back into my lungs, I was aware that Amy's face had turned from the original smile to a more concerned, maybe even apprehensive expression. Debating whether I wanted to ask, I finally landed on yes and said, "What?" And with that, my happiness balloon was once again punctured. Amy disclosed that this woman was not really a friend of hers but a colleague with whom she had worked on various sets, including this latest movie.

"She is a bit 'off' if you know what I mean," Amy revealed.

"How so?" I asked.

"Well, she already has four children with four different men." Amy continued hesitantly.

"What?!" Mason and I exclaimed in unison.

"Yeah, and all the kids have been taken away from her by the Department of Children's Services. She was deemed an 'unfit mother.'"

It was a well-known but not-often-spoken-about fact in the community of set and art designers that she had mental problems, including addiction issues and delusions. She was prescribed a regimen of medications; her coworkers knew when she was, and was not, following that regimen. When she was not, her behavior could become erratic, and she could be extremely volatile and explosive, which was another reason she was not allowed to retain custody of her children.

"Where are the dads to these children?" I asked.

"From what I know, all the men are 'low-life' types who don't want to have anything to do with her or their kids," Amy said somewhat sheepishly, looking down at her shoes. She then raised her head again, looking at me and Mason.

"This is a woman who is fun to have at a party, maybe fun to spend the day with, but absolutely not someone whose genes are healthy to consider having a child with." Amy stepped a bit closer to me, took both of my hands in hers, and looked me directly in the eyes. "I am so sorry, Ram."

11
HOLDING ON WHILE LETTING GO

———❧———

Finding my way in my new life was pretty good. Mason and I were living together after dating for nearly a year. As different as we were in so many ways, so too were we compatible. While Mason was much more "chafing dishes," I was "paper streamer." This was how Sharon and I described the dissimilarities between my new beau and myself. Mason was more formal, more about the looks and presentation, something never at the top of my list. When I gathered with friends, I appreciated the ambiance and the décor, but the reason I was there was to be with the people themselves. The food and the trappings were secondary. Mason appreciated both, maybe equally. At first, I admit it was somewhat intimidating for me to participate in hosting an event with Mason. I was not as meticulous as he, and I knew it was more important to him than it was to me. At the same time, if this was going to be something *we* were hosting together, I wanted it to reflect me as well as Mason. That was one of our main sticking points. You can't have my casual flair alongside Mason's formal staging. I would twist a few colorful paper streamers above doorways and call them the decorations. I would buy colorful paper plates and throwaway cutlery and know we could all enjoy the event without too much hassle at the end of the gathering. Walk around the rooms with a large garbage bag, toss out the partially eaten dips and chips, as well as the used plastic silverware, and most of the clean-up was done. Mason was more about caterers, rented dishes and glasses, and staff. Not better or worse, just different. I was not used to his way; he was not used to mine. I always deferred.

Only through hindsight did I learn that was not a healthy approach for either of us. I built up some resentments, feeling invisible by not getting things to look like me. It was not healthy for Mason since what I was ostensibly saying by my actions was that he got his way every time we disagreed. So, when the time came that I was more adamant, he fought hard to keep the prior equilibrium: he was getting his way. It was as if I were changing the rules unilaterally and blaming Mason for taking a stand for wanting to keep things as he and I had created them previously. And, as most couples do, we found our comfort zone, with a plus-or-minus variance, and together, we entertained, we had our couple friends, we made a life together, and a happy one at that.

One area of our lives that did not connect easily was the family Mason had with his son Ben, and much more so, with Ben's moms. When I moved in with Mason, Ben was nearly three years old. The mommies were quite protective of Ben, not wanting him to lose out on any of his father's attention or love to anyone else, including a partner. Again, with the benefit of therapy, years of life experience, and, if I am honest, years of forgiveness, I learned it was their anxiety and nothing about me as a person. I knew, Mason knew, and they knew not only who I was but the type of person I was in general. I was all about encouraging and embracing family. I happily stepped aside when Mason had time to spend with Ben, with or without the mommies. I knew how important that was for Mason, and I was, in some ways, living vicariously through Mason. Seeing him make time for his son invigorated me. I liked knowing Mason wanted to put family above all else. I believed I would do the same when it was my turn to have a child.

Mason had set days that he would pick Ben up from school, coach Ben's sports teams, and participate in school trips and activities with the other parents, which did not include me. Not at first. Prior to our moving in together, I was slowly introduced to Ben as Daddy's friend, then Daddy's boyfriend, and not until we were certain this was a solid, long-lasting relationship, and I moved in as Daddy's partner. Until that point, Mason and I had to negotiate my existence in Ben's life, sometimes with discomfort for both of us, especially when the mommies insisted that "family time" did not include me. What stung was that they had created a large community of lesbian-parental families, where many of the moms and kids were Auntie This and Cousin That. But I was Rami. Just Rami. For holidays, Shabbat dinners, outings, and family vacations, Daddy was invited to join them and their chosen guests, but I was excluded. Time after time, year after year, Mason felt cornered and restricted, knowing that if he defied the mommies' edicts, there would be a fight. And those fights could get ugly. Loud and ugly. This led to the mommies withholding Ben from Mason for a time until cooler heads prevailed, tempers waned, and life returned to the way it was, with the mommies nearly always winning that round.

Mason and I talked about these events every time one arose. I tried to be supportive, putting my hurt aside, and help Mason talk through what he could say, how he might act, what he might do, but always, always, reminding him in the end that if it meant him not seeing Ben, or spending time with Ben, then it was not worth the fight. Plenty of times, I wanted Mason to stand up for me, for himself really, and insist that the mommies no longer control how he spent his time nor with whom. He was responsible enough, knowledgeable enough, sensitive enough, and loving enough not to put Ben in harm's way. But he seldom did. And again, I deferred. Just like with the chafing dishes rather than the paper streamers, I would go for a hike on my own when it was Family Sunday Brunch with Ben, the mommies, Ben's grandmother, and Mason. This was followed sometimes by time at the park with Cousin No-Relation and Auntie Neighborhood-Friend. To soothe myself, the story I would tell myself was that one day, when I had a child, I would not do that to Mason. I would include him as a family member because he would be my family, and that was what I wanted for my child: a family. Until that time, I would learn to absorb my anger, sadness, and disappointment, try not to take it out on Mason, and trust that things would be different one day.

I tried not to share this with too many people, mostly for Mason's sake and also for my own. I didn't want to make it look as if I were living with an insensitive man, nor did I want to slander anyone's reputation. After all, both the mommies were professionals in the community, both quite known in the Los Angeles gay world. One of the moms, like Mason, was a native Angeleno, and the other mom had moved here as a young professional. The people with whom I would share these events were part of the long history of my newly acquired family, and I opted to keep these events to my pre-Mason, Toronto, and Camp Ramah friends. With them, I could talk about anything and say anything. In the end, I told them that no matter how much shit-talking I did about Mason and the mommies, I was more happy than unhappy and choosing to stay in this relationship, and they accepted it. Full stop.

One exception to this was Scottie. He was a tall, handsome gay man with the twinkliest of blue eyes and the broadest of smiles whom I met volunteering for Jewish AIDS Services. We gave our time and money to an organization that helped educate the Jewish community; AIDS was present everywhere, including among Jews, and that did not make them, or our people as a whole, tainted. Scottie was a lawyer and a native Angeleno as well, and it turned out he went to school with Mason in the same year. They knew many of the same people, both exceedingly proud to be gay and exceptionally committed to helping bring gay awareness into a more positive light. At the time of my first board meeting for this organization, there was Scottie, who was unknown to me at the time but someone I noticed immediately and just knew that I wanted to befriend. Happily for me, he felt the same about me, and from that day forward, we became close. Quickly, we became confidants. Scottie was happy in his committed relationship with Michael. He told me that when he met Michael, he knew instantly that there was a special "something" there.

Scottie was intent on introducing me to his friends and his family and making me part of his crew. I had not yet met Mason for the final time when Scottie and I were developing our friendship; I was a single gay man in the community. Scottie took it upon himself to make sure I met other gay professionals, men, and women, less so for networking and more for making me comfortable being an out gay man. From the start, he was a friend, a mentor, a counselor, and a champion. He wanted me to be happy, whatever that looked like, and never hesitated to answer my phone calls, invite me to gatherings, and just be my friend. A true friend. When I met Mason and shared the news with Scottie, he was hesitant about the pairing. He knew Mason as much more flamboyant and out than I was.

"You know, Mason has been out a long time and has dated quite a bit," Scottie informed me.

"I'm sure he has. He's been out a long time, hasn't he?" I retorted, sounding a bit more defensive than I intended or thought I needed to be.

"No, but when I say that he has dated quite a bit, I mean *a lot of guys*. A lot."

"Scottie, I appreciate you telling me this. But I have to admit that I am kind of flattered that he took notice of me." I heard myself say that and felt a bit pathetic. Still, with Scottie, I could be, and was, one hundred percent honest.

Scottie worried that I was not yet another in a long line of "those" people who had dated Mason Sommers. He also sheepishly admitted that he thought Mason was too "out there" for me in general. Still, with that cautionary warning, he told me he was there for me, supportive of whatever I wanted to do. "And, if Mason does anything to hurt you, I . . . I . . . Well, it won't be pretty!"

As Mason and I grew to know one another, Scottie was the one L.A. person I dared to share some of the difficulties I was having with Mason, specifically around the issues of the mommies. He knew them both quite well and thoroughly understood what I was talking about, including the personality traits I referred to. He acknowledged that what Mason and the mommies had done in creating a child was exceptional in the truest sense of the word. It was an exception to the traditional family rule that a lesbian couple would invite a gay man to sire their child, and the three adults would choose to raise that child together as one family. Scottie also appreciated that Mason's outward bravado was, in large part, used to hide his internal insecurities. The last thing Mason wanted was to lose access to his child and to lose face in the community for having been a pioneer in this unconventional family structure. He encouraged me to stay focused on the bigger picture—that Mason had already done something of particular importance to me. That was one of the many reasons I was with Mason, and not to let some of the thorns dissuade me from staying the course to enjoy the blossoms. Mason and I had much more than just the kid issues in common, and it was up to me to remind myself of those commonalities. As long as the balance sheet showed a net gain rather than a loss vis-à-vis the relationship, I was doing it right. Scottie would remind me of his times of conflict with Michael, the issues that would arise and cause conflict and emotional separation in their relationship, but, in the end, Scottie loved Michael more than he didn't.

One Thursday night, I arrived home at 10 p.m. My routine in those days of my internships was that Thursday night was *ER* night, one of our favorite television shows. Mason prepped a meal and waited for us to eat together as we watched *our* show. I would race home so I could catch the start of the show. If I were late, Mason would start watching without me, and at the time of the first commercial, he would fill me in on every detail I missed. Dinner was on the table, and we sat side by side, both facing the TV and only talking during commercials—sacred time.

After the show, after we cleaned up, and after Mason set up the coffee pot to turn on at 6:15 the following morning with the requisite seven cups of coffee to be brewed by the time he woke up, we would both get ready for bed. We undressed, brushed our teeth, and got into bed. Since Mason had been home for hours before me, he would have listened to the voicemail messages from the day. That night, Mason was already under the covers. I was still in the bathroom, and he called me, telling me there was a message for me from Scottie. I picked up the phone and keyed in our code to retrieve messages, and there it was: the unthinkable. To paraphrase Scottie, he said, "This is probably the second strangest phone call you will ever get. But, I had lunch today with a woman, the daughter of my stockbroker, and she might be interested in having a child with you. Call me for more information. Oh, and by the way, the *strangest* phone call you will ever have will probably be when *you* call *her!*"

Mason and I talked this through, navigating the unknowns of 'this could be it, and this woman could be the one,' all the way to 'this could be another one of those situations like we encountered at Amy's party.' I was happy that Mason seemed excited, and he understood that this call was something that I should do without him, at least at first.

"Do you think that this could all come together so uneventfully?" I asked Mason.

" 'Uneventfully?' What do you mean?" He questioned.

"That after all the asking around, and meeting people at parties, and putting the word out, all it takes is a phone call from Scottie?"

Mason looked at me somewhat quizzically. "How else would it come together?" He leaned in toward me and took my hands in his as we sat on the bed together, facing one another.

"To me, this was *exactly* how it would happen. After all the asking around and letting people know that this is what you, and we, are looking for, one of those people would finally say, 'Hey, I think I have someone for you to meet.'"

I shrugged, not knowing what to feel and not able to identify what, if anything, I *was* feeling at that time. One thing I did know was that Mason and I were in this together.

I debated whether to call Scottie that night or wait. Who was I kidding? I knew that I couldn't wait, but it was also very unlikely that I would reach Scottie, which is what happened. The following day, when I finally got to talk to him, he shared the details of his lunch with Robin with me and told me she was waiting for my call. After a few messages left back and forth on each other's home phones, Robin and I finally set up a time to meet in person. We both thought that, after a brief conversation on the phone, we wanted to see the viability of this scenario, and so a date was set.

I saw what I assumed was Robin's car pull up near the house, a Honda Accord, and park across the driveway. She and I had planned to meet at our house so we could see each other in person, as well as have some privacy to talk about . . . whatever we were going to talk about. Although I had thought about this for such a long time, I never quite grasped what an early conversation would actually sound like. I was about to find out. Tall, full-figured. Brown corduroy pants. Muted sweater in brown tones with an organic pattern on it. Brown, curly, shoulder-length hair that bobbed up and down as she walked toward the door. Green eyes were visible from a distance. Her walk seemed somewhat tentative, but that might be how I was feeling rather than how she was walking. Regardless, she found her way to the door, rang the bell, and I walked over to open it.

Nearly one week earlier, I had called Robin to introduce myself and tell her I was following up on the phone call I had with Scottie after her lunch with him. I had called Scottie the day after hearing his message, insisting on every detail—every single detail—of his lunch. Scottie shared that his stockbroker of many years had wanted to meet with him to go over his portfolio. During that time, they discussed money, investments, and the stockbroker's unmarried daughter. "Now, Scott, isn't it time for you to settle down and start a family?" she asked him. "I have the perfect daughter for you. She's smart, pretty, educated, and ready to share her life with the right man." According to Scottie, he didn't miss a beat and responded with, "If you had a *son*, then maybe I would consider it." Marlene kept her game face on and followed up, telling Scottie that if he knew of any eligible men in their thirties for Robin, he should keep her in mind. "She is ready to have babies." That is when my face came into Scottie's head, making a mental note to call me immediately upon returning to his office, which he did.

Scottie often told me that he would have loved to have a child, but Michael did not. At all. No amount of cajoling or negotiating inched Michael from his firm position of "no children." The truth was that Scottie and Michael were living the quintessential "gay life" of the 1990s: hosting and attending parties, frequent exotic and local travel, and the latest in fashion, real estate, and gadgets. They both worked hard to make good money, and they both knew how to spend their money to make themselves happy. Their life had very little room to raise a child appropriately. Scottie knew this to be true and thoroughly enjoyed his life, but inside, at some level, he felt conflicted. He also knew that his parents, especially Rosie, his kind, loving, less-than-five-foot tall ballbuster of a mother, longed for him to procreate. After all, she had grandchildren from her other son and her daughter, and she wanted at least one baby from her baby, Scottie. It turned out that Scottie once met Robin for lunch, mostly out of curiosity to talk about babies. But, after a frank conversation about having a child, the idea was simply too scary for him. But not so for Robin. From that lunch, Scottie came away believing that Robin might be liberal-minded enough and forward-thinking enough to have a child with a gay man. So my dear friend posed the question to her. Would she ever consider that? Her response was that she was willing to talk to me. So, Scottie assured Robin that he would contact me and relay the information, and depending on my response, either he or I would be in touch with her.

The first time I called Robin's phone number, I heard her voice on her voicemail recording. It was lilting, fresh, happy sounding. What do you say to someone you have never met, and you are calling about a topic so out-of-the-box that no words can sound normal or conventional? "Hi Robin, this is Rami, Scott's friend, and I'm calling you to see if we can find a time to talk about possibly having a baby together." Yup. That was the message I left. I added more, acknowledging that this was a particularly unusual call to make, and I was trying to lighten the message with humor as a way of diffusing some of the awkwardness. I left my phone number and told her I hoped to hear from her soon. In person, Robin's voice was just as crisp and just as melodious as it was on the phone. When she walked in, I was acutely aware of my nervousness and anticipated that she was feeling similarly. After all, it was exceedingly unlikely she had any experience in meeting a gay man for the purpose of having a child with him. I led us to the family room.

"Please, sit down. Make yourself comfortable." I pointed to the couch and gestured for Robin to choose a seat anywhere on the three-cushion sofa.

"Thanks." She looked from left to right and chose the latter side.

"Can I get you something cold to drink? Water? Soda?" I offered, wanting to be a gracious host.

"Water is great. Thanks." Her voice was melodic but somewhat nervous sounding. I imagined it mimicked my own, which I was not paying attention to but could feel all through my body.

With Robin on my left and the light coming in from the French doors, the afternoon sun illuminated the green of her eyes to a cross between the Dunn-Edwards color palette Artificial Turf and Snow Pea. Not quite piercing, unquestionably engaging but at the same time, soft and inviting. Flecks of amber danced in her eyes to create movement and dimension, all the while remaining delicate. I realized I was staring, unsure if Robin was aware of that or not.

We chatted about our professions; Robin was a high school teacher. She was also quite enamored of the theatre, directing school plays and dabbling in writing original musical theatre. Music played a big part in Robin's life, as it did in mine.

"I studied piano at the Royal Conservatory of Ontario in Toronto." I shared. "While most of the music I learned was classical, I am actually a fan of lots of musical genres."

"Wow!" Robin exclaimed. "That sounds pretty prestigious."

"I don't know about prestigious," I followed up, "but it was a step beyond the individual piano teachers that I started with."

Robin nodded her head slightly and took a sip of her water. As she put the glass down on the table which rested in front of us, she continued.

"I'm a big fan of Irish and Celtic music, but I have to admit that Broadway musicals really speak to me."

I somewhat self-consciously revealed that during law school, a student in my dorm building had asked me to accompany her to her ballroom dancing class one evening when her regular partner couldn't attend. One class and I was hooked, becoming a regular dance partner with Janine since that evening. (She dumped the other guy as she preferred to dance with me; I was taller than he was.) We took it very seriously, making ourselves quite well-known to the ballroom dancing circuit, competing, and winning several prizes. Yes, music was in my blood and my hands and feet. Robin grew up in Los Angeles, most of the time in the San Fernando Valley, where she currently lived in an apartment. Her father was deceased, and she was quite close with her mother, Marlene, who lived across the street from Robin.

Robin shared that she was the eldest of four kids, having a brother and twin sisters, one of whom she was close with. The brother and the other twin were not in her life these days, nor in her mother's life. She did not elaborate other than to say there was a falling out with each of those siblings and the rest of the family, and it was best to maintain the distance. I reciprocated by sharing that I was born in Israel, grew up in Toronto, and was now living in L.A. I had both my parents in Toronto, as well as a brother who was four years younger than me. She and I were both the oldest children in our families, and we seemed to appreciate a kinship about that. While I grew up with some religion, Robin identified herself as a cultural Jew. She attended Jewish programs that were more of the cultural and Yiddish variety, whereas I was more of a traditional Conservative Jew. She, like me, celebrated the Jewish holidays by way of custom and ritual but nothing religious.

Robin had dated men and had been in a long-term relationship with a man for several years in her thirties. Over time, Robin believed he was, or at least could be, "the one," but he turned out to want a different life than the one Robin wanted. And he left.

"So there I was, a woman in my late thirties, wanting a family, and I was all alone after such a long time of being in a relationship." She had considered and was still considering being a 'single mother by choice,' which, as she explained it to me, was opting to have a child by way of artificial insemination through a sperm bank. She was capable, had the support of family nearby, and earned enough money that she could aptly care for and provide for a child, and her dream could come true. But she wanted more for her child.

"What I really want is a family."

When she said that, I got it. I really got it.

"To be honest with you, that is what I have always pictured for my child or children."

Even living a gay life, I had hoped there would be a mother figure, maternal inspiration, and women in our family constellation.

"I have always been a believer that both male and female influences are important for children so they are raised to understand what the world at large is like. So they can feel somewhat comfortable interacting with both the male and female energy." I hoped that this was not too weird to share.

I believed, based on my Child Development readings, that an absence of one energy, male or female, could lead to a child feeling timid and insecure later in life. It's as if one needs to 'practice' being around boys and girls, men and women, early on in adolescence and adulthood so it does not seem so foreign. The longer it takes for that to happen, the more potential there is for that child to be anxious. The bottom line is that we were both looking to create a family, not just a child.

I explained to Robin that I was openly gay, living an out yet somewhat discreet life. Being a lawyer was no place for out men. The world at large at that time wasn't either. But, within distinct circles, I was freely me. My parents knew, my friends knew, and my new world of psychology peers all knew who I was. Mason and I had been together for a couple of years by this point, and seeing him in some ways as a role model for a gay man having a natural child was encouraging. I disclosed to Robin the circumstances of Ben's coming into the world, and I was very clear that that was not what I was looking for.

"I don't want to be a 'Disneyland Dad,' that guy who picks up his children for dinner once a week and spends every other weekend with them.

Robin was looking very intently at me. Maybe waiting to hear more of what I was going to say, or perhaps fearful that I wanted more than she was looking to offer.

"I want to be an active, full-time parent, even if it means only having part-time physical custody of the child.

She nodded, yet her face maintained its serious countenance.

"I want to co-parent with the mom and raise the child together, albeit in separate households. It would be like a divorced family without the acrimony."

"That's an interesting way to think about it," Robin spoke thoughtfully, saying each of those words very deliberately.

I was very clear that I wanted to see if something like this was even possible, and the more I thought about it, the more I believed it could work as long as my female counterpart-parent was open to non-conformist approaches. Obviously, this was a big ask of anyone, including me. We would both need some time to consider this, but now that we both agreed, it seems like a viable option to consider. Nearly two hours after she arrived, Robin got up.

"Well," she said, "we both obviously have a lot to think about."

"That's an understatement," I said in response, and we both smiled.

I walked her to the door. And just like she walked toward the house a few hours earlier, she followed the same path back to her car and drove off.

As soon as she left, I wanted so badly to call someone and tell them. Mason was at the office with clients; I would share every detail with him once he was home later. But I also wanted to tell one of my "girls." Debbie and Anita, from high school, in Toronto; Judy, now in London; Sharon. She knew how much I loved children. She saw me with them at camp, she knew me while I was working with the special needs kids at a local synagogue, and she experienced the closeness I had with her kids. All these women knew I could be quite vocal about wanting to have a child, somehow, and they were all in my corner.

What would any of them say when I told them about Robin? What would I tell them? I met a woman for a couple of hours and thought she could be the mother of my child. No prescription of rose-colored glasses could bring this into focus. The way I made sense of this in my mind was to say to myself that right now, there was nothing to tell. My friends knew how much I wanted my own family, and if and when there was something to tell them, I would.

Robin and I met a few more times, the third of which included Mason since he was my partner and, therefore, going to be an integral part of my child's life and, therefore, Robin's life. I was a bit skittish about the introduction, knowing Mason could come off as intimidating to some. Although Robin and Mason were the same age, had both grown up in Los Angeles, and had several interests in common, I was concerned Robin would feel uneasy and Mason would want to dominate the meeting. Mason's way was to take control of situations when he did not feel in control. My having a child was certainly not within his control, although as much as we discussed it, and I assured Mason I was doing this *with* him, he felt ill at ease. I reminded him that he had already gone through a similar process and had created a child. Now, I was doing the same thing, but in a different way. Still, this was not easy for him to incorporate into his vision of what his life was supposed to look like.

"I think this is happening way too fast." He said.

"Way too fast?!" I repeated, slightly insulted and less-than-slightly irritated.

"Well, you and this woman hardly know each other, and you are already seriously talking about a lifelong commitment to one another." Mason was using his therapist's voice with me, the one that drops half an octave and is slower than his usual cadence.

" 'This woman,' as you refer to her, is someone who came to *us* by way of a trusted friend of *ours* for the very purpose of this commitment."

Mason was sensing my defensiveness, and he upped the ante. "I understand, but still, when the mommies and I were contemplating having a child, we spent years before we went forward with it."

That was the wrong tack to take with me. The issue with the mommies and Ben was one that Mason himself was unhappy about, so no matter how much time they all spent together, it still resulted in Mason being relegated to a very part-time position.

"Mace," I began, taking a deep breath, not wanting to escalate this current state of affairs, "All we are doing today is having you and Robin meet. That's all. Where things go from here, well, none of us knows. Please, for me, let's get through today."

I obviously didn't share any of this with Robin. I did not want, or need, for her to know about Mason's insecurities. I would have to navigate this with Mason, just the two of us. While it did create disagreements between us, I was open to listening to Mason's advice but not open to abandoning this opportunity. I blatantly confronted Mason many times, asking him why it was okay for him to proceed with an endeavor that was so unique, with no real road map, but not okay for me. He would often warn me it was not easy and was still not easy for him, and he wanted to protect me from a similar difficult outcome. I often reminded him that I wouldn't know if I didn't try. And my intention was to try.

We all met for dinner at a local restaurant not far from our homes, exchanged pleasantries, and propelled ourselves into a conversation about this unknown and equally exciting territory.

"Robin, where did you go to high school?" Mason asked once we settled into the bread, olive oil, and balsamic vinegar that was presented to the table.

Mason was making an effort, and while I appreciated it, I was still tense that this could be the deal-breaker.

Robin shared that she grew up in the valley, and with Mason having grown up in Beverly Hills, they did not have overlapping friends.

"Rami tells me that you sang in high school," Robin stated.

"Yes, I was a Madrigal," Mason replied. "Not only in high school, but I went to summer camp near Palm Springs."

"Me too!" Robin exclaimed. "ISOMATA."

Now, it was my turn to jump in. "What's ISOMATA?"

Mason and Robin, almost in unison, chimed in. "Idyllwild School of Music and the Arts."

This led down the verbal road of 'do you know...?' and 'do you remember...?'" It turns out that not only did they attend camp in the same summers and were taught by some of the same counselors, but the most unique coincidence was that they both had a crush on the same boy!

Mason, like Robin, was musically inclined and was a singer in high school and during his college years. Just like in Robin's family, where music was a key component of the household structure, Mason's family hosted "hoot-nannies," where friends and neighbors would come over with their instruments, sit in the backyard, and play and sing folksongs for hours. At one point in the evening, as things were humming along quite comfortably, Mason and Robin, at the same time, launched into a full-voice rendition of "General" from the musical *The Pirates of Penzance*. For those who know this song, it's a quick tongue-twister and quite a feat if sung through without error. For those of us who did not know this song prior to that evening, well, it was a sight and sound to behold. Here we were, a gay couple and a near-perfect stranger, meeting to discuss bringing a child into this world, where we three would raise that child as if it were the most natural thing in the world. Mason and Robin, eyes glued on each other as if replicating the child's game of a staring contest, belted out the song with the requisite harmony.

"I am the very model of a modern Major-General,

"I've information vegetable, animal and mineral…"

Lyrics were sung to a song from a Gilbert and Sullivan comic opera from 1879 by strangers in a restaurant in the San Fernando Valley in 1998.

The more time we spent together, the more Robin and I believed there was, in fact, a real possibility this could work. I shared this exciting news with very few people in my life, not wanting to jinx anything and also not wanting to dole out any information that might not, in the end, come to pass. As much as I had joked that this was something I wanted and intended, somehow, to do in my life, this seed was now germinating. I wasn't sure how I would explain it.

The first person I told was Robby, my therapist. It could be my memory playing tricks on me, but I am nearly 100 percent certain that as I revealed the details of the various meetings with Robin, Robby sat more upright in his chair across from me, planted both feet firmly on the floor, shoulder-width apart, leaned in, and ever so slightly, shook his head back and forth. All the while, he was smiling. When I was done, after a pregnant pause, he said, "Well, if anyone can do this, Rami, it's you!"

I also chose to call Sharon and finally tell her the news. "Oh my God, what are you doing?!" Sharon might have been dumbstruck at this news, but if she were, she wouldn't let that stop her from telling me it was a mistake. "You don't know this woman. And you want to bring a child into the world with a stranger?" She told me I needed to "really think about this" and think hard. This was not a game. She was not happy with this or with me.

"Sharon, you know how important it is for me to have a child." I strained to stay composed.

"I know!" She retorted. "But really, who is this person? What do you know about her? This is insane!" She, on the other hand, revealed all of her emotions.

"I've spent time with her, with and without Mason. We have been getting to know each other, and we both seem to want the same thing." My words sounded pathetic and weak.

"Ram," she continued, "you know I love you and want only the best for you. But this does not sound right. It's just not right."

When we hung up the phone, I felt deflated. Maybe she was reacting to what happened to her children now that she was divorced, and her boys don't have both parents together. Or perhaps she was caught off guard by this unconventional, experimental idea of mine. Or maybe she knew something I didn't know. She was not on board.

When I told Robby about Sharon's reaction, he suggested Robin and I go see a therapist, a family therapist, together. We could discuss our plans and see if there were issues we needed to be alerted to and consider before moving any further.

I put forward the idea of our going to see someone to Robin. I told her I could do some research and find someone with a specialty in unconventional family structures, and she agreed. Robby found me a few names, and after interviewing them on the phone, I chose Sally. She was young but not too young, hip but not too hip, clinically experienced but not too stodgy, and had a background in non-traditional family structures. Robin and I sat on the couch across from Sally, and like a good game of ping-pong, we lobbed information, one at a time, to Sally. Every once in a while, she would interject with a question, asking how we saw ourselves navigating issues of X or Y, who we might want to be caretakers of our child should something happen to both of us, and how we intended to resolve conflict or differences. None of this was earth-shattering, but it did leave us both with many important topics to consider and flesh out. As we were leaving, we said we would spend some time on this homework and reconvene in a couple of weeks. Both Robin and I felt good leaving Sally's office, but definitely a bit less excited.

"Well, what did you think?" I asked as the elevator doors closed, and we were on our way down from the eighth floor.

"I like her," Robin said.

"I'm glad. I do, too."

"But you knew her from before, right?" Robin asked.

"Only by name. She was referred by my therapist, who knows what I have been wanting." I replied, hoping that Robin did not fear that I had some agenda that I did not share with her. She quickly disabused me of that fear.

"Oh, ok. She seemed really tuned into what we were talking about. I thought maybe you had already prepared her for some of this."

"No. Met her today for the first time."

Maybe this situation was made a bit too real for us, a level of reality that we had not, until that point, really contemplated.

Robin and I spoke a couple of times throughout the following two weeks, the second time confirming that we would meet at Sally's office the following afternoon. Robin's voice seemed a bit shaky, maybe nervous, maybe tentative, but something seemed off. I asked if she was okay, and she responded that she was. "See you tomorrow." In the waiting room of the therapy office, Robin's body language and energy echoed what I sensed in her voice the previous day. Again, I asked if she was feeling well and if anything was going on that I needed to know, and she said she would tell me in Sally's office.

"Sorry to be a pest, Robin, but I can tell you're not yourself." I turned to look directly at her. My anxiety was getting the better of me.

She did not return my gaze. "I'm fine. Really." She was trying to sound confident, but it was not working.

She sat upright, back straight, with her fingers interlocked in her lap. She looked stiff, apprehensive. She was not sharing any more out here.

My heart felt heavy, but I chose not to speak anymore. All would be revealed in a few minutes.

Sally opened the door into the hallway that led to her office, nodded, and smiled but said nothing as we walked through the door. We took the same seats as last time, but the quiet seemed oppressive. Sally was the first to speak, asking us how these two weeks had been and how we had been. I looked to my right, where Robin was seated, but she didn't return my look. She looked directly at Sally, smiled weakly, and said she had been busy with work, but overall, she was well. Sally turned slightly to me, indicating it was my turn, and I answered similarly. Busy with school and work, but overall fine. Sally asked us about our last session, how it felt, and if we had given thought to the session itself and to the homework she offered. Robin did not jump in with a response, so I did, saying I found the session helpful and important. I spent time considering the bigger questions of what it meant to have a child with someone, as well as speaking about it in my therapy and to a couple of close friends. I admitted it was more daunting after facing some of the more complicated questions of parenting. However, I was still excited to move forward and wanted to see if there was a chance to make this a reality, one that would work for all of us, including the child.

When it was Robin's turn to speak, she finally revealed what her nervousness was about.

"Last session was very helpful." She began. "It gave me a lot to think about."

"I'm glad to hear that, Robin," Sally replied.

Robin continued. "I talked to my sister about all of this. She is my closest confidante, and we both agree that there are lots of reasons to go forward with this."

I looked over at Robin, whose eyes were on Sally, not on me.

There was a bit of a pause in the dialogue, and Sally stepped in.

"Go on."

"Well, I guess I still think of myself as a more traditional person, which is funny because, in so many ways, I'm not. But I keep thinking of the fairy tale of meeting someone, falling in love, getting married, and having a child that way." Robin sounded more genuine and less guarded than in the waiting room.

"If I went ahead with this, not that that couldn't happen, but it would pretty much be the end of that as an option." She sighed and lowered her head. I was reading a sort of resignation in her words. What she was saying was that if we proceeded with this, it would preclude her from making that dream a reality. She was scared.

"Robin, thank you for that openness." That was Sally, not me. "Everything that you say not only makes sense but is truly how you feel. You have to trust that and honor that."

I didn't like where this was heading.

Sally continued. "Is there anything more to this that you want to share? Now would be the time to unburden yourself with all of your thoughts and feelings."

Slowly, Robin turned her head toward me, and I could see that she was teary. She probably saw the same in me.

"Well, there is someone that I recently met, and we've gone out on a few dates. It's really early, and I don't have any idea if this will go anywhere, but it makes me think that I need to give myself more time to pursue what I want in the way that I have always thought it would."

Robin finished by saying that she was profoundly sorry, but was putting our baby pursuits on hold, and she was going to see what transpired with this man.

12
WHERE FEAR AND FAITH MEET

C rash! I could not believe what I was hearing. Robin hadn't given me an inkling that she was going to reveal this. What happened two weeks ago when we were last in therapy, talking about the ins and outs of making a family, untraditional as it would be, and today? Obviously, a lot! I just wasn't made privy to any of it. The inside of my head felt like a pinball bouncing off all the rubber barriers in its way. With each collision, I heard a loud "bang!" causing me to feel and hear thumping in my skull and my vision to go blurry. Not again. I could not believe that this was, again, the end of my possibility of becoming a father. It had felt different this time; Robin seemed different from the others. She and I met for the sole purpose of this undertaking, and she knew what she was getting herself into. No secrets, nothing manipulative or disreputable. We both wanted a child in the frame of a family, and we both were up for the challenge of making it come to life. Until one of us wasn't. Throbbing. My head was throbbing, hammering on all the parts of the inside of my head that were usually the calm, rational, thinking parts. We'd talked on the phone about this. We met in person—a few times. I introduced Mason into the mix. We agreed to go to therapy to identify elements we needed to consider.

Was I not entitled to know before showing up here that there was a monumental change in the plan? Of course I was! And should have been! Why do this to me? Hell, why do this to herself? Why not tell me on the phone, prior to making the trek to the office, that plans were on hold? None of this made sense to me.

I think Sally was talking, but I wasn't processing. The English language was, at that moment, as foreign to me as it was all those years ago when my family arrived in Canada from Israel. I was a boy of less than six years, not understanding the sounds coming from those around me. Robin was teary. I do remember that, but I couldn't connect to any compassion for her at that moment. We sat in the office a while longer until it was time for Robin and me to leave. Sally wished us well, and I, dazed, stepped aside to allow Robin to leave the office first. Always the gentleman, I guess. In the hallway, Robin said, "I really am sorry, Rami." Heading off to the elevator, I had nothing to say. We rode down to the ground floor in silence. Robin was proceeding toward the front door, presumably toward the parking lot where she likely left her car. I walked next to her, neither of us speaking, until Robin was about to turn toward the parking structure.

"I'm really, really sorry, Rami."

Yeah, me too, I thought. "Robin, you have to do what feels right. Better now than later. Take care." I was able to get those words out as we both walked away in different directions.

Life continued after that day, and I was busy. Each day, I increased my odometer's totals by 40 or 50 miles. I had classes in Marina del Rey. My four part-time jobs spanned the far reaches of Los Angeles County. Every day was spent crisscrossing the freeways of L.A., knowing I would inevitably get stuck in some traffic crunch that could cause me either to be late to my next stop or, at the very least, to stress over it. Even with the meticulous calculations of plotting out where I needed to be and how to get there in the most efficient way, the greatest unknown, as I am sure it is in every metropolitan city, was the traffic.

Rather than give in to the tension and worry, I made a deal with myself. Drive time would be time to catch up with friends and family by phone; it would provide me with time to gather the local and world news of the day from the radio, and it would help me hone my ability to be patient. I am one of the most patient people I know. Not to brag. It's just who I have always been. Patience would undoubtedly be a needed trait to bring into the therapy room with clients, to model for them how being patient can allow them to change their negative thinking and create a healthier approach to living their lives. To learn to appreciate the process of getting "there," wherever "there" is as opposed to only appreciating the destination.

During my time in the car, with the radio quiet and the phone in the off position, I focused on my breathing, inhaling deeply through the nose and exhaling through the mouth. I did that ten times in an attempt to clear my mind and cleanse my airways. I visualized scenarios, ones in which I could place myself and enjoy the experience, like the beach. Imagining walking along the threshold of sand and water, enjoying the lapping of the waves against my feet. Feeling the sun overhead and the smell of the salty air. Sometimes, I pictured walking in the snow, bundled up with multiple layers of clothing so I could feel the cold on my nose but enjoy the toasty warmth against my body. I visualized walking in the cold, still air, seeing the pure white of snow blanketing the fields and hills around me, and reveling in nature. Every once in a while, I went back in time to Israel, in the idealized world that might have been my childhood. There, I explored the neighborhood of my youth, swinging on the swing set outside our apartment building, pumping my legs harder to reach the heights of the nearby trees and balconies. The breeze blowing across my face was warm, somehow familiar, affectionate. Delighting in these images allowed me to feel at rest, to know, on some deeper level, that all would be fine. Life would turn out the way it was supposed to, to use a ubiquitous expression, but in these moments, it really did feel true. In each of the mental movies I created, I was at peace. I was calm, happy, patient. I trusted that the time spent doing this would teach me both stamina and serenity—perseverance leading to peace.

As I worked my way through the required courses in the master's program, I found myself choosing from the developmental psychology options for my electives. I wanted to learn more about child, adolescent, and adult development, understanding which and how early childhood experiences shape us into the adults we become. I also hoped for a greater clinical comprehension of how to help clients address their early childhood issues in their adulthood, to make some sense of them, and hopefully, overcome them. The more I studied human development, the more I believed that understanding the child self was a crucial component of all adult behavior. To no one's surprise, once again, I was drawn to children. Through serendipity, one classmate shared that he was training with a group of clinicians to become a shadow for children with special needs. The organization coupled a psych trainee with a family who needed assistance with their child. Some of the children had mental challenges, some emotional. Some were on the autism spectrum, while others were identified with impulsivity issues, conduct disorders, or general disruptive attitudes. The seasoned therapists in the group mentored newly licensed ones and those in training, to address the needs of both the family and the kids. They helped integrate these children into everyday life activities, including school, daycare, social and academic extracurricular activities, and even basic social interaction. My classmate was generous enough to share the name and phone number of Nicki, the leader of this group, whom I contacted, and arranged to meet at their next meeting. Once there, I learned more about the specifics of the group and the expectations of the trainees, and, as a bonus, I found out that these gigs were paid. I had assumed that since I was unlicensed, being supervised, and accumulating hours toward my total needed prior to sitting for the licensing exams, this work would be done on a volunteer basis. But I was wrong. Happily so. Nicki gave me the names and numbers of two families, both with boys with autism, and suggested I call them, have them interview me while I interview them, see if we were a good fit for one another, and go from there. She was sensitive to the fact that I was quite nervous about taking on this type of work and offered her time to help out along the way.

Julian was the first of the boys I worked with. Three years old, autistic, with two young parents who were both in the entertainment industry. They felt wholly overwhelmed with how to help their firstborn with a cherubic face and a sweet disposition. He had a vocabulary of about ten words, made almost no eye contact with others, had a calm demeanor, and could stand at a sink or hose for hours, letting water spill over his hands and through his fingers. But, when Julian became frustrated, he would screech as if he were being tortured. The sounds could be deafening, scaring anyone around him, and consoling him could take seconds, minutes, and sometimes much longer. This was the most heartbreaking for me, seeing this little boy angry or exasperated, not able to communicate his needs, and we, the adults around him, not understanding how to support him during this episode. His parents, of course, were used to this, taking it in stride. They were aware that social situations were challenging for Julian and the other kids around him. Add to the mix his aggravation, the noises, and the volume of those noises, and Julian was almost always invited to leave and not to return. Heartbreaking.

Julian's parents hoped to find a preschool for their son where the environment would be welcoming and nurturing enough to allow a boy with special needs to learn how to integrate into some semblance of regular life. They had narrowed the list down to two places and wanted me to take Julian to both of them as a trial run to see how he fared without them. They knew Julian might have a difficult time going off with a stranger, which is why I would need to come to the house a few times before our experiment to familiarize myself with the boy and to have him scrutinize me. Assuming that went well enough, we could move on to Phase 2, where I would take Julian with me and have his dad follow in his car, without Julian's knowledge, to observe me with his son, his son in unknown territory, and the two of us as a team.

Julian and I became fast friends. In fact, after the first time I visited his house and stood at the kitchen sink with him, him on a stepstool and me to his left, letting the water from the faucet run down, I knew he accepted me. For a while, neither of us made any sounds. Then, casually, with my hand next to his and the lukewarm water streaming, I began to count. "One." I touched his thumb with my thumb. "Two." I touched his index finger with my index finger. "Three." My next finger touched his corresponding one, followed by "four" and "five." Julian made no movement, no reaction. I waited a minute or so and did the same again. The third time I did it, after saying the word "one," I turned off the water. Julian looked at me, perplexed. Not angry, certainly not happy, but puzzled. "One," I said again, and with my dry hand, I pointed to Julian, touching him gently against his chest. "Now you say it. One." Julian looked up at me. Eye contact. A breakthrough. "One. Now you say it. One." I did this five or six times. And then, I heard Julian's little voice come through. "One." He said it! "Great job, Julian!" I yelled, maybe a bit too loudly, and turned the water back on. Julian's lips turned up ever so slightly at the ends into a mini smile, presumably that the water was back on. I was elated. We stood there a bit longer, and then I tried again. "One. Two." Turned off the water. Again and again and again and again, but after the seventh time, Julian repeated the numbers. And again, I allowed the water to come back. By the end of nearly 50 minutes, I had bonded with Julian enough for him to trust me. Dad came back into the kitchen, and we showed him what we had been doing. I pointed to Julian's thumb, and Julian uttered, "One." Then, "two." "Three. Four." And finally, "five." Dad became teary. I became teary. And while we had no idea what Julian was feeling, I was sure we were both hopeful this day was the beginning of a new chapter for this family.

I was hired, and the next step was to take Julian to the two preschools for a trial run. While both of them had kind caregivers, one was considerably more comfortable for Julian than the other. Coincidentally, the one Julian seemed to like more was run by Sara, an Israeli woman. At first, I did not reveal my heritage to her. I asked her questions about her program for the kids, her food, and how she would help a special needs child fit in with the other children. I wanted to know her credentials and if she would allow me to be present with

Julian, sitting on the floor with him, at the table with him, doing art with him, etc., so I could help him be, and hopefully feel, like one of the group.

She didn't flinch. "Of course!" she said in a somewhat husky, accented voice. "Why not?" It was as if this were the most natural thing in the world of preschools to her, to have an adult man sit with the kids and participate as if he were one of those kids himself. And she did, with seemingly no hesitation. I was stunned, happily, to see her ignore me at times when she was engaging with the other kids, setting up other activities, preparing lunch, and attending to any specific needs. Periodically, she would ask me if Julian would like to try a game or an art project, which I always agreed to. She spoke to Julian as if he were any other three-year-old, always following that by looking at me to see if I had anything to add or to tell her. I appreciated that she respected my position there and wanted to ensure that what she was doing was in Julian's best interest.

On our first day there, Sara had cut out construction paper rectangles approximately two feet long by eighteen inches wide. Red, green, blue, pink, one by one, she placed one sheet in front of each child at the big table she had in the main room. The other two assistants who worked with her were at the ready, and I was seated next to Julian. She poured different colored paints onto paper plates, which were just beyond the reach of the children. She informed us that we were going to put our hands in the paint, palms down, and then one of the adults would help each child press down the kids' hands onto the paper, leaving their handprints. Each child was asked what color paint they wanted, and if they answered, they got it. If they were too young or didn't respond, a color was chosen for them. One assistant stood close by, with the plate of paint in one hand, and helped the child place their clean hand into the paint and press the hand down onto the paper. They did the same with the other hand. Once both handprints were on the page in front of the child, they were ushered to the other assistant standing nearby at a spigot with a black hose attached and a yellow plastic bucket nearby. That was the "let's wash-our-hands" station, where the kids would rinse off the paint into the bucket and dry their hands with a nearby towel. Once the prints were on the page, Sara collected the papers, and with old-fashioned wooden laundry clothespins, she hung them up to dry on a line in her backyard.

When it was Julian's turn, he seemed a bit apprehensive. He did not like to be touched, which is a common characteristic of people with autism. I explained to the assistant that I was watching what she was doing and that I would help Julian since he was more used to me touching him than anyone else at the preschool. No problem. I presented red and green plates of paint to Julian, hoping he would, on his own, choose one of them. Either would look good on his yellow construction paper. Julian made no moves toward either of the paints, so I decided he would go with green. I, too, had selected a yellow sheet of construction paper, wanting to mirror what all the others were doing. As I slowly moved my right hand toward the plate, I narrated what I was doing, allowing Julian and anyone else to listen and pay attention and know what was happening as it was happening. I gently pressed my hand down, raising it and showing Julian my green hand. "Whoa, look how green my hand is!" Julian didn't look. "Look what I'm doing now, Julian. I'm going to put my hand down on this paper, and look what happens!" As I flattened my hand onto the yellow sheet of paper and then raised it, a stark contrast of green in the shape of my hand remained on the page. "Coooooolllllll!!! Now I'm going to do my other hand." With the same level of exuberance and narration, I imprinted my left hand onto the paper, showing the results and saying, "Now it's your turn!" With my green-stained right hand, I reached over and gently took Julian's right wrist and quickly spread his fingers open, laying them into the green paint on the plate. I don't think Julian knew what to expect or that touch was about to happen, but he didn't fight me. He seemed intent on looking at the plate where his hand was, and I raised it toward the yellow sheet of paper in front of him. "Let's do what I did and set your hand down on the paper, Julian." My right hand was still holding Julian's right wrist, so I took my left hand, spread Julian's little fist open, and placed it down onto his paper. I pressed firmly on the top of his hand, trying to ensure his entire handprint would show. Once we were done, I lifted his hand and loudly called out, "Fantastic! Now, let's do the other hand!" Just as methodically, with narration and fairly quick and fluid movements, I repeated the steps with the left hand, getting two good handprints on the page. "Amazing, Julian!" Immediately after both of Julian's hands were being held by mine, Sara removed the page, and Julian and I got up and walked over to the water and bucket. "Let's wash our hands, Julian."

Julian was beginning to register what was going on and was starting to show his displeasure. He made some unhappy noises, not too loud, but definitely ones I knew could escalate into something scary for the other kids. I did my best to steer him to the hose, saying out loud, "Look, Julian, water." Before the noises intensified, Julian was in one of his happy places. Water. I purposely waited to be the last one to do the art project, knowing Julian might need to stand in the water for a while, and I didn't want to impede the other children from cleaning up. As soon as the water began to pour over Julian's hands, all his utterances ceased, replaced only by periodic faint humming. Julian was happy. Or at least relieved. He stood there, motionless, while I held the hose over both of his hands. We both watched the green paint drip into the bucket, Julian's hands becoming cleaner and cleaner. I inserted my hands, too, needing to clean up myself, and each time my hands were over the bucket, I rubbed some more paint off Julian's hands. And, not to miss an educational opportunity, when I touched Julian's thumb, I said out loud, "One." And when I touched his index finger, I said, "Two."

Later that week, once the paint had dried and the kids had put some stickers on their pages and drawn with crayons whatever patterns they chose, Sara laminated the construction paper. She sent each kid home with a unique and special placemat they had made. On the back, she put their name and the date, creating a keepsake for as long as the parents chose to hold onto it. And there was one made by Julian.

I worked with other children, too. Each one has its distinctive features, and intuitively, I created a rapport with each, understanding their needs and addressing them, all while pushing them out of their comfort zones to expand their lives. All were boys, and most showed some traits of autism. I spent time in first grade with one boy, facilitating his integration into a group setting socially, as well as helping him learn how to structure his time, do his homework, and communicate more effectively. Another boy whose family I worked with needed practical modeling of patience. The boy, age eleven, had some nonverbal learning disabilities, manifesting in poor results in his grades. The parents knew that their son was smart and could be doing better. They wanted him to study harder and take school more seriously—my work with them involved meeting with all three of them a couple of afternoons each week. We sat at the homework table, where I showed the boy where his strengths were and praised them. I also pointed out to the boy that his inability to focus or stay calm was his way of expressing that he was having difficulty in that area. Rather than having the parents tell him what to do, I attempted to show them their boy was telling me what he needed.

"Maybe we should all take a quick break," I said enthusiastically.

All three looked at me as if they had never conceived of stopping other than because of a familial disagreement.

I continued. "Let's all stand up and shake out our bodies."

This time, the three of them looked at me as if I had lost my mind. I turned to the boy.

"You know how you told me that you and your friends like to chase each other during recess? Show me what your body looks like when you run, but stay in one place."

I began jogging in place, shaking one arm, then the other, then both together, from my sides, up over my head, and then down again. The kid laughed.

"Now you!" I called out. "You too, Mom and Dad."

The boy immediately mimicked what I was doing, exhibiting an even more exaggerated flailing of the arms. The parents just stood there.

"Now let me see your legs swing out from side to side, like this." I contorted my legs, from the knees down, to rotate out to the sides, making me look like perhaps I was devoid of cartilage, or I had never run in a straight line before. Regardless, this brought out laughter in all three of the family members.

"Come on, let's see *you* do this!" I did not identify which 'you' I was talking to, hoping that any or all three would join in. The boy did, swinging his limbs wildly all around his body, and to his credit, Dad began to shake out his arms a bit.

"That's funny, Dad!" the boy called out. "That looks so weird!"

"No weirder than you!" Dad said back, his voice less stressed than I had ever heard it.

"Mom, now you! Let's see you shake your body." Son was now engaging with his parents in a way that was obviously foreign to them all. They were having fun in the midst of what was usually a situation fraught with a power struggle.

Mom eventually joined in, and after what seemed like a long time, but it was probably no more than 90 seconds, I took the reins back.

"Thirty more seconds of this, and then we wind down, take a few deep breaths and get back to math. Deal?"

"Deal!" they all shouted in unanimity.

More frequent breaks, less time on each particular subject, and positive reinforcement. That was not the system the parents were familiar with or comfortable with. Yet, in time, this new tutoring approach proved to them all that the boy was capable of better grades. And the fighting decreased dramatically. With each family, I found the "hook" I believed would be the way to shift the child and the parents and siblings, if necessary, to feeling better about the way their family system was functioning. I found myself doing pseudo-individual, pseudo-couples, and pseudo-family therapy without fully understanding why I was doing what I was doing or the exact theories behind it. But it worked.

School, full time. Four part-time jobs. Happy new relationship. And I was back in regular communication with my parents. Those waters were still thawing, but at least there was movement. After nearly four years of iciness between us, during which I gave them the time and space they requested, I decided to call my parents for their anniversary. It was September 14, shortly before the Jewish New Year, then Yom Kippur, followed by my father's birthday on the 30th, and then my mother's birthday on October 11. I calculated my chances for a happy autumn versus a sad one, risking them either not responding at all or hanging up on me.

To my complete surprise, my mother answered the phone, and when I told her it was me on the other end, she genuinely sounded happy to hear my voice.

"Hi, Ima. Happy anniversary." I was cautious but wanted to sound confident.

"Thank you." She responded.

"Have you had a nice day?" I asked.

"It's been very nice. Aba brought me a beautiful card and flowers when he came home from work." She said.

"That's nice. I am glad that he did that." I wanted to tread lightly, not to say anything that could sound or be interpreted as judgmental or negative.

"Did you hear from anyone?" I asked, hoping that she would share with me that family and friends had remembered and reached out.

"Sure! From friends and from Israel, too. And now I heard from you, too."

I asked if I could speak to my dad, but she said he "was busy," but she would pass along my good wishes. "Thanks." At the end of the call, I told my mother I was very happy she answered the phone, and I would try and catch them again for Rosh Hashanah later in the week.

"Okay" was all she said, but it was enough. An indication that she would not only expect my call but that she would pick up the phone when I did. I called again a week later.

"Happy New Year, Ima," I said into the phone.

"Oh, hi!" she exclaimed. "Thank you. The same to you!"

Again, we had a somewhat strained but still agreeable conversation, wishing for all of us to be healthy and happy and back in each other's lives. "Same to you," was how she responded. Over the next two weeks, I made calls for each of the calendar events until my father finally got on the phone and broke the moratorium.

Like the first call with my mother, this one was short and superficial in the sense that we only talked about unimportant things, but it was anything but superficial in any other sense of the word.

"Hi, Aba," I said.

"Hi." I could not determine the tone of this exchange.

"I didn't get to talk to you for Rosh Hashanah or your birthday, but I wanted to make sure that you know that I wish you all the best for this new year." I took my time saying this, wanting to make sure that it was clear that all I was doing was wishing him well.

"Thank you. Happy New Year to you too." His response sounded sincere. At least, that was the way I was choosing to hear it.

It was hugely significant that he took the phone receiver and that we talked at all. From that point on, the relationship softened, certainly from their side and happily from mine. It would take nearly another year for my mother to actually talk to me about my being gay and ask me if I was happy, safe, and healthy. AIDS was still very much in the news, and "gay people were getting AIDS." She was scared I would get it and not tell her.

"I'm healthy, Ima. I promise you." I said, attempting to reassure her.

"So many gay people are so sick, and they suffer so much with it." She sounded sad.

"I know. It's really awful how much pain people are going through with this disease." I said.

"And it's only gay people who are getting it." My mother was either not thinking as she said that, or she was poking at me.

"Well, that's not true," I said. "You are right that the majority in North America who have AIDS are gay men, but all over Africa, it's straight men and women."

"But we are not in Africa!" Her voice sounded sharp.

"Ima, I don't want to fight with you about this. About anything, actually. Listen to what I am telling you. I am careful. I am educated about this illness. And I am healthy. I promise you that if I ever get sick, I will tell you. But you have to trust me that if I don't say it, it means that I am fine."

"Ok." She said, and happily, that was the end of that topic.

In time, I shared more of myself with my parents much more with my mother, including men I had met and was dating. Once Mason came into my life, my parents and I were communicating regularly again, but only for the past year or so. I felt at ease telling them about him, that he had a son, that he was a Jewish professional, and that we loved each other. When I informed my parents that I was moving in with Mason, they were concerned and fearful, that if anything went awry, he would kick me out, and I would be unable to take care of myself.

"You are giving up your apartment and moving in with him. What if it doesn't work out?" I was disappointed that this was their way of thinking, but a part of me was appreciative that they were sharing their love with me again.

"I am not jumping into this without thinking or lots of conversations with Mason." I tried to reassure them.

"But he is the one with the house, not you. And he is the one with the money. Not you." Ouch. That stung.

"Yes, I am moving into his house, and he does have more money than me. Still, I have lived in my own house before and have been living in my apartment for a while. I have been earning my own money for years now. I know how to take care of myself." I needed to remind them of this.

"So why do you need to move in with him?"

"Because we love each other, and we're in a relationship, and we want to move it to the next level." I knew this would sound odd to them, maybe even hurtful, given their feelings about having a gay son. What they wanted was for me to buy a house and have a nice Jewish girl move in with me.

"Can you afford it?" my father asked.

"Yes, we talked about how to make it fair for both of us. I will be paying Mason rent, the same amount that I was paying for my apartment." It had been many years since I had discussed personal matters with either of my parents, but especially my dad.

"If you need to do this, why don't you buy something so that you both own it?" Obviously, my dad was uneasy about my not being an equal partner in the assets of this relationship.

"If, after a while of living together, we decide that we want to buy a house together, we will do that. But now, I am at the beginning of a new career, and my income is not enough to afford to buy a house."

"So maybe wait." Again, my dad is negotiating with me.

"I will wait to buy a house, but not to move in with Mason." With that, I was definitive.

No matter how much I tried to assure them that he was not taking care of me and that we were both able to support ourselves, they did not believe it. For them to accept me as their gay son, who left the legal profession to pursue psychology, now moving in with his boyfriend, was apparently their limit. Thinking of myself as capable and self-sustaining was too much. Still, this was immense progress in our relationship, and I was going to accept it.

I reminded myself, almost mantra-like, that as I had always done, I had to keep moving. Moving forward. Always forward.

13
WHEN LIFE TAKES A DETOUR

A few weeks after the last time I saw Robin, neither of us having contacted the other, I was making peace with the outcome of yet another loss. I was better able to understand Robin's decision, at least intellectually; but emotionally, I was still reeling. Maybe not reeling, but I was profoundly disappointed. Each time, there was what I hoped to be a reasonable option or potential to move forward with this endeavor, but it failed. I knew this was not a conventional approach to, well, anything out there. There was no template that identified the basic rubric of a gay male seeking out a woman, gay or straight, who would have a child with him and raise that child together. The closest I got was Mason, whose two-mommies-in-control-of-the-situation was not in the least ideal, but it was something. The only other option for me was surrogacy, which was out of contention due to its financial magnitude. Adoption was still not what I wanted since I hoped for a biological child. And then it hit me. That was the same situation in which Robin found herself. Just as I knew adoption could provide me with the outcome I was seeking, having a child, emotionally it did not satiate the craving I had for a child with my genes.

Robin was saying that as much as she was open to the idea of having a child with me, she still craved the image of mother, father, and child all in one household, raising the child together as a traditional family. We both wanted what we wanted. Robin was not ready to give up on her dream.

I had resigned myself to the experience of having my child with me part-time. Not that I wanted that, but it was seemingly the only realistic way I could create what I wanted. I had no dream to hold out for being the full-time sole parent, so for me, to share custody of my child was as good as it was going to be. And I could be very happy. I was already in my mid-thirties, and waiting until I might be able to afford surrogacy could take years. I did not want to be too old a dad; I wanted to be able to play and run and ski and skate and rough-house and enjoy my child. The expression I frequently recited quietly to myself helped me get through the days: Man plans and God laughs. My hope was that God was only laughing because He knew that when I was least expecting it, He would surprise me.

One evening, when I returned home, I found a phone message from Robin. When I heard her voice, a bit of a shiver went through me. Why was she calling? The last communication we had was at the therapy office a few weeks back, and everything I needed to know was said at that time. I couldn't tell what she wanted to say to me from the message; her voice was upbeat, and all she said was that she hoped I was well and to give her a call when I had a chance. I called Mason to the phone and replayed the message for him, asking what he thought it might mean. Of course, he had no more information or insight than I did, so we decided I would wait until after dinner and call her back.

At first, we exchanged pleasantries, and we'd both been busy with work, had been well physically, and were enjoying the spring weather.

"I have to say, Robin, I was very surprised to get your message." I couldn't hold back any longer. "What did you call about?"

That question opened up a conversation that would forever change both of our lives, including the lives of those around us. The man Robin had alluded to in our last therapy session, the one she had recently begun dating, did not seem like he was "the one" for her. She was likely going to end things with him. However, the more important issue for her since we parted ways a few weeks ago was thinking about having a child and a dad for that child.

"I know it was very hard for you to hear what I said the last time we saw each other. I really am very sorry." She said.

"I appreciate that." I didn't know what else I should say.

"To be honest, I've been thinking a lot about what I want. When I think about what *I* want, selfishly, it's a traditional family. But when I considered who would be a good father for my child, I didn't see the guy I was dating as that person."

Not knowing how to acknowledge this statement, all I was able to muster was, "Hm."

She continued. "Truth is, as a father, I kept thinking of *you*."

This time, I didn't even have a 'Hm' in me. Of course, I was happy, flattered even, to hear this. But where was this going?

Robin told me that it was absurd to her to think she would be a single woman sharing a child with a gay man. But each time she thought of other options and alternatives, including going it alone by way of artificial insemination with an unknown sperm donor, she realized that was not what she wanted for her child either.

"All the back and forth of single mother and child versus part-time mother with a father for my child has kept me spinning."

She closed with what I will never forget, words that were so sweet and caring, gifting me with a feeling that, for so much of my life, I did not get from others. "I can't think of a better man to be the father of my child, Rami."

14

THE COST OF FOLLOWING YOUR HEART

O ff we went on a wild and mysterious ride. Robin made an appointment with her gynecologist to ensure that, physically and physiologically, she was healthy to move forward with trying to get pregnant. She also asked him about fertility clinics and got recommendations from doctors and facilities that could help us with artificial insemination. Perhaps naively, neither of us thought that I should be checked to confirm that my sperm was viable. We both assumed it was, I guess. We met after her appointment, and somewhat sheepishly, Robin said the only thing Dr. Charlie told her to be aware of was her weight. "If I were starting forty pounds lighter, I would have an easier pregnancy." Robin had a history of being overweight her entire life and struggled, as so many do, with issues of body image and self-esteem. She and I commiserated that, as children, we both felt embarrassed when wearing bathing suits in public since we both had excess flab on our bodies that we did not like, or want. I told Robin that my weakness was sweets; hers was butter.

We shared stories of escapades of making poor food choices throughout our lives and laughed. That being the case, we both had to admit that a baby coming from the two of us might have to deal with food issues. True. I did manage to get my eating under control by the time I was in my twenties, and since then, I have kept myself in good physical health. Sometimes, I would exercise more, sometimes less. But my overall appearance was a tall, slender man. It didn't bother me that Robin was heavy. One's physical appearance doesn't mean they have any particular personality traits. Maybe that was me being an empath; I knew how I felt looking and feeling overweight, and I had compassion for Robin. From what I was able to discern, Robin was a generally good person, so to judge her on her weight would be the antithesis of who I was as a person. As long as her doctor said she was healthy to go ahead with a pregnancy and she wanted to do it, I was on board.

We also set up an appointment for genetic testing. Robin was forty-two, and with both of us being Ashkenazi Jews, there were risks involved. Sitting in a room with a counselor, answering what seemed like thousands of questions, filling out copious amounts of paperwork, and then having to wait at least two weeks for the results seemed like torture, but we did it. Fortunately, neither one of us was a carrier for any genetic mutation, and from a cellular perspective, we were healthy. Robin's age was a factor, though. Statistically, the chances of women over the age of forty having healthy pregnancies and delivering healthy babies were rare. Possible, but statistically more exceptional than common. The closer a woman got to menopause, the longer it would take for her to become pregnant. And once over forty, there was a sharp decline. Again, statistically. While that was not in our favor, Robin's physiology was. We were still hopeful and decided to proceed.

The more emotionally difficult conversation Robin and I had after meeting with the genetic counselor was how to address if we were pregnant with a child who had chromosomal abnormalities. In our hours-long meeting, part of it was spent discussing the various possibilities of child defects, in general, and the ones more prone to women over forty: Down syndrome, spina bifida, and heart defects. There was also a higher likelihood for older women to miscarry than their younger counterparts. There is so much to think about, such consequential considerations.

Sitting at a coffee shop after our meeting, Robin and I leaned in over the small, round table between us, each of us holding our thermal paper cups steaming with coffee—Robin's with decaf—and processed what we heard. We were both undaunted by Robin's age and believed that if this were meant to be, it would happen, and all would be fine. Fortunately, we both felt the same way about conceiving a child who might have birth defects. We both approached the topic gingerly, wanting to appear respectful and sensitive.

"So.... " I began slowly, "If we were to hear that our child would be born with Down syndrome or another major defect, we would not go through with the pregnancy. Right?"

I waited.

"Right." She responded. "I hate to say it, and I hate to think of it but to raise a child on my own and know in advance that it has special needs, I don't think I want that."

To be honest, to hear her say that she would be raising a child 'on her own' was a bit of a sting, but I had to put that aside and trust that she meant it in the best possible way.

"The way I think about it," I continued, "is that this situation of ours was going to be unique enough with a healthy child. You a single woman, me a partnered gay man ..."

Robin was nodding her head, looking down into her coffee.

"This child will have enough differences to live with."

"I agree. Completely." Robin was now looking back up, straight at me, seemingly much more confident than just a few seconds ago.

"Not to mention that we, the adults, are going to have to navigate how the world will look and act given our *exceptional* arrangement," Robin said with both sadness and assuredness.

I jumped in. "To add severe medical issues to that scenario just doesn't make sense."

We both sat for some time, me nodding slightly, my mind a million miles away. I would have bet that Robin was equally distant. She then put both palms down on the table, bringing me back to the diner.

"Are we saying what I think we are saying?" She asked, smiling.

"I think so."

"O.k. I guess our next step is for me to call the fertility clinic and see how we proceed." Robin's voice was a bit shaky. Her hands were still on the table, palms still down, on the outside of her coffee cup. I brought my hands up from my lap and placed them on top of hers.

I was building a family! I had a partner whom I loved and who loved me. We were making a home together. I was maturing in a new career and looking forward to a profession that felt more cohesive with who I was. Now, I'd finally found a woman whom I trusted and believed in to create a baby with, to bring a child into this world together, and to raise that child as *ours*. Not mine or hers, but to give this little person, who would grow to become an adult person, a mother and a father and a stepfather, Mason, and maybe another stepfather, if Robin were to later partner with someone, and a local grandmother and aunts and uncles and grandparents and cousins and life experiences from two very different perspectives. In other words, we would be doing what every traditional, heterosexual couple does, only doing so from a particularly atypical starting point. It was hard for me to believe this was actually happening. Step by step, we were advancing.

Thinking ahead, I needed to talk to Robin about the legalities of what we were doing to the extent that I understood them myself. Matters of physical custody, decision-making, vacations, and a host of other topics that I knew from other couples who did not live together but needed to be addressed. I was also keenly aware of Mason's family constellation; the mommies had a say, and Mason took what looked like the leftovers to me. They decided what they and Ben were doing, when, where, and with whom, and once that was all arranged, they might inform Mason of it, and he might be invited to join. That was not what I wanted, not at all. Robin and I were two separate people who had two complete lives prior to meeting one another. But now that we were going to be bonded for the rest of our lives, we would need to be considerate of one another, just as any two people in a relationship have to be. In this case, of course, we needed to have the child's best interests in mind. But who would decide what those best interests would be? I wanted to spare us both from too much argument and disagreement over if, and more likely *when*, that would come up.

Using my legal skills, after conversations with Robin about as many topics as we could think of related to parenting a child together, I drafted a document, a contract of sorts, to enumerate and itemize our specific intentions. As the biological parents, we each had a 50-50 say in the raising of the child. But to show good intentions on both of our parts, we delved into uncomfortable territory.

"I really want our baby to feel comfortable and safe in both of our homes." I began. "So I hope that we can come to an understanding about how to do that. I know that in the first couple of years of life, Mommy is often the primary parent." Although I hated saying this, I knew it to be true.

Robin nodded. "I think it's really important if the baby had one primary home, at least at the beginning." What I knew she was not saying was that that primary home should be hers.

"I agree. It is best for the baby to be with you at your place much of the time. As long as you are okay with me bringing the baby to my house for blocks of time so that they can get used to both being away from you and in a different environment."

"Sure," Robin said with less enthusiasm than I had wanted.

"And I think that sleeping at your house for the first several months is probably the best." Again, I was reluctant to agree to this, but I knew that it was best for the emotional health of the newborn.

"Great. That makes sense." Robin's tone and voice perked up, and she sounded happy again.

Robin was planning on breastfeeding and taking time off from work, so it made the most sense that the baby would live at Robin's at first. We agreed that I could and would visit often, and that I would be able to have the child spend the occasional night at my house as long as we arranged it in advance. This way, Robin could pump breast milk to keep the baby on the same sustenance.

"What about traveling with the baby?" Robin asked.

Robin's sister and her family lived in San Francisco, and Robin was close with them, especially with her young nephew.

"I would like to be able to let my sister and her family get to know my growing family." Robin continued.

"Of course!" I responded. After all, this is why we are doing this: to create a family.

As for my family in Toronto, we agreed the baby wouldn't travel before the child was eating foods other than the mother's milk. Knowing that Robin wanted to take at least one year off from work, more likely two, which we both believed was ideal for the child, I agreed to help support Robin financially during that time. After all, she was going to be nurturing my child too. We agreed to revisit the length of time Robin would be home and the monthly amount I would help with. As long as Robin understood that I was not in a financial position to support her fully, she would have to participate in that. While Robin did not ask, I stated that it was my intention to support the child in all ways, including financially, for the life of that child.

"I will start asking around for good pediatricians if that's ok with you," Robin said.

"Sure, good idea. I can do that too if you like. But I am also happy to let you take the lead on that." I wanted to show that I was open and willing to step in and step up, but I also wanted to give Robin the feeling of being in charge. I sensed that that was important to her. And, if I am being completely honest, I also wanted her to be happy so that she would not pull out of the deal. I would pick my battles, as the saying goes. Not that this was a battle by any means.

Regarding decision-making of the child's health and welfare, we agreed we would do that equally. Realistically, of course, I would discuss everything regarding this child with Mason, but each bio-parent would have an equal say. Robin and I understood that we each had a wealth of knowledge from our worldliness and each of us working in the world with children. Still, we would not always agree, and on those occasions, we would do our best to come to a compromise or seek out assistance from other professionals before coming to a final determination. We established that vacations would be discussed, but neither of us would preclude the other from taking the child on adventures and excursions.

We also understood that holidays were important to us, both secular and Jewish.

"Thoughts about the holidays?" I inquired.

"Which ones?" Robin asked.

"All of them. Rosh Hashanah, Hanukkah, Thanksgiving, Passover, Christmas, Fourth of July?" I listed some of the holidays that came to mind.

Robin shrugged.

I continued. "Maybe we can see how things go and sometimes spend the holidays together. I'm sure that you're going to want to take the baby away to San Francisco, especially for Christmas. That's fine with me. Unless they come to L.A., and maybe we can all be together? Celebrating as a family?"

The last of the big headings of our Family Documents was in the case of the death of one or both of us. Neither of us wanted to think about death. We only started thinking about creating a life! But life does happen in a nonlinear way, and we have to be adults about this. Naturally, we agreed that if one of us predeceased the other, the remaining parent would be the sole caretaker of the child, promising to maintain a relationship between the child and the deceased parent's relatives. In the unimaginable catastrophic event that both Robin and I died while the child was still a minor and in need of physical support, Robin wanted her sister Lisa, the one in San Francisco, to be the child's guardian.

"I think Lisa is the best choice since she will likely be the closest family member to our baby. Don't you think?" Robin asked, somewhat hesitantly.

"I agree," I responded, "that she will be the closest of your family members, but what about Mason? He will be a consistent adult in her life, like a second parental figure."

Robin did not like that. It showed all over her face. "But Mason won't be her parent."

"I know, but neither will Lisa." I retorted. We were getting into some difficult territory. I didn't want this to end before it even began, so I made the following suggestion.

"What if we leave this for now? Let's see how things move along; let's get pregnant, and have this baby, and see who, in fact, is in our lives."

"Ok." That was all Robin said about that.

As hard as it was for me to think about relinquishing custody from anyone on my side of the family, I knew that I would acquiesce. I could see that Robin was anguished even considering this topic, not to mention that she might have to surrender her child to someone outside of her family. The maternal tugs existed before there was anyone to be maternal to. And, as hard as it would be for me not to have Mason as the guardian, which I knew would be hurtful to him, I knew that I should trust my gut that Robin should feel secure about this. After all, she, too, was becoming part of my family.

As those parts of my family were growing and strengthening, unfortunately, my relationship with Mason was becoming rockier. The more time I spent with Robin, getting ready for each new step, the more it seemed that Mason was becoming more distant. All the talk of us, specifically me, having a child and all of his verbal support seemed to be more lip service than sincere excitement. Each evening when Mason and I were home for the night, after both of our workdays, we would catch up on our activities and goings-on.

Mason would tell me about friends and family with whom he spoke that day, and I would share the same, usually including the latest information I received from Robin. Had she seen her doctor? Did she get a prescription for fertility medication, or was she going to wait until after we attempted a round or two of insemination? Robin had begun tracking her ovulation cycles to maximize our chances of becoming pregnant, and she would remind me of the upcoming dates so both she and I could arrange to be free on those days, or at least flexible with our schedules, for the time we would need to get to a clinic. At this point of our conversation, Mason's demeanor and affect would change. I could see it on his face, turning from whatever it was previously, traveling through stoicism, and ending in anger and resentment.

Often, he would challenge whatever I told him I had learned.

"Did Robin say that she spoke to a specialist, given her age?" Mason asked.

No, she didn't say anything about a specialist, but she did…" Mason interrupted me, sounding exasperated.

"Why not?"

"I don't know. But I do know that Robin wants this as much as we do. I am sure that she…" again, he broke in.

"I don't get it! I just don't get it!" He looked directly at me as he raised his voice in frustration.

"What don't you get?" I asked now I, too, exasperated, only not with Robin, but with Mason.

"It seems to me that you are both assuming that this will *just happen*." These last two words he said with a pejorative, disparaging tone.

Seldom did I have an answer to his questions. I sat and listened, tried to engage and explain, but I was forever interrogated and confronted. I was frequently told that that was not how Mason and the mommies did it as they pursued having Ben. Intellectually, I understood that Mason was less angry than scared. Maybe even threatened. Mason was used to being the boss and in control of his life. Even in our relationship, it was much more often Mason's way or no way. I would defer, much more regularly than I felt comfortable, to keep the peace. That was, and is, one of my ongoing therapeutic issues: low self-esteem. In my family of origin, as long as I did what was expected or what I was told, I was 'good.' I tried to be the good brother, the good friend, the good student, and the good everything in order to have those around me like me. And when I was not, because I disappointed someone or did what I wanted, which was different from what they wanted, I would be shunned. Dismissed. Rejected. All I wanted was to find a balance between doing what I wanted *and* having those around me accept me. I didn't need to be right all the time, but I did want to feel *heard*. Sometimes, I knew what I wanted, whether it would yield the desired outcome or not, and I wanted to be supported in my pursuit. I was fine if others felt differently, but I was still hopeful for their support. Mason was not particularly good at that.

Mason would tell me that he and the mommies spent years getting to know each other, spending time really digging deeply into what a family would look like if they, as three gay professionals in the community, were to pursue such a rare project. I had only known Robin for months, not even a full year yet. Mason believed I needed to wait longer before moving forward. When I asked him why he was now acting so differently than prior to meeting Robin, he responded that he didn't think it would happen so quickly. Mason brought to me a parental voice, and not in a good way. How was I going to afford this? Why the rush? Why not wait until I am more settled in my new career?

Why Robin? Why not keep looking for someone else? Question after question, challenge upon challenge. Nearly every night was a repeat of the night before, where I would feel like the boy caught with his hand in the cookie jar, and a voice of authority over me would sit me down, chastise me, shame me, and send me to bed without dessert. It felt awful. I felt awful.

Another specific area of dissonance between us was money. Mason had it; I did not. Mason earned a lot of it; I did not. And while Mason was already living a "grown-up" life when we met, I was still in student mode. It was enormously important for me to pay my way. Mason and I split our bills evenly, everything from going out to restaurants to household bills. Because I moved into Mason's house, I paid Mason's rent rather than split the mortgage. Otherwise, everything was equally split. But, with money comes power and control, and Mason was exerting his.

What became clear to me years later was that Mason was feeling insecure and that my attachment to him was weakening and growing with Robin. This would-be child we were talking about was the primary focus of my life, replacing Mason. In truth, the primary focus of my life was my education and therapy career; it had to be since that would be the one area of my life that I could somewhat control, and rely on. Relationships were not indestructible, and I had no guarantee that Robin *or* Mason would remain in my life. If my parents could reject me, certainly anyone could. Still, the threat to Mason was real, and the friction it caused in our relationship escalated. The conflict spilled over into almost every aspect of our lives, with Mason believing that I was not ready to do this.

Mason began wanting to go out more frequently to more expensive restaurants. I would oblige periodically but reminded Mason that I was not in a financial position to spend large amounts of money on a meal, and certainly not several times each week. We had also been talking about finding a house to buy together, which would inevitably be less expensive than the house Mason owned, but it would be *ours*, not just his. I had some money saved up toward a down payment, but it had to be the right house for both of us, including its monthly affordability for me. At this time, Mason began upping the list prices of homes for us to look at, and when I shared my inability to pay for that, he again told me that perhaps I was rushing into having a child.

One Sunday evening at bedtime, after a weekend of nonstop fighting, I told Mason we needed help.

"Mace, what are we doing?" I asked. "Actually, what are you doing?"

"What do you mean? He replied.

"All this fighting. All we seem to do is fight about my wanting to have a child with Robin. And you keep pushing back against it."

"I am not pushing back," Mason replied. "I am just trying to help you."

"Help me?!" I said this louder and with more scorn than I intended. "How is any of what you are doing helping me?"

Mason looked directly at me from a few feet away as I sat on the edge of our bed, but it felt as if we were miles apart from one another. "I've been through this before. You haven't. I know what it takes to do this. You don't."

"That is all true," I said. "But you're not only questioning me and not only challenging me, but you are also telling me *how* to do this. You did it differently. I get it. But this is how *I* am doing it." I composed myself to some degree so as to share with Mason how I was really feeling. Defeated and deflated. Because of him.

"Yeah, but you are not on your own here. I am a part of this, too. That's what you seem to be ignoring."

And there it was. Mason was feeling left out. Not primary. Not in control. And he did not know how to deal with it.

"Maybe we need to see someone to help us through this. A couple's counselor." I heard myself say this, feeling both empowered and scared. This current situation was untenable for us both, and either he could ask around for a recommendation, or I would. I had worked too long and too hard to feel like I mattered, going so far as to lose my parents in coming out. I was not going to succumb to what felt like his bullying and give up my quest for parenthood. Nor was I going to tolerate any relationship where I did not feel valued.

Later that week, Mason and I met at noon in the waiting room of the therapist he found for us. She came highly recommended by a few of his colleagues, and I trusted he knew more seasoned clinicians than I did. I also secretly knew that no matter who I would suggest, Mason would need to be the one to "win" with the therapist, so while I did get a few names, I never truly considered that we would see any of them.

Elaine was a woman probably in her later forties, maybe early fifties. She seemed a little "Beverly Hills" in her physical appearance and in her office décor to me, but hopefully, she would help us plot our course through this morass. She was tall with light brown hair and big blue eyes. She wore a flowy, floral outfit, which she accessorized with large gold hoop earrings. Elaine offered us coffee, which we both declined. She announced she was going to have some and ducked into what looked like a small kitchenette, where she reached for a large ceramic mug and filled it with steaming coffee straight from the coffee maker. "Right this way." She pointed with her right arm, the one holding the aromatic coffee, further down the hall and to the left. Mason gestured for me to proceed, with him following and Elaine coming in last, shutting the door behind her.

Since we were all familiar with a therapist's office setup, I identified which chair was likely Elaine's. I had to decide whether to sit on the two-person loveseat or the slightly oversized chair. In that split second, I assessed what it would look like if I sat in the chair, which is where I wanted to sit; I didn't particularly want to sit next to Mason. However, I concluded that it would show me as possibly resistant or angry or defensive, and I did not want to be prematurely judged. I was feeling those things, but I didn't want to present myself that way to the therapist. I sat on the couch, tucked closely to the side so I could comfortably place my right elbow on its fabric arm. Mason sat next to me. Elaine did, in fact, sit in the chair across from us, and we began.

Mason went first, introducing himself as a clinical psychologist in practice for many years and explaining that Elaine's suitemate and colleague, a psychiatrist, was a longtime acquaintance of Mason's. He was clear and accurate in his articulation of why we were there, from the perspective that he, as my partner, wanted what was best for me. He believed that in my haste and desperation, I was not considering the potholes on the road to this outcome, and he, as my partner, was already affected by my actions and would continue to be.

When it was my turn, I also briefly introduced myself, reminding Mason and sharing with Elaine that one of the main reasons I went out with Mason three years earlier was because I was fascinated with how he, as a gay man, had been able to create a family and have a child. It was no secret and not a whimsical impulse on my part. This was part of me before Mason. Just as he joined me in my pursuit of leaving one profession and starting another, he also knew he was joining me in leaving being a childless individual in pursuit of becoming a parent.

One of Elaine's first questions to me was, "What's your hurry in doing this?" That felt a bit harsh, the word "hurry." It seemed judgmental. I explained that "hurry" might not be the correct word, but I was already in my mid-thirties. I had wanted this for a long time, and I had been looking into it for years prior to meeting Mason. Mason and I had been pursuing it together, and now, finally, when there was an opportunity to do it, Mason was no longer on board.

"Well, since Mason has gone through this process, perhaps he knows something that you don't, and maybe this is his way of shielding you and protecting you."

"Perhaps, but it also feels very controlling, a tendency that is part of Mason's personality." And with that, I saw on Elaine's face that I had lost her impartiality. She did not like that I was labeling or maligning Mason. She put her large coffee mug down on the small side table on her right, leaned slightly forward in her chair, and straightened her back, catlike, similar to a pre-pounce pose. "Sounds to me like you are being rash about this."

What the fuck? I was screaming those words inside my head, behind my eyes, which were stinging from the swell of tears forming. This wasn't what therapy was supposed to be like. While I had never personally been in couples therapy before, nor had I yet counseled a couple, this just did not seem right. It definitely did not feel right. Where was her compassion? Wasn't she supposed to process why this was so important to me? Where was her objectivity? Why was she not asking Mason what was coming up for him in my pursuits? This started from our first session as a venue where I did not feel seen. Again. The fact that she disagreed with me was nowhere near as important to me as her dismissal of me. Unless I did things the way others wanted me to do them, I would not be accepted. Again.

I let Elaine tell me how she felt about what we were discussing.

"Elaine leaned back, looking directly at me. "To me, you are acting in a passive-aggressive way."

My eyes widened, feeling curious and stung at once.

"The way I am experiencing this, Rami, you present yourself as someone who wants to work on his relationship. But, when you don't get your way or hear what you want to hear, you shut down or lash out." This was her assessment of me.

"I'm sorry, Elaine, I have to say that I just don't ..." Once again, I was interrupted, halted actually, from continuing to speak. Elaine raised her left hand to indicate for me to stop talking.

"You see? You didn't like what I had to say, and you were already starting to protest." There was a smug look on Elaine's face as she said this to me as if to say, "Aha! You see! I was right!"

Elaine was clear that I had someone in my life who loved me so much that he wanted to protect me from what he was experiencing in his unconventional family formation. With all of the care time and investigations that Mason had done, this was still nowhere near a perfect scenario. So, embarking on something even more unknown seemed reckless. I hardly knew Robin, and we had no way to know what she was really after.

When I tried to explain to Elaine that I was not looking to replicate the template Mason and the mommies had devised since that was obviously not working well but that I wanted to forge my way, Elaine and Mason both said that was an error on my part.

"Now, *I* would like to say something." I spoke up. "In any relationship, heterosexual or gay, when two people meet and decide to create a couple and then a family, there are no guarantees. We have very little tangible control over making a relationship work, as evidenced by the divorce statistics." I was feeling good, finally getting a voice.

"Lots of people get into relationships, expecting and hoping they work out. They adopt dogs and cats. They have children. And then, along the way, things don't work out. One household becomes two."

I saw Mason turn his head toward me, and I sensed that he was about to speak. I pre-empted that by mirroring Elaine's image, the one of the raised hand, only this time in his direction.

"Children have to balance their lives between sometimes two very different households, between two parents with very different personalities and ways of living in the world. They end up lugging their backpacks back and forth, asking why their parents couldn't work harder to prevent this from being their lives."

"Exactly!" Said Mason. "And I want to help you *not* create two such different households!"

"What I'm trying to do is bypass that in a way. From the start, there would be two households, two separate parents living separately, but without the acrimony that tore them apart. We would be *choosing* this life for ourselves and would be as sensitive as possible toward our child's needs." To me, this made sense. But somehow, it was not translating to the other two in the room with me. Still, I continued.

"Instead of lugging the schoolbag from home to home, we could arrange to have duplicates of textbooks and school supplies. And, if need be, one of us parents would drive to the other's house to get what was needed for or to our child without involving him or her so that it wouldn't be presented as a burden. It's just what a parent does. Of course, there are unknowns. That's called life. Yet, going into a situation with the understanding that we *both* didn't know how to do it but had the support of the other, *that* was what could help make this a successful venture." There! I got that out. No interruption. If nothing else, I said my piece.

We continued to see Elaine for several more sessions. In addition to talking about the baby issue, we also addressed the inequality of our financial means. Elaine tried to help me understand that Mason was offering to do nice things for me, reiterating what Mason had always said about wanting to take me out to a nice dinner or to pay for a nice vacation for both of us. I explained that to me, it sometimes felt conditional. Mason would pay for the restaurant he wanted to go to. Mason would pay for the holiday retreat, which made him happy. And when I suggested something else, I would be met with resistance. So, to me, it was not that Mason wanted to take care of me; it was Mason wanting to do what Mason wanted, with me there to keep him company. That was not "us" together; that was Mason taking care of Mason and me, once again, unseen and unvalued.

We talked about buying a home together, and it was important to me that we both put in the same amount for the down payment and that we both make the same monthly payments. If the real goal was for us to do something together, then why was it me who had to do all the compromising?

"Why don't we look for a less expensive house, then, one that I can afford?" I posited.

"Why should I have to scale down my life, in a material way, just because you can't afford what I can afford?" Mason retorted, looking over at me with some bluster.

"Rather than looking at it as scaling down your life, maybe look at it as compromising in a relationship. And, once I can afford more, we can move forward together." To me, as I said this, it all sounded very logical.

Mason looked exasperated, now turning away from me, raising both hands and slapping them down on his thighs.

"Why can't I do this for *us*?!" He questioned.

I pointed out, that since Elaine could not or would not, Mason was quite selfish and had a fragile ego. Not only did I know that, and not only did I accept that, but I also *loved* him for that. Whether he knew it or not, Mason was a healthy role model for me, showing me how one could be successful in all aspects of life while not doing so at the cost of one's self-worth. Mason pursued his sexuality, his professional choices, and his philanthropic and social participation unapologetically. On the outside looking in, Mason Sommers was a big, bold, sometimes brash success. Maybe he was identified by those who did not know him well as narcissistic, but those in his inner circle knew him as loving, caring, doting, and insecure. I did not *need* to be with Mason; it was my choice. I was able to learn from him, as well as learn how to be less of a doormat. More often than I liked, I caved. So often, I gave in to those around me so they would like and accept me. But that was not the real me. I thought that in my relationship with Mason, I would have the opportunity to speak up for myself. Even in times of conflict with him, I hoped that I would still feel seen and heard. And, at the end of the day, we would both get into bed together, trusting that tomorrow was another day, and we would have to find a way to make it work, whatever the 'it' was. With Mason, I could be gay, I could be not a lawyer, I could be silly, I could not know things, and I was still seen. Until now.

Throughout the course of our sessions, Elaine sided with Mason. She wanted me to be more open-minded and less stubborn. During our seventh meeting, once again, the topic of Robin and me and insemination was the key theme. Mason wanted me to slow down and do things his way.

"Wait at least another couple of years," he said. "That's what I think you should do." And with that, I felt I had no more options. Nowhere to go with this conversation. I turned to Mason, with Elaine's gaze on us both, and I said very calmly,

"Please don't ask me to choose between you and a baby. Because if you do, I am telling you now that I am going to choose the baby."

In response, Mason said I was threatening him, and of course, Elaine agreed. Maybe this time, they were both right. I assured them both that this was not a power play on my part. I was doing what I saw Mason doing for himself: trying to get what he wanted. I was not dependent upon Mason in any way other than emotionally to some degree, from which I would heal if he needed to move on. I would find another place to live. I would continue with school and traineeships and eventually get my license to practice therapy. I would proceed with life, as I had done prior to meeting Mason, and I was certain he, too, would do the same. He had dated extensively before me, so there was no worry on either of our parts that he wouldn't find someone to date and hopefully to partner with. But, as I reminded them both on our first date, I told Mason how important this was to me.

"You do remember me telling you at dinner that night how fascinated I was that you were able to create a family, with a biological child, as a gay man, right?" I asked rhetorically.

"Of course I do." He puffed.

"And you have known all along, since we met, that what I wanted was to create my own family, with a partner and a child."

"Yes, I have known that all along," Mason said with a tinge of sarcasm in his voice.

"So why is this so difficult for you now?" I said irritably.

With his participation, I thought *we* had found the right person. But because I was not doing things *his* way, he was unhappy. I did not want to give in and feel resentful toward Mason. I was not going to give up this opportunity. I intended to proceed with Robin, and I wanted him with me. But that would be his choice.

15

BULLY FOR ME

—❧—

Willowdale was a northern suburb of Toronto when I was growing up there in the late 1960s, and it has continued to be so for several decades. However, as Toronto's population grew, so did its northern borders. Willowdale still exists today, but it is no longer considered the northern anything of Toronto; in fact, the city stretches out for miles and miles to the north, east, and west, and all the way south to Lake Ontario. In the vein of so many older people, I think to myself, "When I was a boy. . ." But yes, when I was a boy, Willowdale was our little city within the bigger city, referred to as one of the more Jewish areas, and certainly an immigrant community. I don't remember any hostility between us kids that had to do with ethnicity, religion, cultural practices, or even elitism based on financial achievements by the families. We were one big neighborhood, living happily and peacefully in the high-rise apartment buildings, commingling our languages and the odors of our native foods. Many a time, I remember stepping off the elevator to smell curry followed by boiled cabbage, which ended in chicken soup by the time I reached my door. It wasn't judged; it just was. And, beyond the rows of multistory residences that bordered the main streets, there were single-family dwellings, duplexes, and townhouses that shared similar experiences as I did, only with more distance for the aromas to waft from house to house.

As an immigrant first grader, six-year-old me did not speak any English and sat in the back of the class with the other two Israeli newcomers, Rachel and Rachel. None of us understood what the teacher was saying, so we huddled together: safety in numbers. I don't know how they felt, but I still remember feeling vulnerable. Not quite intimidated, and not bullied, but certainly exposed. What if a teacher spoke to me and I did not understand? What if some of the other kids approached me, talked to me, and waited for a response? Fortunately for me, one of the Rachels knew a bit more English than either the other Rachel or me, so she could periodically step in and be our mouthpiece. After school, in Miss Hanson's English as a Second Language class, Rachels and I, along with so many others, attended daily sessions until we caught up to the native English speakers in our classes, at which time I hoped the vulnerability would end. Unfortunately, it did not. Yes, I was now able to speak the language spoken around me, but I still felt odd. I was a tall kid, chubby, not athletic. While the other boys ran and chased each other and played sports at recess and lunch, I sat on the side of the yard against the brick building near the metal-framed glass doors. All I wanted was to be inside, where I could feel more protected, not stand out as the "weird one" as much.

After elementary school, when I left public education for a private Jewish middle school, again, I felt different. Still chubby, now also wearing glasses, still not athletic, but a good student, I tried to find my place in academics since I knew athletics would never be the talent for which I would be known. I was smart, and enthusiastic about studying and doing well. Some called it a bookworm or a geek or a nerd, and while those labels certainly did not make me feel accepted in any way, they were not as harsh or hurtful as the other names I was called: Faggot. Sissy. Weirdo. Always being the last one chosen in gym class for teams, being laughed at for always missing the football toss, never connecting the bat with the baseball, barely dribbling the basketball a few yards before it was stolen away from me by a better player, these were the staples of my P.E. experience.

Anita was one of my first friends in junior high and remains one of my closest friends today, along with her husband and children. She liked me regardless of what others said or how I looked. We lived near each other, walked to and from the bus together, talked, laughed, and commiserated that we were both the older siblings, she having a sister and I a brother. We invented a "disorder," we both lived with OCS. Oldest Child Syndrome. Somehow, no matter the circumstances, we, the eldest children in our families, were responsible for all the things that went wrong, while our siblings seemed to get away with everything. After all, they were the "babies." With more than a foot of height between us, we must have looked a bit funny walking together, but I always admired Anita because she kept up with me. She would tread alongside my legs, at least twice the length of hers, seldom falling behind. When her bookbag was so heavy that it slowed her down, I would get behind her, place one hand on her back, and proclaim, "I'll make a man out of you yet!" pushing her along to keep pace with my strides.

I admired Anita for many reasons, the main one being that she didn't seem to care about how others might perceive her. She always had friends, she was a good student, she was eager to find part-time jobs, and she never complained when she had to be at Mr. Bagel, a local coffee shop in our neighborhood, at 7 on Sunday mornings to prepare for the bagels and lox crowds. Anita was, and still is, my Voice of Reason. She and I could talk about anything, anything I was willing to discuss anyway, and she always gave me an honest and direct perspective. Always kind and compassionate, she was, and is, a straight shooter. She never entertained going to the "dark side" of the mean girls or the bullies; that was not her. She was empathic, and even though she did not officially know of my struggles, she intuited them. She took care of me as a big sister might, constantly reminding me that I was loved and safe and had a friend in her. Unbeknownst to her, she was my shield.

The bullying continued, sometimes more overtly and other times more nuanced, but I felt it. In high school, with my few close friends, I was well-liked enough, but that was when I began to bully myself. While I did not know or understand what homosexuality was at that time, I often cursed myself and chastised myself for thinking about men in a sexual way. Not for religious reasons and not to judge those who might engage in those practices; it just felt "wrong." There was no world in which I could explore that aspect of myself, nor did I want to lead girls on. So, the only ethical option was for me to be platonic friends with those around me. I was genuinely happy for my friends who found partners, soulmates, and sex buddies. I lived vicariously through them. But at the end of the night, when the couples would want their alone time to make out and have sex, I would go home alone and castigate myself for being peculiar and odd.

Why couldn't I be normal and feel what I was *supposed* to be feeling, affection and lust for girls, and get on with my life? Was it so difficult to put these disruptive thoughts and feelings aside, commit to a particular way of life, and proceed? In so many aspects of my life, I succeeded. Why not with this, too? But every time I met a nice girl and befriended her, and we began to move out of the "friend zone" and into the physical, I felt conflicted. Physical yearning versus integrity. The times I pushed myself beyond the initial stages of my honor code, seeing if there was a place somewhere deeper inside of me where being with a woman could feel "right," I always found my answer. The longer I was with that particular woman, the more I ended up hurting or offending her by saying, "It's not you; it's me." I was not ready to disclose the real reason for my need to disconnect, and so again, I would walk away feeling profound sadness for the pain I caused and for the wretched behavior on my part. For the boy who was always soothed and more comfortable around girls, the boy who was more of a feminist than many of his friends who were girls, I was not treating women respectfully. I was championing my girlfriends to pursue activities or endeavors they believed were beyond them. "Go on!" "Why not?!" I challenged them. "You can do it just as well as anyone, male or female!"

And then to be that guy who lies and mistreats women, well, that did not sit well with me at all.

The negative self-talk that went on inside my head when I knew I was living a lie became so oppressive that in my mid-twenties, I decided the bullying I was engaging in toward myself, trying to become someone I am not, had to stop. I respected women, and people for that matter, too much to continue to contort my emotional self into something I just was not able to sustain. As much as I could, and did, functionally engage sexually with women, the emotion was not there. Not the emotion I wanted from an authentic relationship. With a man at some point. But if not, then alone. I committed to be kinder to myself, which meant to stop dating women. Until I was more comfortable to share with those around me that I was gay, I would not date.

This decision enlightened me to the fact that I was no longer willing to accept being bullied by others. I had been mistreated and victimized plenty in my younger life, and then I took over the role of tormentor. I felt it from my parents when they expelled me from their lives, but I found the strength to stand up for myself and be me. I was hopefully not going to allow anyone again, certainly no friend or partner, to take those reins. If people were not going to like me or accept me, then that would be their choice, and I would find a way to live with that choice. I learned to know myself well enough by this point in my life to appreciate that I was patient and tolerant but not long-suffering. I would always be willing to talk things out, listen to others, and genuinely consider their points of view. And, if it turned out I had missed their perspective, I would be open to change. As stubborn as I was, I knew it was a self-protective mechanism. It wasn't because I *needed* to be right. I stood my ground so as not to let another push me away from what I believed. In fact, I have always been quite forgiving, but if pushed too far, I, too, finally had a limit, including my own thoughts. Therefore, for others to tell me what I must do or what I was allowed, was no longer an option.

At this point in my life, my relationship with loneliness became clear. I would choose to be alone, and lonely, if need be, rather than to feel trapped in a relationship that did not see me for who I was and what I was able to offer. I kept myself company well enough when I needed to. I could read, I could hike, I could watch television, and I could lose myself in thoughts and fantasies that would take me away from the very issues that triggered any particular bout of aloneness. I enjoyed being around others but did not need to be. My long-term self-respect was more important to me than diminishing my self-worth for someone else's pleasure or need. Working during the week and meeting the needs of the lawyers in the firm, I did what I signed on to do. Volunteering with the special needs families on Sunday mornings and being there for them felt right to me. Saturday was errand and household chores day. By my choice, not anyone else's. But in the downtime, I began feeling comfortable going to the movies alone. Driving down the coast and stopping along the way on my own. Exploring new hiking trails in Los Angeles was a fun activity, sometimes driving way too far for what turned out to be a dud of a trail. But I did what I wanted to do. At this point in my life, I must have decided to stand up to any bullying I was faced with and not back down. Even if it meant that facing that bully would leave me with a bruised face or ego, as long as I would stand up for myself, I knew I would be the victor.

Thinking back to the days I arrived in Willowdale, Ontario, Canada, with my immigrant parents made me stronger. They must have been scared, but they did it. They must have felt vulnerable, but they overcame it. Fear and anxiety can be bullies, and there was no way that my parents did not experience those emotions. Not that I saw it or knew it, but now, as an adult, I believe this existed. Their determination to make a better life for themselves and their family kept them going. I remember that some of the other families who lived near us, also originally from Israel, returned after a few years. The story was often the same: they just couldn't make a life here. Even as a boy, I remember thinking to myself, 'What do you mean? You just have to try harder.' That's what my parents did, and that is what was modeled for me. Now it's my turn.

16
THE WAITING GAME

———— ❧ ————

"Hi, I'm Rami Aizic, and I have a 9:45 appointment." I stood at the desk, feeling both sheepish and excited. This was my second time at the clinic, with the same woman behind the desk as last time. Not that I expected her to remember me; she greeted dozens of people every day. But for me, to show up at a facility where it was known, I would be led into a room to masturbate and leave my sample. Well, that was still somewhat embarrassing.

"Hi, is all your information the same as last time you were here?" she asked. I acknowledged that it was, and she invited me to sit down since I was a bit early. I looked around and saw two other men, seated, and I projected my discomfort onto them and assumed that they, too, were finding it difficult to make eye contact with anyone else in the room. They each had their eyes glued to the magazine pages in front of them, but if I were to guess, I would say neither of them was absorbing a single word of the articles on those glossy pages. There was also a couple in the waiting room, and they were whispering to each other. I assumed they were there for a preliminary consultation with one of the doctors, perhaps to find out why they weren't becoming pregnant. There were a few doctors in this particular practice of fertility specialists, so it made sense that men, women, and couples would all have reason to be here at different times for different reasons when it came to the issue of procreation.

Just as I sat down, one of the two seated men was called. As he stood, I noticed what a handsome man he was. Tall, swarthy, olive complexion, rugged build. He had a head of thick, dark hair, wavy, parted, and swept to one side. He was wearing a very flattering and expensive-looking suit, dark navy blue, with a faint but present grey pinstripe. A crisp white shirt, starched collar, and a navy, lavender, and white patterned tie completed the outfit. Not to mention the highly polished black Oxford lace-up shoes. He might have been Mediterranean, perhaps Middle Eastern. I couldn't tell by the name. I remember thinking that whoever had his babies would likely have extremely attractive kids.

As was the custom in most, if not all, doctors' offices, due to privacy and confidentiality, little of the identifying features of patients was to be revealed. So, it was not uncommon for a nurse to call out a first name only and wait to see if only one person responded. If that were the case, no more information needed to be spoken aloud in the waiting room. Mr. Swarthy closed his magazine and placed it face down on the empty chair next to him. In one seamless movement, he stood up and nodded in the direction of the nurse. He followed her through a door with a light wooden frame holding within it a vertical piece of white frosted glass. I would be going through that door at some point, too, since that was the procedure last time.

After my last session of couples' therapy with Mason, he and I had a rough patch together. Since the meeting with Elaine was in the middle of the day, we each returned to our respective offices and finished our days. That night, once we reconvened at home, tension surrounded us as we made, ate, and cleaned up dinner. We made small talk, neither of us broaching the topic from earlier that day. "I think we need to talk about it, don't you?" I asked Mason as we were putting the last of the glasses in the dishwasher. He agreed. We sat down at the kitchen table, a round, wooden table we'd found at an antique stall, which was the first piece of furniture we purchased together. It was a style neither of us would have looked for, but for some reason, the look of it, along with the chairs that had both ample seats and high rounded backs, making them quite comfortable, convinced us to come out of our individual comfort zones when it came to design, and to purchase something different, something novel for us both.

"I didn't appreciate the ultimatum you gave me," Mason said.

"No, I'm sure it didn't feel good," I responded. "But now you might understand how I have been feeling throughout this entire process."

I expressed to Mason that ever since we actively began moving forward with me having a biological child, as much as his words were encouraging and positive, his actions were not. Not that there were too many actions prior to Robin coming into our lives. I pointed out that to me, it had felt very "ultimatum-like" that if I did what Mason found comfortable and familiar, then he was supportive. But, whenever I departed from his familiarity, the support was gone, and I was either scolded or shut out. Anger would come out of Mason, and to me, it looked and felt like petulant behavior. I gave Mason examples of his conduct being less than a model, none of which I enjoyed, nor did he.

"Why do you do that? Why do you bring up the past? We're talking about the present." He challenged me with this statement, one he had pointed out to me in prior disagreements. Mason's contention was that I hold onto the past and "throw it in his face" when we argue or differ on topics. My counterargument to that was that instead of throwing it in his face, I was trying to show him this pattern. And, I would show him how often I had accommodated and acquiesced to his ways. My error in letting Mason get his way so often. I told him that night, "I have my limit. And having a baby is not something I plan on letting you dictate how to do." I reminded Mason that his situation was far removed from ideal, and mine might be, too. But rather than do things his way, especially since they didn't turn out particularly harmonious for any of the three adults or Ben, I was willing to try something else.

"Yes, it's a risk. I know. This is all unknown. Just as your approach was unknown to you and the mommies. But what other options do I have?" While that was meant as more of a rhetorical question, Mason came up with suggestions, all of which had to do with waiting. Waiting for another woman. Waiting for the ability to do this via surrogacy. Waiting for me to be more settled in my career. But I suspected Mason was offering these options so he could become more comfortable with the idea, or, in my more cynical moments, maybe I would give up the entire idea altogether. Mason does not like to feel inferior to anyone, not when conditions are similar. Here, I was in some way 'challenging' Mason's ability to create a family, and I felt that he was feeling threatened. I might get it 'right.' My way might not produce the difficulties that arose for him.

From my early childhood, I had learned to shut up, blend into the background, and let others take the spotlight. I did not welcome attention because it so often led to me being seen in a negative light. The fat kid. The unathletic kid. I became quite comfortable, unhealthily so, with self-deprecation and self-minimization. Mason needed to feel like the winner, and I was content with feeling the loser. A perfect pairing. Yet, once pushed to my limit, I often said, "You were off the list." No more. As patient as I was, and I was very patient when something was of particular importance to me, I went after it. I broke it down to Mason.

"Look, Mace, I want to be direct and honest and transparent with you. I will have no hard feelings if you decide this is not what you want. Really."

"What does that mean to you?" he said, with equal tones of therapist and apprehension in his voice.

"I plan on going through with this. With you, which is my preference, or without."

"Really?" He sounded surprised. "You would just walk away from this? From us?"

"Is there really still an 'us?'" I asked, looking at Mason squarely in the eyes, honestly wanting to know how he was feeling about that.

"What do you mean?! Of course, there is an 'us.'" I believed that he truly believed that.

"And maybe that's at the core of this."

What I was not willing to live in or with was resentment and a power struggle.

"If you choose to stay in this relationship, you need to support me in my pursuit. Whether it's Robin or someone else, this is going to be about me first, not you. *Me* in the spotlight, and you in the supporting role."

During this time, I obviously didn't share anything with Robin about what was going on at home. I was still following the trail that seemed to be unfolding in front of me. Where it would lead, I didn't know, but I had to follow the breadcrumbs. Robin arranged for her gynecologist to attempt to inseminate her rather than for her to go to a clinic. She felt comfortable with Dr. Charlie, who had been a part of Robin's family for years, and although he did admit he wasn't set up to do this as a fertility clinic was, he knew the basics of what needed to be done, and he would try. Robin had spoken to medical professionals about the best ways to track her ovulation, keep track of her body temperature, and find the best day or days for insemination. Once identified, I was told where to go and what to do, and we would see if things worked. Unfortunately, but not surprisingly, Robin's first attempt did not take. She had her period two weeks later, at which time she, Dr. Charlie, and I all decided it made more sense for us to do this at a fertility clinic. The reality was that for me, not much would be different. I had to appear at that facility and leave my sample. When we did it the first time, Robin picked up my sample and took it with her to Dr. Charlie's office. This time, it would be left at the fertility clinic, and Robin would come in later in the day for the insemination procedure.

I must have lost track of time or not paid any attention to it, but at some point, while I was still seated in the waiting room, Mr. Swarthy came back through the same door he had entered. Only now, he was no longer that same put-together, composed gentleman. He was holding his suit jacket over his right shoulder by his right index and middle fingers. His once-crisp white shirt was extremely creased and wrinkled from the chest down, with the top two buttons of the shirt undone and the knot of the tie loosened, askew, leaning left. His hair was rumpled and messy, tousled really, but nothing like it looked earlier. This man looked like he had been in a ferocious windstorm. Or a fight. Or engaged in a fight while out in a windstorm. What went on in that room? How aggressive does one have to be while masturbating? After all, he wasn't at home, in the privacy of his environment where he could fantasize about whatever scenario he chose, act it out, role play, use costumes. . . He was in a clinical facility, where others would also need to use the same room. It fascinated me to contemplate what was going on in that room, both inside and outside this man's head. I didn't know how many rooms there were for us men to use, and I speculated as to whether I would know if the room I would be called into was the same as the one just used by Mr. Swarthy.

Jolted from my reverie, I heard my name, and I trekked the same path as he, and so many others, had done, through the door that led to the rooms in which couples became families. I did what was expected of me and informed the nurse on my way out that I left the sample in the designated area. I asked her what time Robin was due to come in. I hoped that day would be the day that would change the rest of my life. Two weeks later, we found out we were not pregnant.

Robin and I were determined to try again, which we planned for the following month. As Robin monitored and tracked her body, the day for our subsequent insemination was set for November 9, 1998, which was not at all a convenient day for me. On that particular Monday morning, I was scheduled to be a guest lecturer at the University of Southern California. I had been approached by a veteran psychologist and psychology professor at USC to speak on the implications of corporate culture on the psyche and how individuals and companies could better prepare for what they might encounter. This professor had heard I was a former lawyer, now practicing psychology, and asked around about me both at my school and my traineeship. He had heard that I was quite knowledgeable about the corporate structure and how psychology can affect it, both in negative and positive ways. He wanted to help his students understand that regardless of where they ended up in their professional lives, appreciating the fact that psychology could be a useful tool in helping them navigate those lives would keep them more centered and mentally healthy. My task was to educate the students about "family systems," any communal construct in which one lives. These systems can be one's family of origin or chosen family but also include the dynamics of one's friend group, workplace community, or any team or congregation of people one chooses to participate in.

A "family" is much more than those related by blood or marriage in psychological terms. It is a collection of people joining together for a common purpose, each of those individuals bringing their history and life experiences and their baggage. Being cognizant of that prior to entering the fold allows one to be their better "self." Also, recognizing that one seldom knows in advance the backdrop and background of others is another issue to prepare for. It sounds like a bit of a conundrum, to prepare for the unknown, but to the extent that one can do that, that is precisely what will help make life smoother.

Coincidentally, that was exactly what was occurring in my own life as I was about to lecture on it. Robin, an unknown, and I were embarking on an adventure whose outcome neither of us could know. There would definitely be an impact on those around us, again, with the lack of knowledge as to what that impact would be. We were creating a family system of Robin, me, Mason, Robin's mother Marlene, my parents, the mommies, and Ben . . . concentric circles that had no end.

The clinic opened at 8 a.m.; I was to be in the classroom at 9 a.m. The driving distance between the clinic and the classroom was 23 miles. That did not take into account my time at the clinic, getting lost, looking for a place to park, parking, walking to the building itself, finding the classroom, and, of course, traffic. Los Angeles traffic. Whatever you have heard about L.A. traffic is either true or worse than you imagine. Monday morning rush hour traffic is particularly harsh, with more and more people on the road, all trying to get to destinations that inevitably are the exact ones you need to get to. At the same time as you. But, this was the day Robin's body was going to be most primed for insemination, and we weren't going to forgo it. With every month that passed, Robin was getting older, and we were more susceptible to unaccounted events to derail us from our decisions. I could have requested to teach my class on another day, but being a new clinician and feeling exceptionally honored to be asked to do this, I did not want to appear cocky or arrogant. I shared with my host what I needed to do that morning and said that I might be a bit late. I gave him the option of suggesting a change to the date, but that didn't come, so on with the plan. My goal was to be waiting at the front door of the clinic when it opened, get in, do what needed to be done, and then get on the road.

I was already parked in front of the door of the clinic at 7:45 on that morning, waiting at the door on the fourth floor of the building, hoping someone on the other side of the door would open it early and I could benefit from the extra few minutes. I was unaccustomed to such anxiety. Once I heard movement on the other side of the door, I knocked, and a familiar face opened the door. I explained that I needed to be downtown, asking if there was any way I could get in a bit early. Without hesitation, she accompanied me through the waiting room, down the hall, and to the room assigned to me for my task. "I will leave you here," she said at the door with a smile on her face. "Sample cups are on the counter."

I was already familiar with the interior of this room and the magazines and videos to "help" me along in the process. I opted for doing it cold turkey. It was yet another of those bizarre moments in my life where I found myself musing on my existence at the moment. I was in a fertility clinic, about to leave a semen sample to be inseminated into a woman, a straight woman, who might become the mother of my child, a child I intended to raise with her and my gay partner.

Who was I? Yet, at that moment, it was all so normal. Not ordinary. Certainly not conventional. But normal. This was where my efforts and my determination led me to be. The people pleasing, the acquiescing, the placating, and the foregoing were no longer present. Not at this moment in time. This moment was for me. *Me!* Unapologetically.

Once I was done, I hurried back to my car and did my best to get to the next event of the day, another unique one for me, but oh-so-different from where I had just been. Somehow, with the traffic gods looking down on me, I moved along the freeway faster than at crawl speed, yet not at full throttle. I reached my destination, took in a giant breath, and entered the classroom. After the presentation and appreciation from the students and the professor, I was heading back to my car. I had to stop and laugh to myself. What a morning! I had to perform two disparate tasks in two disparate rooms. The former could reveal the next stage of my life in a personal way, taking me from childless to parent. The latter could lead me down a professional path, moving me from novice to expert. From student to teacher. From one iteration of myself to a more evolved, more established self. Such unknowns, and they were both so exciting and terrifying.

It would be a couple of weeks, again, before we would find out if this insemination would take. I called Robin to let her know I had been at the clinic and left the sample. Later that day, she informed me that she had arrived at her appointed time, and according to the nurses, all went well. Now, we would wait.

Over the next few days, Robin and I checked in with each other. Robin shared that she was trying to "listen" to her body, trying to intuit what it was telling her and if it was revealing any news. In reality, the same sensations that might be indicative of pregnancy could be those of her upcoming menstrual cycle. We were both cautious. Optimistic, hopeful, but cautious.

These days were also ones where Mason and I were getting along much better. Something changed in, or for, Mason, and he was much more sensitive and caring with me, as opposed to the emotionally detached partner he had been. He asked, from time to time, how I was feeling, wanting to hear about the latest insemination. He wandered down the fantasy road with me, envisioning what life might look like for us having a baby in the house. I contemplated asking him what changed, but I didn't want to come across as challenging or unappreciative. Still, a part of me held back my total outpouring of excitement and fear, worrying that I might, once again, feel abandoned by Mason. I opted to talk to him rather than ask him questions. I did share that I was feeling happy he and I were getting along better and that I was grateful for his increased curiosity and attention toward me and the process.

"It feels really nice, feeling like I have you back."

While he did not respond with words, the glistening in his eyes, with tears trying to peak out, told me that he felt the same.

One evening, Mason and I had decided to treat ourselves by going out to dinner in the middle of the week. We were both homebodies of sorts, me more than Mason. But, between my finances and Mason's busy schedule, we enjoyed and valued the time we spent together at the end of each day. Standing together in the kitchen, prepping whatever we were going to make for dinner that night, and catching up on our days was always a treat. It seemed so natural for us. That night, as we both looked in the fridge, wondering what we wanted to make to eat, Mason suggested we go to a nearby local restaurant, have a quick bite, and come back home to watch TV. To my credit, at first, I bristled slightly on the inside, but I soon realized it was not about money or anything other than convenience. So I pushed myself happily out of my comfort zone, and off we went.

Less than two hours later, we parked in our carport and headed for the back door, continuing to talk about whatever we were discussing in the car, when I noticed a small gift bag on the stoop. I pointed it out to Mason, who wondered what it could be. As we moved closer, I picked it up, a small, shiny bag that looked and felt more like mylar than paper. The rope handles were loosely tied together with a small string attached to a gift card. With Mason standing at my side, I looked inside the bag, and removed two cigars and a small yellow rubber duck. When I read the card, I began to cry. "Congratulations, Daddies. Love, Robin."

17
CHOOSING FATHERHOOD AGAINST THE ODDS

The pregnancy was, happily, uneventful. I went with Robin to the first few ultrasounds, as well as to some of the early doctor's appointments. The baby was growing nicely, and thankfully, after the genetic testing and the amniocentesis, we learned we would not need to make any unthinkable decisions. We were moving forward in the same way the baby was: vigorously. We knew the highest risk to any pregnancy was throughout the first trimester, so we all decided we would not announce the news until the start of the second trimester. Of course, I knew Robin would share the news with a few people, as I would too. But, to the general population connected to our world, the revelation would come later. During those early weeks, Robin, Mason, and I spent time together being social. I hoped Mason and Robin would find more common ground and interests so I would not feel as responsible for making them more comfortable around each other. Again, happily, they did. Mason had decided to be with me, and this was a part of me that was happening in real time. Robin knew nothing of the stress between Mason and me regarding moving forward with a child. What she did know, from that first day that she and I met, was that Mason was a part of my life, and if she was uncomfortable with that, for any reason, she held all the cards. It was ultimately her choice to move forward with having a child with me or not, knowing what she knew about me. I was Israeli-born. I grew up in Toronto. I went to law school and lived in England for three years. I was moving from one profession to another. I was a social person. I was liberal and progressive in my politics. I was musically inclined. I was gay. I was partnered. Along with the many more facets of my life that she learned prior to deciding to continue down the path of creating a family, it was her decision to do so.

I had to believe she was sincere; after all, why would she burden herself with all this cargo if all she wanted was a child? As she and I had discussed many times, and she reiterated just as many, she wanted a family for her child, a father for her child. She could be a single mother by choice, but she didn't want her child to have no other immediate family. She seemed to like the idea of having my extended family, especially since both of my parents were from Romania, and one set of her grandparents were also Romanian. She appreciated that Mason and I could expose our child to aspects of life not within her wheelhouse or expertise or interest. This child would be greater than the sum of its parts. Part Robin, part me, and all the other parts of our respective lives, including family and friends, create an expansive world for this little person. And yes, this child would be a product of a less-than-conventional family organism, but by choice. All the members of this child's life would be there because they, we, wanted to be. There would be nothing accidental about how this child came into the world.

Once we got the "all clear" from Robin's doctor that the baby was healthy and we had entered the second trimester, I wanted to tell my parents that they were going to be grandparents again. My brother and sister-in-law had two little girls to whom I was as close as was realistic, given that they lived in Toronto. The nice thing was that my parents, known as Saba (Grandpa) and Savta (Grandma) in Hebrew, had the opportunity to be active, hands-on grandparents. Dana's entire family was in Germany, where she was from, so my parents had very little competition for primary family time.

I discussed with Mason how and when to tell my parents, and I decided I wanted them to be the first of the family members to hear the news. I picked a date, and wanted Mason by my side when I told them. We opted for a day after work for both of us, one when we were both done relatively early, so it would not be too late in Toronto. I would go to Mason's office, and call them from there. Mason had more privacy in his office than I had in mine, and I wanted to ensure that in case things went badly, I had the space to gather myself. So many iterations went through my head as to what to say. Should I lead with a backstory, or start with the news itself? How much should I share about who Robin is and how we met? What should I tell them about why *she* was choosing to do this? No one in our orbit could truly share the same narrative as the one I was about to share with them. They knew Mason's history of bringing a child into the world, but that was different from this. Still, I could use its template in case I needed to help them understand some of the logistics. To the extent that I understood the logistics myself. This was all unexplored territory to Robin, to Mason, to me, to our friends and acquaintances: we were pioneers. Like my parents were when they arrived in Israel after World War II, they suffered through the labors of learning a new language, working the land, and fighting for the rights of immigrants so there could be a place they could call home. In a way, I was doing the same. As a gay man wanting my biological child, I was undertaking a path not yet clearly identified but risking it because if it were to succeed, I could find my "home," my own "family." That was the home I was choosing to build.

One fear I had about sharing this news with my parents was that they would, once again, abandon and reject me. It had happened before, and it could happen again. I, and we, worked so hard to get through those years of silent anger and hurt that I did not want either side to have to endure that again. It was difficult enough for them to come to terms with having a gay son and then having family and friends find out about it. As far as I know, for the longest time, they did not tell anyone, but after a while, they had no choice but to acknowledge it. I had heard that my parents said to those who found out that they were 'broken,' 'devastated,' 'embarrassed,' 'depressed.' "How could he do this to us?" was how they put it. Still, I stood my ground, creating the life I wanted to have, making room for all who wanted to be part of my life to remain a part of my life. Sadly, there were some, including my parents, who chose not to accept me for my authentic self, leading to divergent lives. I dreaded this materializing again. I wanted this to be joyful news, but my trepidation got the better of me. I didn't want to have later-in-life memories of telling my parents about one of the most euphoric moments of my life, and have it tinged with negativity and scorn. This would be one of the most monumental moments of my life, telling my parents they would be grandparents again, this time by their other son, the one whom they had resigned themselves to never having children. I did not want it spoiled.

I walked over to Mason's office, literally hearing beats in my ears, coming from the profundity of my heart beating like I had never felt before. The walk from my office to Mason's was less than five minutes, but shortly into it, I was perspiring. Obviously, it was not due to the strenuousness of walking on a flat sidewalk but to the adrenaline gushing through my bloodstream. It was a sunny but cold day in early February 1999, with people bundled up as only seen in Southern California. Women in short skirts, bare legs, T-shirts, and fuzzy scarves wrapped around their necks and clunky woolly boots on their feet. Some of the men in suits walking in Beverly Hills had their jackets buttoned and their hands in their pants pockets, causing the bottom of the jacket to splay out like wings. With plenty of activity on the street, everyone was engrossed in their existence, and nobody paid any attention to me. I thought, "What if some of these people knew what I was about to do? What was I about to say to my immigrant parents? That their gay son was having a child with a straight woman while happily making a life with his male partner? And we were all planning to be one big happy family? Would they stop in their tracks? Would they at least stop what they were thinking about and show me compassion and support?" I was worried about losing one set of parents, so I guess I was looking to find substitutes. Replacement parents, alternate or stand-by parents, until my birth parents would hopefully return.

When Mason came to get me from his waiting room, I lunged at him and held him tightly. I was scared. Very emotional. He held me, saying nothing. No words could calm me, but his presence could. We walked into his office, and he closed the door, pulled out his desk chair for me, and sat down next to it.

"Do you know what you're going to say?" he asked.

"I think so."

And with that, I dialed the ten digits needed to connect me from Los Angeles to Toronto, waiting for the receiver on the other end to lift and for me to hear an accented voice, either male or female, say, "Hello?" My mother answered, and she sounded happy yet surprised to hear from me. It was not common for me to call at this hour on a weekday as I was usually working. The first thing she asked was if everything was okay. I assured her that it was, that Mason and I had both finished work early, and I wanted to call to say hello, see how they were, and share some "very exciting news." I asked her to get my dad on the extension, which he picked up quite quickly—still feeling my temples throbbing as if to the beat of a metronome, I soldiered on.

"You know how family is very important to me, and how much I always wanted children." I began.

"Yeah." My mother said in response.

"And you know that even though I'm gay, I know other gay people, like Mason, who have children."

"Of course, we know Mason has Ben!" My mother sounded a bit exasperated, probably wondering, 'Where is this going?'

"Mason and I have met several gay people who have created their own families. It's happening more and more these days." I continued.

"Ok." My mother again.

This was it. I was about to get to the core. "For the longest time, I've been saying to friends that I wanted to have a child, so if they knew anyone who might want to have one with me, to let me know."

At this point, I went through the story of Scottie, whom they had heard me mention, and how he met a woman and introduced us. Her name was Robin, and we talked about how we both wanted children.

"She's not married, she's straight, and she doesn't have any children, but she does want them. Over the past few months, Robin, Mason, and I have spent time together, getting to know each other. After a lot of talking, we decided we wanted to go ahead and have a child together."

I paused, thinking that maybe my parents wanted, or needed, to say something. But, the silence on the other end directed me to continue.

"Well, she's pregnant! We just finished the first trimester, and the baby is healthy. Mazel tov! You're going to be grandparents again!"

I closed by telling them that I loved them, and that I would talk to them again soon.

I did it! I said what I wanted to say! I actually did it! I was shaking, and began to get teary-eyed. Mason took my hands in his and smiled, and we sat there in the quiet for a while. Even though the same thumping was happening in my head, somehow, my brain was interpreting it differently than earlier. The messaging now was elation, accomplishment. I had taken on a seemingly impossible quest and conquered it. My parents said very little on the call, but what they didn't say was most significant to me. They did not tell me that I was making a mistake, nor did they say anything negative at all. They let me share my news, they listened, and we finished off the conversation with a friendly tone.

Mason asked, "What did they say?" but for some reason, I wasn't responding.

"Were they happy? Did they have questions?" Again, I said nothing. Mason looked at me for what felt like a considerable amount of time and asked again. "Ram, what did they say?"

When I finally spoke, all I said in response was, "They're not mad at me."

No matter how old I was and how accomplished I became, at the core, I still wanted my parents' approval. Not that they said anything particularly approving of my news, but they didn't dismiss it. Or me. There was no rejection of me, the one thing I feared most. I still had my family as I told them that I was creating my own family. I dreaded thinking that now that I had a child on the way, I would have to give up my parents. The repetitive experience I had suffered so many times already, this time, did not arise. When I came out as gay, I feared having to give up a family. When I found a woman to have a child with, I fought to keep my partner. Now that I had both my partner and the baby, I was jeopardizing grandparents for that child. So far, everything was still in place.

A few days later, when I spoke to my parents again, they did have more questions. My mother told me that it was a shock, but not in a bad way. She admitted that at first, she and my dad sat in their self-allocated seats at the kitchen table, shaking their heads, wondering why I was doing this to them. Hadn't I put them through enough already? What were they going to tell people? How were they going to explain that their gay son was having a baby with a woman while in a relationship with a man? What would become of this child? Would the mother let me see that child? Who was this woman, anyway? My mother obviously needed to unload her fears, anger, and insecurities on me before getting to the other side of our exchange.

I remember thinking that so far, everything she had identified was about her and my dad, not about me or the fact that there was going to be another member of our immediate family. The content was negative. Would I jump in at some juncture and point this fact out, or would I sit there, listen, take it all in, and swallow the pain, as I had so many times in the past? Before I had to make that decision, though, my mother did reach what seemed like a moment of a different perspective.

"Aba and I *are* happy to hear that you are having a baby. We know how much you want that."

"Thanks for saying that," I said in return. I really appreciate that."

She continued. "Maybe you told us, but I want to know some more about this woman. Is she Jewish?" There was something oddly comforting about that question. It reassured me that she was still my Ima.

She asked who the woman was, how we met, what we were planning to do about where the child would live, who would take care of the baby, and what my financial obligations were. And she even asked if we had a name picked out. I answered each and every one of her questions, leaving airspace between sentences so she could interject or ask a follow-up question before we moved on. When we reached the conclusion, she again asked about a name.

"The three of us have not picked a name yet. It's still early. But, of course, Mason and I have been thinking of some."

"If it's a girl, maybe Jessica. Jessica is such a happy name." That was my mother's contribution, which I took as a prominent sign of approval, or at least acceptance.

As my heart swelled with happiness, I responded, "I will add it to the list."

The next family members to meet were Robin's mother, Marlene, and her then-husband Stuart. Robin had shared the news with her mother, and according to Robin, her mother, a liberal, progressive, independent woman, was initially surprised at the unexpected news. This quickly turned to excitement and happiness: her firstborn was going to have her firstborn soon. Admittedly, Marlene wanted her daughter to experience this more traditionally, with a husband, or at least a man in Robin's life, but again, according to Robin, her mother was thrilled.

Robin and her mother were extremely close. They lived across the street from one another, Robin having lived with her mother at various points in her adult life. Marlene was one of the first female stockbrokers in Los Angeles. She was married to Robin's father, with whom she had Robin and Robin's younger brother. That marriage did not last, and Marlene went on to marry her second husband, Syd, the man who Robin referred to as her dad. He was a marriage and family therapist, like I was going to be, and Robin always spoke of him with tremendous love and admiration. Syd was blind, but that did not keep him from consuming knowledge, mostly by way of listening to the radio. Twin girls were born to Marlene and Syd, making a total of four children. Unfortunately, when Robin was a fairly young woman, Syd became ill and died.

When I met Robin, her brother, Mark, was not in the picture. He had a falling out with the family, and although he lived in Los Angeles and was married with a child, there was no contact with him. Equally absent from the family's life was one of the twin girls, Judy. She had her share of issues with the family, and although she trained and worked as a doctor in Los Angeles, she was not in communication with the family. Robin was close to the other twin, Lisa. She was married to Robert, had a son, and became pregnant with a girl a few months before Robin did. According to Robin, Lisa was her main cheerleader regarding whether or not to become involved in this atypical family setup. Weighing the pros and cons, Lisa came down firmly on the side of the pros. She knew how much Robin wanted to be a mother, and this was a way for Robin to realize that dream while having the support she would undoubtedly need. We arranged for Robin, Marlene, and Stuart to come to our house, where Mason and I would host them for a Sunday brunch, and we could all become acquainted in a private setting rather than a public restaurant. This would give us all the room for discretion in discussing whatever would arise.

All three arrived a few minutes after 11 a.m., the agreed upon time for brunch. Marlene was shorter than I expected her to be, given that Robin stood five-foot-seven or so. With honey-brown short, wavy hair, she had fair skin and was smartly dressed. Either it was her history of being a corporate woman, or she wanted to make a good impression on the man who would be the father of her soon-to-be-grandchild. She arrived with a bouquet in her hand, a racetrack cake, a pastry, which she said was one of the standout pastries of all her years growing up in Los Angeles. Stuart, also shorter than Robin, had a head of white hair and was a nice-looking, fit older man. Marlene was, in stature, thickset, and I could see some similarities between Robin and her mother. At first glance, Robin was in some ways a taller, larger version of her mother in her physique, yet Robin had a youthful radiance, especially through her luminous green eyes. We made our introductions all around and sat at the table that Mason had set for the five of us.

As I knew he would, Mason wanted to feel "primary" in some way at this meeting since it was really going to be about me. We expected that Marlene would scrutinize me, making sure I was in no way considering taking advantage of her daughter. I thought of Mason as my "plus one." He was not under the microscope. I let Mason plan the menu and set the table. He was much more attentive to aesthetics than I was, and I had no concerns at all that he would arrange a table fitting for a positive first impression. One thing I did insist on was making a particular salad that I grew up with, an Israeli potato salad. My mother would make this salad on special occasions, and this seemed the right nod to my mother since she could not physically be there with us to meet Robin's mother. It was not a salad for formal events, but it was, as my mother would say, "a labor of love" to make. My mother learned to make this from her early days in Israel, on the kibbutz where she lived, and it reminded her of her early years of life after leaving Romania. Even though she was only fourteen, she had to become somewhat "adultified" and self-sufficient, and this salad was, for some reason, one of the early memories she had of that time of her life.

The salad itself consisted of cubing potatoes relatively small and boiling them in salt water. Added to that were peas, cooked carrots, cut about the same size as the potatoes, chopped pickles, dill, and a sauce of mustard and mayonnaise. The salad took on various flavors if it sat overnight, so I made it Saturday afternoon, covered it tightly, and left it in the fridge to do its magic. In addition to the salad, we also prepared bagels, cream cheese, Spanish onion cut into rings, tomatoes, scrambled eggs and sausages, coffee, orange juice, and champagne for mimosas, along with sparkling cider for Robin. Mason had also baked his famous and delicious chocolate brownies, bringing his past to the present, using the pan that had been in his family for decades. This recipe was his aunt's, but he perfected it over the years, resulting in one of his "known for" treats whenever we entertained. People expected his brownies.

I was less nervous than I thought I would be, yet I was aware of Mason's nervousness. I tried to reassure him that the hard part was already over-telling *my* parents. In the end, as much or as little as Robin's mother would favor this arrangement, it was done. Robin was pregnant, and she and I were going to be parents. Mason was going to be my partner in parenting, and I would soothe my parents' anxieties, and Robin would be responsible for her family.

As we sat around the table, Marlene opened up the conversation by saying that she was quite stunned at Robin's declaration, but "After all, there are all sorts of families these days, aren't there?" I was so happy to hear her say that. She was just as Robin had described her: progressive. One curious behavioral trait that I noticed very quickly about Marlene was that she was very similar to Mason in many ways. She was smart, direct, less-than-subtle at times. Her frankness could be disarming, yet it could also be quite brash. I interpreted this, as I did in Mason, as some insecurity that she lived with. Perhaps anxiety. Some traits that she hid quite well by presenting herself as capable and accomplished on the outside. Inside, there was still a vulnerable girl trying to hold it all together.

One curious statement that Mason, Robin, and I all remember is Marlene asking, in earnest, "Since you're Israeli, what's to stop you from taking the baby to Israel, never letting any of us see him or her again?" I didn't know how to respond to that. Should I smile and brush it off as a poor attempt at humor, or acknowledge how offensive it was. I found some middle ground.

"Well, that would negate the whole purpose of creating a *family*."

I did notice that Robin and Stuart, both of whom were sitting across the table from me, looked quite uncomfortable at Marlene's statement. I dared not look over at Mason for fear that he might pounce in response as a way to protect me from that comment. We were able to navigate our way out of those waters, and the rest of the brunch was friendly.

Other topics covered that day were politics, music, theater, ancestry, family histories, and professions. Robin sat quietly while Marlene did most of the talking on their side of the table, and it was fairly equal between Mason and me. Mason was able to share his history of Los Angeles; he and Marlene reminisced about restaurants no longer open and the divide between the city and the valley. Mason shared that his family was a musical family, as was Marlene's, so they had that in common, too. Since I did not grow up here, I had very little to contribute to the "olden days" part of the conversation, but I did enjoy seeing Mason and Marlene, along with Robin and Stuart, romanticizing over the days of yore.

Still, I was not off the hook.

Marlene asked me, "So really, why have a child this way and not by a surrogate?"

"For one thing, I really do want a large, or at least larger, family for my child."

She continued. "Did you consider surrogacy?"

"Yes, I did. I actually interviewed a few agencies that provide surrogacy services. Through the process, I realized that that is not what I want. I really do want something more traditional."

That seemed to satisfy Marlene for a moment until the next question, directed squarely at me, came.

"What's your vision for this child? And how does that vision fit into the construct of a larger family?"

Wow! It's as if she had these questions lined up and ready in advance.

"That's a great question. To be honest, I guess I have to think more about that. What I can tell you is that I grew up with cousins, aunts, uncles, and other immigrant families, and where I called my friends' parents Aunt and Uncle. Their kids were like our extended family."

Before I could continue, Marlene interrupted, leaning forward toward me across the table, eyes slightly tearing.

"That's what saved so many of the immigrant communities, the bonds that they clung to." She said.

I nodded slightly and continued. "And that is the template that I want for my child. A large, eclectic assortment of people who we all love and admire and trust, and those people will be our family.

On that, Marlene and I agreed wholeheartedly. As a gay man, I was both privileged to and penalized from being able to have two families: a family of birth and a family of choice. I shared a bit of my story of my family of birth, specifically my parents having such a difficult time accepting my homosexuality.

"So, for a while, it was as if I had no parents."

That punitive measure led me, like so many other gay men and women, to seek out a family of choice, friends who accepted me for who I was. This was my chosen family, which, thankfully and happily, included not only my gay and straight contemporaries but their parents as well.

"Having had the experience of an assortment of people being part of my family, I know it works. It helped me move from Israel to Toronto. It was a great comfort when I came to California. The concept works as long as we all agree to it from the beginning. I have no problem with that for my child."

"*Our* child," said Marlene, which I took to mean this assortment of people around the table.

After more than two hours at the table, all of us having eaten sufficiently, the meal and the visit came to a natural close. Stuart shook my hand and Mason's hand while Marlene was open to hugs. Robin seemed calmer now than when she arrived, more relaxed, and as we hugged each other goodbye. I whispered in her ear, "I think this went well." I could feel her head nodding against my neck, which made me feel happy.

When Robin told me that at her next appointment, we could find out the sex of the baby, I immediately knew I did not want to know. I wanted to savor the anticipation for as long as possible. In truth, it did not matter to me what sex the baby would be as long as it would be healthy. Of course, I had images of a little girl, dressing her up, letting her educate me as to what little girls are like. I had memories of my cousin Dalia's kids, the little girls, and how much fun we all had. I imagined my baby girl growing up to be a little kid, then an adolescent girl, knowing and trusting that I had already had some practice and experience being around girls of that age with Anita and Debbie, my two closest girlfriends. A little girl then grows up to be a woman, and how fantastic that would be. After being such an advocate of girls being equal to boys in nearly all ways, to have a daughter would mean she has a built-in support system and cheerleader at home.

If a boy, that, too, would be fantastic. I knew I could foster healthy self-esteem and be a present dad. I would not be one of those dads who worked all the time and was not emotionally available, like the dad I had. I could encourage a boy to pursue sports, art, music, or anything he wanted without judgment and without limitation. Again, I could be his built-in support system and cheerleader. I knew that I would need to nurture whatever this boy presented, no matter how uncomfortable it might be for me. While I would not be the soccer or baseball coach, I would be at every game. Neither would I be the dance instructor if he wanted to learn ballet. But I would be there, wherever *there* was for *him*.

I imagined watching a boy grow up into a young man, knowing some of what he would be going through physiologically and psychologically, helping to shepherd him through his maturation process to the extent that any boy allows his parents to do that. Eventually, my young adult son would find a partner, boy or girl, and I would wish them both a lifetime of happiness.

Either would be perfect. But Robin wanted to know, as did Mason.

"There is so much uncertainty about all of this," Robin said, "that knowing the sex of the baby is one thing we *can* know."

"I agree." Mason chimed in. "Why not know?"

"There is something very exciting to me about making this experience last until the birth of the baby." That was me, sharing the thoughts in my head out loud.

Robin smiled, but it was one of those polite smiles that is usually followed up by a "yeah, but."

"I want to know," Robin said again, adding nothing more.

Mason took a step toward Robin, turning to look at me. "I think we should know. We'll know better how to plan the baby's room and clothes to buy."

"Maybe that's part of it." I countered. "Jewish tradition is that we don't prepare too much in advance."

"But that is so impractical," Mason said.

"I don't even think I knew that that was a Jewish tradition." Said Robin.

Mason had an idea. "Well, if you don't want to know," he said again, looking at me, "Robin could let me know, and she and I can know, and you can be surprised."

That was not going to work for me. "No," I said. "I don't want to feel left out of this." I was not going to allow myself to venture so far into new territory only to be left feeling like I was on the outskirts of my own life again.

"Ok. We'll all know," I said.

The following day, Robin left a message on our phone to call her when we were free. "I have some news."

That evening, once Mason and I were both home, we stood in the kitchen, put the phone on speaker mode, and dialed Robin's number. We stood shoulder to shoulder, holding hands. Once Robin answered the phone with her usual melodious 'hello,' we exchanged appropriate pleasantries.

"You said you had some news," I said.

"First of all," Robin began, "everything is fine with the baby. My check-up went well, Uneventful."

"*Uneventful* might be the irony of the day." I couldn't help myself.

Mason smiled, as I am sure Robin did.

"And….." Mason moved the conversation along. Robin responded with four little words, which were the biggest four little words of my life up until that point. "We're having a girl."

18
SHOWERS OF LOVE

When Robin was well into her second trimester, it was time to share the news with not only the inner circles of our lives but the outer ones, too. One person I wanted to tell in person was the man who really made it all possible: Scottie. After all, if he hadn't called me on that fateful day to tell me about his lunch with Robin and their discussion of me as a possible option for her to have a baby with, then none of this would be taking place. Once every several weeks, Scottie and I planned on meeting for lunch halfway between our two offices, within walking distance for us both. On this particular day, we met at the same place, and as was our ritual, as soon as we saw each other, we hugged. Scottie said he liked hugging me because it forced him to stand on his tippy-toes. He was used to being tall, but at just over six feet, he was nearly four inches shorter than me. To look each other eye to eye, he had to stand on his toes, stretch his back to its fullest extension, and still hope I would slouch a bit. I never did. Once that was complete, we sat in a booth, as we always did, and ordered the same meals we always did. Creatures of habit.

We told each other how good the other one looked, which, as far as I was concerned, was always true about Scottie. He always looked refreshed and bubbly, the twinkle in his blue eyes announcing his impending arrival into a room before he ever entered it. And his broad smile below his bushy mustache always made me smile, too. Since we both had to get back to work, we talked while eating and over one another to ensure we said all that we wanted to say. We asked about each other's families, and I inquired about his powerhouse of a mom, Rosie. Standing less than five feet tall, Rosie was larger than life in so many ways. In her intellect, her business savvy, and her capacity to love her family, both blood and adoptive. Rose was ahead of her time. In a world of homosexuality hardly being widely accepted, she proudly walked into any room talking about her three children and their spouses. She included Scottie's partner as one of her children-in-law, just as she did with her son's wife and her daughter's husband. And she always wanted Scottie to have children, or at least one child. She knew that child would be loved, as her other grandchildren were, but Scottie was her baby, and she wanted her baby to have a baby. She praised me and encouraged me in my pursuits, telling me not to let conformity stand in my way. More than once, she looked directly into my eyes, her luminescent blue eyes, the same ones she passed down to Scottie, intent when she said, "If I waited around for people to let me do what I wanted to do, I would still be waiting." She would go on to tell me that some little old Jewish lady like herself was not going to *act* like some little old Jewish lady. She was going to be whoever she wanted to be, and that was what she tried to impart to her children. And when her beloved husband died quite suddenly, at the cemetery after the burial, those of us who were there witnessed her older son walking off with his wife and children, her daughter with her husband and her kids, and Rosie was flanked by Scottie on one side of her and Michael on the other. Conformity be damned.

Scottie and I caught up, shared, and gossiped, and as we started to say our goodbyes, I leaned in close over the table, took his hands, and said, "I have a bit of news to tell you before we leave. Congratulations! You're going to be a godfather." In my head, that made perfect sense since I had been thinking about Robin and pregnancy and Scottie being the one who brought us together, and now we were far enough along that we even had a name. Poor Scottie, though, had no idea what I was talking about. "I don't understand." That was all he said when I launched into the story, with as many details as I could fit into one long run-on sentence.

I recounted everything from the voicemail that he left for me through meeting Robin, talking to her about having a baby together, going to therapy about it, doctors' appointments, insemination, and now being pregnant with a girl. Later, as I thought about how I told Scottie all this news, I had an image in my head of his head blasting off his shoulders. Too much information all at once. But, to his credit, all he did was stand up, signal for me to stand up from my side of the booth, and give me a long, firm bear hug. In the middle of the restaurant, not caring who was looking, two grown men stood hugging one another for what seemed like minutes. Scottie rocked us slightly from side to side, all the while not lessening his grip on my torso. It felt so good, and I felt so loved. Other than Mason, here was the first person I had told who gave me what seemed like unconditional love as a response. No questions, no hesitations. No concerns about any of the what-ifs of the future. Scottie was happy because I was happy.

As the months progressed, life continued as if nothing had changed. I had to straddle both sides of the world I was living in. There was the one in which I woke up every morning, showered, dressed, and drove to one of my part-time jobs, followed by a few nights of school to finish off my master's degree. And then there was the other part of my life where I would wake up, shower, dress, and remember that in a few short months, I was going to be a father! A baby was forming and growing, and it was half of my DNA. She was already so precious to so many, and she hadn't even set eyes on the planet yet. She had no idea what was in store for her once she arrived. Robin continued to work and wanting to finish her academic year of teaching so she could bank a full year before taking time off. Since the baby was due in August, that was easy to do as long as Robin continued to feel well. And she did.

She had her regular doctor appointments, and we checked in with one another at least once every four or five days. One day, after not seeing one another for a few weeks, Robin and I met for coffee. I saw her. Pregnant. Very pregnant. She looked wonderful. I am sure that what I was seeing was not only the "glow" that people talk about pregnant women having but the additional "glow" of how happy both she and I were that this was coming to fruition. Two strangers from two different worlds found each other less than two years earlier, now going to be tied together for life by way of a new life they both created.

Robin confessed that she had gained a considerable amount of weight, but the doctor was not concerned. He did tell her some of the weight, of course, was the baby. The rest of the weight was Robin. I empathized, and came clean that I, too, had gained weight, anxious about the future. We both acknowledged that we knew what the other was concerned over since we had both struggled with being heavy all of our lives. "Yeah, but you have yours much more under control than I do. Or did before getting pregnant." Robin seemed nervous that since she was heavy, to begin with, this additional weight gain was in some way going to make her less . . . what? Certainly, it is no less desirable as a mother for our daughter. It didn't seem to me that Robin was thinking of herself in terms of dating right away, but who knew? Maybe she was hoping that once the baby was born and a routine was in place, she would be out in the dating pool again. That was something we rarely discussed, but I decided we needed to do it. I wanted Robin to know that I wanted her happiness, whatever that looked like. Obviously, if she were happy, the baby would be happy. Equally with me, as long as I was doing what was making me smile every day, moving forward in my new career, and building my relationship with Mason, I was happy, and our daughter would see me happy.

"Do you think about dating again?" I asked her. "Not necessarily right away, but at some point in the future?" I could see that I caught Robin more than a bit unprepared for this question and perhaps for this topic. Not wanting to put her on the spot too much or to make her feel too vulnerable, I quickly followed that up. "Because whatever you want in the future, Robin, I want to support you. Why shouldn't you have a partner if you want one?" Maybe I was looking for it, or perhaps it was actually there, but Robin's face seemed to relax a bit, and her eyes began to mist. Here was a woman who was pursuing an extremely unconventional path, leaving behind the traditional course of events, at least for now. As someone who was doing the same thing, maybe even more so as a gay man having a child altogether with a straight woman, let alone while partnered with a man who has a son with a lesbian couple, yeah, I knew that conformity was about as far away from me as Mars. "I get it. We're both doing something that neither of us has any knowledge of other than our intuition. We'll figure it all out. We've got this."

The mist that had been forming in Robin's eyes now turned to full-on tears, and as she cried, I stood up from across the small bistro table, slid the chair over to her side, leaned into her, and hugged her. She wept quietly, with her hands on my back and her head on my shoulder. As her body pulsated, I allowed myself to release what I was also storing inside: the dread of the unknown. Intellectually, I knew how to take care of a child. Emotionally, I was not ready to experience the avalanche of feelings at the top of this experiential mountain. What was I doing? What were we doing? At least Robin lived across the street from her mother, a woman who had four children and could be physically present for Robin in less than five minutes should Robin need her. I, on the other hand, lived 3,000 miles from my mother, a mother who, at best, was still coming to terms with me being gay, let alone having a child. Mason's mother had died when he was in his twenties. While we had women in our orbit who were mothers and upon whom we could rely, it was not the same as having a mother present. My mother. And as Robin composed herself, feeling calmer about her future, I was becoming more and more unsure of my own. How was a gay man going to raise a daughter with another man? I kept these apprehensions to myself;no need to dump all of this on Robin. We would figure it all out. We had this.

We were given three baby showers. One for Robin and the women in her life, hosted by her mother and her sister Lisa. This was no small affair; it was a "high tea" at the Ritz Carlton, which Lisa had arranged from San Francisco, and Marlene did the legwork in town. Mason and I were going to show up at the end, as was often the custom when the soon-to-be dad arrives and allows the well-wishers to flood him with words of happiness and good health and good luck getting sleep. At this event, Mason and I finally had the opportunity to meet more of Robin's family, including her sister, her nephew, her newborn niece, and our baby's cousins. Robin's aunt and cousins were there, along with a few friends of hers and Marlene's. Robin's maternal grandmother was there, too, but by this point in her life, she was a bit hazy on facts. Robin had told me that her grandmother did not understand Robin was having this child as a single woman, and certainly, there was no mention of the baby's father being a gay man. I was asked to play along and not cause any distress to her grandmother, to which I happily obliged. When I met Sadie, she smiled and told me how much she loved Robin. Robin was her first grandchild, which made her that much more special, and now her first grandchild was having a child of her own. "You take care of her," she said to me in a tone that I so enjoyed hearing. It had the notes of emphasis and bluntness, but just beneath that austere instruction was a depth of feeling so filled with affection and love that all I could do was take her hands in mine, smile, look her directly in the eyes, and tell her, "I will. I promise."

Scottie also wanted to throw a party for me and Mason. He admitted that he had never thought he would be the host of a baby shower, certainly not for a gay couple, but why not? Michael, Scottie's partner, like so many others of the gay men we shared this news, seemed both perplexed and titillated. Not only was it uncommon for gay men to be having children, but to flaunt it in such a way as to call others to celebrate such a dubious endeavor was, well, uncommon. Exceptional. Rare. Still, to his credit and true to himself, Scottie, along with Michael, opened their home to two dozen of our male friends, having organized food and drink and games and music and laughter.

Mason had prepared a big blank scrapbook for guests to write their good wishes and thoughts in, and after the event, once the photos were developed, Mason put them together as a keepsake of the day. What a fun afternoon that was, me being the center of attention, which was hardly my "happy place." Still, the reason for that attention made it all worthwhile.

All of the men we invited came, not one declined. They were friends from my recent past as opposed to my old life, though. Sadly, despite all that I had gone through to declare my homosexuality and live an out life, I still felt uncomfortable reaching into my past, those from my Camp Ramah days. Camp Ramah was probably my primary reason for choosing to move to Los Angeles. It was there that I discovered I was likable and funny, sought-after, and of value. It was also there that I had my first inkling that I was gay and that it might, just might, be acceptable. It was there that I "fathered" dozens of kids over several summers, all day, every day, breakfast, lunch, and dinner, praising them for their accomplishments and attempting to educate them when they had erred. Camp Ramah had provided me with an internal fulcrum, one that I could depend upon in times when my life seemed to sway too much in any one direction, causing me to feel as if I were about to fall. Camp Ramah held me and contained me until I found my footing again. Yet none of my friends from that time of my life were part of my current one. I was nervous, and I am ashamed to admit, ashamed, that I had not shared my truest self with those friends once I moved to California. I compartmentalized my life in such a way that those who were truly the principals in my young adult life were tucked away in a box labeled as Important Keepsakes, yet placed in the back of the closet. Incorporating them into my present felt far too intimidating.

Friends of mine from my psychology program, from the neighborhood, and mutual friends of mine and Mason filled Scottie and Michael's home with cheer and laughter, filling the scrapbook with loving congratulatory wishes and complimentary sentiments. Gifts of all sizes also made their way into the house, which surprised me. I was so lost in the enormity of what I was doing that I forgot to think that for these men, whether this was ever a consideration for their own lives or not, they were bearing witness to a rare phenomenon. True, I was not the first openly gay man to have a child; after all, my partner had already accomplished that. But it was different in this way, as an equal partner in parenting, as opposed to a sperm donor or the kindly "uncle" figure who would be marginal at best in the life of the child. I was forging new territory. The fact that I was doing this with a straight woman, who knowingly entered into this arrangement by choice and with excitement, well, that was novel indeed both in the gay community and the straight one. I was sure Robin was interrogated as to why she was doing this since she could easily have found an anonymous sperm donor and proceeded independently to create her family. I don't know how she answered those interrogators. What I do know is what she told me when I was one of them: she wanted more than just a child. She wanted a father for that child. She wanted a family.

Gifts. Lots of gifts. A beautiful, engraved silver picture frame and Beatrix Potter baby china, Dr. Seuss books and children's books specific to dads and kids, a one-of-a-kind rocking horse, and scores of the softest stuffed animals I had ever touched. And the gifts kept coming. Clothing, an activity center for baby, blankets and toys . . . all for me to take home to my baby so she would want for nothing. And all delivered with love. I could feel that love; it was palpable in the house that day. Just as Mason and I made an appearance at the end of Robin's shower, we had arranged for Robin to come and say hello at the end of this one. And, of course, Scottie's mom, Rosie, would not hear of not attending, too, in the end, to *kvell* over the hospitability and graciousness of her son and to wish Mason and me all the very best for the future.

The third baby shower was thrown by other dear friends of mine and Mason, hosting it in their backyard on a summer evening. Again, more love, more good wishes, and this time, a real mixture of straight and gay people. At Robin's shower, there were all women, all straight, some married and some single. At the party hosted by Scottie, it was all men, all gay, all in some state of incredulity at the prospect of a gay man choosing to have a biological child. This time, couples and singles, older and younger, gay and straight, some with kids and some never having them, were all seated around in a backyard together. To me, it was as if this were the most natural scene in the world, a gathering of people on a warm July night, some meeting for the first time, some reminiscing of other times together, all celebrating a baby's imminent arrival.

While the majority of the guests were friends of mine and Mason, we invited Robin to the party rather than just coming at the end, along with Marlene, Stuart, and a few of their friends. Marlene was thrilled to be included, sharing with me at one point in the evening how much she was enjoying meeting some of the guests "since these will be the people in our baby's life." Again, like at brunch when we first met, Marlene referred to the baby as "our" baby, which sounded and felt odd to me, but I said nothing. I told her I was happy she was having a good time, and of course, "the more good people in the baby's life, the better!" as far as I was concerned. She smiled and hugged me, and when she leaned back, I could see her eyes filled with tears. I hoped they were tears of happiness. As the evening proceeded, small groups of guests approached me, revealing their happiness for Mason, me, and Robin. When one of the hosts spoke on behalf of the group, she referred to us as "the unconventional conventional family." She explained that as unique as this was at the start, all we were doing was what so many others had done and continued to do every day, all around the world: create a loving environment in which to bring children. There was nothing more normal and more heartwarming than that.

19

BUILDING A FAMILY MY WAY

———❧———

The Hollywood Bowl is an iconic outdoor music venue in Los Angeles. Tourists and locals alike know of its existence, an amphitheater with exceptional natural acoustics situated in the middle of Los Angeles, an area called the Hollywood Hills. Centrally located near Downtown L.A., the San Fernando Valley, and West Los Angeles, it is a destination like no other. Few experiences are more quintessential than an evening in the summer, under the stars, watching and listening to a concert at the Hollywood Bowl. It was called "the bowl" because of the natural cavity in the hills where it was built. The open-air setting was used to present concerts and hold Easter productions and was made available to the masses. On July 11, 1922, the Hollywood Bowl presented its first official season as the newest performance site in the city. Back then, it was basic, to say the least. Patrons were invited to sit on temporary wooden benches and watch the Los Angeles Philharmonic play. After that first season, residents looked forward to recreating the experience the following summer, which they have done every summer since.

In 1926, permanent seats were built, replacing the provisional ones, as well as a band shell, a set of concentric arches, and a façade in front of which the performers performed. The shell, as it was called, was also fixed, remaining in place until the 1970s, when part of it was replaced, and then again in 2004, when a larger, acoustically improved shell was installed. The original design of the shell was inspired by famed architect Frank Lloyd Wright, whose work is renowned worldwide. One of the original tenets of the Hollywood Bowl was that it be accessible to the public, allowing all who wanted to experience the arts the opportunity to do so. Prices varied, depending on where one sat, but even today, it is still possible to purchase a ticket for $1.00, assuming one is willing to hike up to the back of the amphitheater. When the venue is at capacity, all 17,500 attendees can declare that they experienced an evening at the Bowl. Today, there are boxes for two, four, and six occupants closer to the stage, where one can sit more comfortably and experience the staged event a bit more privately than on the benches, bleacher-style. Picnic grounds lie adjacent to the theatre, where hundreds of patrons bring their food and drink and create an entire evening out of sustenance and a show. As for who has performed at the Hollywood Bowl, a better question is, "Who has not?" All genres of music are offered at the Bowl, religious and secular events, sometimes sing-alongs with movie musicals projected onto large screens, and even staged productions of legendary and celebrated plays.

Mason had long been a supporting patron of the arts, dating back to when he was a little boy, and his parents would regularly take him to see plays. He was a season ticket holder to two theatres, as well as to the Hollywood Bowl. When he and I officially became a couple, we changed from the box of four, which Mason shared with a friend, to one of our own, and we enjoyed inviting friends to join us in the box, and in return, they brought dinner. The box accommodated four people snuggly, but it worked. With two folding tables affixed to the sides, we could bring picnic baskets and set up the food on the tables, knowing that at the end of the meal, we could pack up the leftovers, fold down the tables, face the stage, and enjoy the show. We had the Saturday night season, which was often contemporary music or shows, sometimes classical, and often with a fireworks display at the end. Color and sound would fly high above the bandshell, lighting up the night sky with beauty. Since parking was always extremely difficult at the Bowl, we often would invite our friends to meet at our house and take one car from there. That way, we got to enjoy the entire experience together, from the drive to the Bowl through the conversation after the concert itself.

A dear friend of Mason's, Greg, partnered with Rob about a year prior to me meeting Mason. Mason and Greg dated once or twice but quickly realized they would be much better friends than anything more. Greg, a Louisiana boy, brought out the silly and the fanciful in those around him, while Rob was the more grounded civil servant type. Together, they made an extremely compatible pair, and we always enjoyed spending time with them. We invited them to join us for a night at the Bowl one particular Saturday night, August 7, 1999. The show was Movie Music Magic with the Los Angeles Philharmonic, which was scheduled to play various themes of well-known Hollywood movies. The night would end with a fireworks display, which I always enjoyed, and Greg was a big fan, too. Both Greg and Rob are good cooks, and they offered to bring jambalaya, cornbread, and an assortment of other Southern food for our meal, along with drinks and dessert. Greg never disappointed with his food, and neither did the Bowl. It was going to be a wonderful night. Mason drove, with me sitting beside him, Greg and Rob in the back seat. We could smell the goodies in the trunk wafting into the car itself and could hardly wait to be seated and start feasting.

The parking situation has always fascinated me at the Hollywood Bowl. There are so few parking spaces relative to the number of potential attendees, but the powers that be have managed to navigate this beautifully. There are several physical tiers and monetary tiers of stacked parking. Therefore, once parked at the Bowl, there is no way out until the end of the show.

Allowing the 17,500 patrons to leave the event, not all of whom have driven, takes time. Some walk down to the main streets and take buses back to the designated parking lots where patrons can pay and leave their cars. Others park a fair distance away and walk the thirty or so minutes back to their cars if they are able to find street parking in the nearby residential neighborhoods. And some drive and park on the site itself. One hopes that everyone will be respectful of this parking situation once the show ends. It is almost essential that the owners of the cars in front of you, behind you, to your left and right, return to their vehicles before you can drive away. Yet, it is almost always the case that there is one car that is sitting dark and empty while those around it are idling, ready to return home, but are wedged into their spaces, unable to move. More than once, I have witnessed a car attempting to maneuver itself like a contortionist from Cirque du Soleil, only to end up scratched and dinged and still trapped. One learns from one's own experiences and others' experiences that patience is needed at the end of a show at the Hollywood Bowl.

For the four of us, it was a Saturday night out, nowhere to be until Monday morning, so we were in no hurry. We gave ourselves plenty of time to enjoy the whole experience of a night out under the stars with wonderful music and equally wonderful food, not to mention friends. The boys in the front of the car asked me how I was feeling about impending fatherhood.

"Nervous and excited." This had become my standard response over the last few weeks. " I'm ready for the 'talking about it' phase to be over and the 'actually living it' phase to start."

"How is Robin feeling?" Greg asked.

"She's actually doing really well," Mason responded.

"And, if she's not, she's not telling us or showing it to us," I added.

We were approaching the official due date, but as we knew from so many others, and as Robin was told by her doctor, first pregnancies are often late. Robin was ready to deliver the baby. Like so many mothers-to-be, almost stereotypically, her feet were swollen, her back hurt, and she could not sleep for any real length of time at night because she could not find a comfortable position. And once she did, she would wake soon thereafter because the baby was pushing on her bladder, and she had to pee. It was summer, it was hot, and Robin had stairs to climb each time she left her apartment or returned, which did not help. And she was anxious. Excited, of course, but also nervous. When we spoke in the early afternoon, Robin told me that she was not feeling great, but it did not seem as if the baby was coming. "It doesn't feel like time yet," I told Robin that Mason and I were going to the Hollywood Bowl but that I had my pager with me. If there was any news, she could reach me. She had hers, too, and we both had our cell phones, the brick-sized plastic blocks that weighed almost as much as the rectangular clay blocks they resembled, just in case. We wished each other a good night and said that we would check in with each other the next day.

Greg, Rob, Mason, and I settled ourselves into the box and out came the food. Lots of it. All smelled even better than what came wafting into the car as we drove. Greg, who has a flair for the flamboyant, set out tablecloths with matching napkins, of course. Next came the plastic wine goblets and the separate plastic water glasses, followed by the fancy plastic cutlery and table decorations, including short white candles in slightly taller clear glass hurricane containers to protect the flames from reaching out. Our plan was to dine, not just eat. We had plenty of time, so why not enjoy the entire experience? We would start with appetizers, followed by a main course, then watch the first act of the show. At intermission, we would indulge in the desserts and coffee, which the second act would follow. The authentic Louisiana cuisine tasted just that: authentic. We savored every morsel. With the announcement of the ten-minute warning prior to the start of the show, we collected the scant few leftovers, returned them to their Tupperware containers, and gathered the used plates and other trash into a plastic bag. Since I was the closest to the entrance to the box, I volunteered to throw it out and stop in the restroom before the show began. Rob joined me, leaving Mason and Greg in the box. Once we returned, we all settled ourselves into position, the four of us facing front. The orchestra marched onto the stage, with the men in white tuxedo jackets and black trousers and the women wearing white blouses and black skirts. The conductor followed, and he motioned for the musicians to get ready. With that, the start of the national anthem rang out from the shell of the amphitheater, causing all 17,000-plus of us to rise to our feet, many of us singing along. This was the start of every show at the Hollywood Bowl.

Just prior to intermission, my pager buzzed in my waistband. I had silenced it so in case a call came in, usually from a client calling my office number, it would not disturb the concert. I looked down at the small screen and saw that it was Robin. Although it was still dark and the music was playing, I knew I would not be able to concentrate if I did not call her back.

"I'll be right back," I whispered, and I quietly excused myself.

I walked over to the side yard near the concessions and restrooms, where I could return the call.

"This is it." Robin was heading to the hospital.

From that point, things seemed like they played straight out of an Abbott and Costello movie. I whispered to Mason what Robin had told me, and the adrenaline hit us both. We had to go. The first half of the show was just ending, and I shared with the gang that Robin was going to the hospital, and we were going to have a baby!

Mason and I tried to figure out how we were going to do this, with the car parked among thousands of others and no way to retrieve it. We decided that Greg and Rob would stay for the second half of the concert, and they would drive our car back home for us, leave it there, and take their car home. Mason and I collected our things, said our goodbyes, and trekked through the throngs of restroom-goers and intermission coffee-seekers, snaking our way from our seats to the entrance. Bumbling and fumbling, we reached the main gate, where we asked one of the police officers directing traffic if there were any taxis to be called. She began asking questions.

"Why do you need a taxi?" She enquired.

"We need to get to the hospital." Mason blurted out.

"The hospital?" She exclaimed anxiously? "Is everything okay?"

"Yes, everything's okay. We just need to go." Mason reined in his excitement and nerves, wanting her to direct us to the nearest cab.

"Do you need medical attention? Is anyone hurt?" she continued.

I wanted to yell *stop*! But I couldn't find the voice to do it. Mason spoke up, telling this well-intentioned uniformed officer that we were having a baby, the mother was on her way to the hospital, our car was lodged in the stack parking lot, and we needed to get home to retrieve our other car so that we could get to the hospital.

"What hospital do you need to get to? Is anyone with the mom?"

Why was she asking all those questions? I wondered, still unable to utter a sound. This didn't concern her. All we wanted to know was if a taxi was nearby that we could summon.

"Please," I was finally able to say, "we really are in a hurry and need a taxi. Do you know if there are any around?"

She began to respond, but I stopped paying attention almost from the beginning once I saw her raise her right arm, pointing with her index and middle finger in the direction of a short-term parking lot across the street. I remember thinking that she looked like she was a flight attendant during the safety announcement, pointing out the exits on an aircraft. Or an air traffic controller signaling incoming planes onto the runway. I think Mason was still talking to her when I turned around and began walking.

This was the beginning of a chapter of my life that I had longed for, prayed for, fantasized about, and almost resigned myself to never having. I was about to have a baby. My baby! The throbbing in my temples made it nearly impossible for me to pay attention to much. The images flooding my brain were all-encompassing. What would she look like? Would she have that smell so many babies have? Would her voice be squeaky or strong? Hair or bald baby? My eyes burned a bit from the salty tears collecting in them, but I didn't want to cry. I wasn't sure why I didn't want to cry, but I remember wanting to maintain composure. It had often been said of me that I was not a demonstrative individual with my emotions, to which I would respond, "That doesn't mean I don't have them." I did. I do. I just prefer to keep them private, away from full view, and certainly not to be shared with the masses. I was extremely selective to whom I revealed my feelings. This was a self-protective mechanism I learned very early on in my life.

My role in the family was to be the placater, the keeper of peace and harmony. I was supposed to be Switzerland. From my early days in Israel, seeing my mom sad that my dad was away, whether in the army or Canada, I took on the position of making her happy, easing her load, and caring for Gil so she could take care of the other necessities. Then, in Toronto, my responsibilities included being the mouthpiece until my parents learned the English language well enough to communicate. Then, to be the "helper" to Mom with Gil while Dad worked six days a week and Mom herself had immeasurably long days. I was to be the good student, the good brother, the good son, the good cousin, the good neighbor, the good one. There is not much room in that prototype to show anger, sadness, fear, or disappointment. I adapted and censored myself, allowing those around me to see what I believed they wanted or expected to see. All the rest I suppressed, revealing those other emotions only to my imagination late at night, in the dark, quiet privacy of my bed. There, I would cry. And feel brave. I could stand up to bullies and say whatever the hell I wanted without fear of repercussion. Nighttime was always the safest time for me since I was alone, sometimes with another person next to me, but almost always feeling alone. Falling asleep has always been an obstacle for me. No matter how much I tried or wanted, I had what I call a "busy head." Thoughts and issues and images and conversations and experiences and dilemmas and outcomes that span the continuum, all happening once anyone and everyone around me is asleep. It is then that I am left to partner with the quiet. The quiet is where I have always felt safe. Emotionally safe. Now, in the next few hours, hopefully, some of that would change. With the birth of my child, I wanted to be different, more open and accessible. I wanted to model for her that with me, she would be eternally safe to share her feelings and emotions, whatever they were. I made her that promise that night that I would be there for her. Always.

When Mason and I arrived at the hospital, Robin was in her room, outfitted in a pale blue gown with a black diamond-shaped pattern on it, attached to a fetal monitor. Around her were Marlene, Stuart, and her best friend Linda. Robin seemed as relaxed as a first-time, over-forty, single, expectant mother could be, and when she saw me, she beamed. She shared with us the events of the day and how, as the morning hours turned to afternoon, she could feel something was different. She couldn't identify with any clarity what the "different" was, but she knew that whatever was happening, she wanted it to happen in the hospital rather than at home. She had been out to dinner with Marlene and Stuart, and they decided to head to the hospital.

Only once before had I been in the room with an expectant mother, my friend Sharon, as she prepared to welcome Adam, my godson, into the world. Her parents were notified that she was going into labor, but since they were in Tucson, it would take some time for them to arrive in Los Angeles. Sharon's husband at the time was there, but he was both nervous and annoying as Sharon tells the story, so she wanted him out of the room until it was actually time to push. I was the person she wanted sitting by her side. I remember with Sharon that it all seemed surreal. She, too, was lying in bed, connected to wires and tubes, but she and I were talking about television shows and plot lines. She was about to have a baby, yet she was commenting on one of our favorite shows of the time, *Life Goes On*. We both loved that the creators of that program had a special needs child as one of the leads, a boy with Down Syndrome named Corky. Sharon and I often lamented the fact that life was not more fair to Corky.

Here, with Robin, she, too, was laughing and chatting with Linda about their days as teachers together in a local high school and the musical shows they both worked on throughout their years teaching.

Where was the gravity, the importance, of this moment? Was it unrealistic of me to be looking for more? Mason, too, shared his time in the delivery room with the mommies, remembering that they, too, talked and reminisced as if they were at a cocktail party or an outdoor café. It didn't hurt at all that Robin had opted for an epidural, allowing for pain relief until it was time to push.

Mason and I arrived at approximately 10:30 p.m., and together with the others, we made ourselves comfortable. There was no way to know how long this would take, so we indulged in snacks that Robin had prepared, we shared stories, many by Marlene, of Robin's childhood, and we sang. Robin, Marlene, Linda, and Mason were all good singers, followed by me, and then Stuart. That did not matter. To while away the hours, we revisited folk songs from the 1960s, madrigals, with which Robin, Linda and Mason were all familiar, and even show tunes. Throughout the hours of that night and into the early hours of the following morning, nurses came in and out of the room to check on Robin. Each time they did, they all marveled at the novelty of never before having seen a woman in labor, surrounded by her posse, singing songs. If they only knew that was the least novel thing about this entire situation! We appreciated their vivacious energy and attention up until 6 a.m. when we were told that it was time.

Stuart, who seemed as if he could not wait to get out of that room, quickly excused himself, and Robin asked Linda to join him in the waiting area. I had previously asked Robin who she was comfortable having in the room with us when she delivered, and she wanted her mother. I, of course, was going to put my Lamaze class skills to use, which meant I was going to be in the room. We had talked about whether or not to document the birth with photography. This was not important to me, knowing that as soon as the baby was safely swaddled, we would begin with the cameras. It was somewhat surprising to me that Robin wanted both video and stills of the birth, and the only person she and I trusted to be able to do this was Mason. Again, surprisingly, she agreed to have Mason in the room with us if he would be responsible for the photos.

Dr. Charlie arrived, gowned and masked, said hello to us all, and exclaimed, "Let's have a baby!" With Robin in position on the bed and me to her right, I held her head with my left hand and her right hand with mine. Marlene was seated off to the side in a chair, looking nervous. Mason was at the foot of the bed, with a camera strapped around his neck, holding a video camera in both hands. Dr. Charlie was to his left. *Was this really about to happen?* Robin and I looked at each other, and I looked over to Mason. Here was my new family. My strange, unconventional family and I were about to welcome the next generation. Something both Robin and I had dreamed of for years. Not together and not with each other, but here we were. Fate has brought us together, as it does most couples. Only we were both bucking the system, living life on our terms. We were both about to close the chapter of our lives where we just *wanted* to be parents.

Labor went quickly. Robin began the official pushing shortly after 6 a.m., and at 6:31 a.m., on August 8, 1999, Bailey Suzanna was born. Eight pounds twelve ounces, twenty-one inches long, with a full head of jet-black hair. She was perfect. And beautiful. And our reality. I was offered the honor and task of cutting the cord, which I happily and nervously did, after which Bailey was wrapped in the quintessential white blanket with a blue and pink stripe that every hospital maternity ward seems to have, and she was handed to Robin. For the first time in her life, Robin was called by a different name: Mom. Nestled in the crook of her arm, Robin held Bailey, looking down at her face, with me standing over the two of them. "We did it."

Once Bailey was officially introduced to her parents and the select few others who had spent the night waiting for her arrival, it was time for her first bath, handprints, footprints, and then some rest. For mommy and baby. That was our cue to leave. Mason and I walked back to the parking lot, surreptitiously letting our fingers touch as if to say to each other, without actual words, we did it too. Not only did Robin and I create a child, but Mason and I went through this process together. While Mason would not be Bailey's biological father, he would be my partner and, therefore, Bailey's other parent. Whereas

Ben came into Mason's life prior to my being in the picture, Bailey will always have Mason as another adult who knows her story and walks the uneven steps of the path to bring her into the world with both of her parents. It was August, but I was shaking as we approached the car. Maybe it was the air conditioning in the hospital, followed by the heat outside. Perhaps it was the fatigue of having been awake all night. Most likely, it was the combination of adrenaline and euphoria hitting me all at once. I handed Mason my car keys and once buckled into the passenger seat, I began to cry. The further away from the hospital we drove, the harder the sobs became. All the way home, sadness and joy and anticipation and a myriad of emotions living inside of me for decades were released. No longer did I need to be stoic. No more did I need to worry about what others needed or wanted from me. Finally, I had someone to protect and help because I chose to.

20
A LEGACY OF LOVE AND RESILIENCE

———⚬⚬———

In the Jewish tradition, when a baby boy is born, on the seventh day of his life, a *bris*, or ritual circumcision, is performed. For girls, tradition holds that within the first thirty days of her life, a baby girl is named and brought into the Jewish covenant. This is ceremonial and is open to however a family wants to create it and present it. There is often a rabbi who will bless the child and name her both in Hebrew and in whatever other language the family wants, in our case, English. The rabbi will also share some of the history of why such a custom is performed, share the meaning of the name, and ask that those gathered help the new parents not only in welcoming the new child into the world but to embrace all those who are part of this new family, help them and guide them and support them as they begin a new chapter as a new assemblage of family.

Since Robin's side of the family was not at all religious, yet both of us were traditional Jews, we decided we did want such a ceremony. We agreed we would find a rabbi who could speak to our collection of family and friends in a tone in synch with who we were. Someone who would not only accept our less-than-traditional arrangement but who would celebrate it. We interviewed two rabbis, one gay, one straight, who was gay-friendly, and neither of them seemed "right." I suggested to Robin that we both talk to my friend Anat, Rabbi Anat, with whom I interned at the Jewish Federation. She was young, very progressive, warm, and friendly, with a smile that lights up a room, to use a cliché which, in this case, is almost literally factual. Once we did, it took us no time at all to decide that Anat would be our officiant.

The party room in Robin's mother's condominium building was where Robin and Marlene wanted to hold the party, which was fine with me. We discussed food, decorations, and the number of attendees, and before we knew it, the Baby Naming Ceremony was set. It would be two weeks after Bailey was born, on Sunday, August 22, 1999. It would be an afternoon gathering, primarily for close family and close friends. Robin and Marlene put their list together, as did Mason and me. I let my parents know about it, and told them that I really wanted them to be there, to meet their newest grandchild. To my slight surprise, they made no fuss about it, booked their tickets, and arrived a few days before the date, making sure to spend some time with Robin, Marlene, and the baby before the official naming.

My parents, Mason, and I arrived slightly earlier than the arranged time to make sure we could greet the guests as they made their way to our celebration. Shortly after that, Marlene, along with Robin's sister Lisa and her family, came in, and a bit later, Robin and Bailey arrived. Robin seemed either nervous or tense or exhausted . . . whatever she was, this was not her best mood. As she walked into the party room, cradling Bailey in her arms, she immediately made her way to me. With a strained look on her face, she extended her arms as if passing the "hot potato" and said, "Here. Take her. She was up most of the night." That likely explained Robin's mood. Selfishly, I must admit, I was happy I could be the one to hold our little bundle as our well-wishers arrived. Even more, I was happy to have a moment to share Bailey with her paternal grandparents without Robin or Marlene present and with the grandmother, whose own mother is Bailey's namesake. One of my brother's kids is named for my father's mom, the grandmother we grew up knowing best, my Savta Golda. (Savta is the Hebrew word for grandmother or grandma.) I wanted my child to at least have the first letter of my maternal grandmother's name, which in Romanian was Bette. We grandchildren grew up knowing her as Savta Bette, or Savta Batia, her Hebrew name. And Batia was the name we chose for Bailey's Hebrew name, again, to honor my maternal grandmother. We figured Bailey was a good compromise all around. Robin's love of all things Irish. Mason's grandmother Beatrice and my grandmother Bette, both names starting with the letter B. Mason was the one who suggested the name, so even though he isn't biologically linked to Bailey, he is truly connected in a very profound way. And all three of us liked the name.

My dad, always stoic, smiled at Bailey, crooked his right index finger under her chin and on her tummy, and said, "Hi Bailey" several times but made no motion toward wanting to hold her. This was typical for my dad: showing love the way he knew, in a demonstrably limited way. Yet, we all knew there were, in fact, feelings deep down inside him. In this way, I was very much like him, having many feelings yet publicly showing only a few of them.

Placing Bailey in my mother's arms will be an image I will carry with me for the rest of my life. There it was, an event my parents believed they would never experience, one where they were holding the child of their gay son. And a biological child at that. For so many years since I came out to them, after the years they were hurt, then angry, then sad, they lamented the fact that *I* would be sorry because I would not have a child, something they knew was so important to me. And, even though I insisted that somehow I would make it happen, they were skeptical at best. Truth be told, while I was not skeptical, I was faking my external certainty since, on the inside, I had no fucking clue how this was going to happen. But there we were: my parents, me, and my daughter. Never underestimate true determination and tireless perseverance. Watching my mother cradle Bailey in her arms, beaming down at her little face, whispering to her, "Hi, Maideleh," brought tears not only to my eyes but to my mother's eyes as well. (Maidel, or Maideleh, is the Yiddish word for "little girl," often associated with endearment.) It was as if Bailey was completely inducted into our family in those few moments; her grandmother was talking to her in Yiddish, Romanian, Hebrew, and English. Sharing with Bailey how she felt about her and how happy she was to meet her. My mother whispered to Bailey how she was looking forward to many years of imparting to Bailey all the history that preceded her, yet which was also a part of her and which she would carry forward to future generations. There was so much to tell her, so many stories she would find hard to believe. But, the more she got to know us, the more she would understand that we were a hearty group, we came from peasant stock, and we did not collapse under the weight of hardship.

Once the room was filled, people snacking and schmoozing and smiling and chatting, we were ready to begin. Anat called Robin and me to the front, where a small table was set up with a newly polished but old kiddish cup, containing wine, for the traditional blessing. I was once again holding Bailey, having taken her from my mother, who sat proudly in one place while others came to her to meet this newest member of our family. Anat recited a few blessings, sharing both the literal and figurative interpretations of their meaning. She revealed her colossal excitement at meeting Robin, and heralded her for pursuing her dream of becoming a mother, albeit in a unique way.

"I have known Rami for such a long time and know the person he is. For him to have found you, and for the two of you, with Mason, to be doing this, well, it's *beshert*. This was all meant to be, and therefore, Bailey was meant to be."

Anat commented that any two people, Robin and me, along with our supporters who were gathered in the room, were clearly part of a larger story than the one currently present. We were pioneers, and visionaries, and we were destined for bigger outcomes.

"This doesn't have to be anything grand or public." She said. "Not all great public outcomes begin with great public announcements. The quiet determination that you both manifest into creating this family will not end with you."

Anat looked out into the room, smiling in the direction of the grandparents.

"We might not all live to see how this union plays itself out, but it is surely going to be notable. That is the story of the Jewish people. From generation to generation, through times of abundance as well as scarcity, wars, and peace, we persevered, we showed grit and moxie, and we kept going. What we were all witnessing on this day was a tiny slice of our 5,000-year-old history."

At the end of her oration, Anat blessed Bailey, wishing her a long life to the age of 120, a life that would hopefully be filled with good health, happiness, laughter, and internal peace. She named her Bailey Suzanna, the B for my grandmother, and the S for Sidney, Robin's father. And in Hebrew, she welcomed her into the covenant of the people of Israel, where she would be known as *Batia Shayna*. Literal translation: beautiful daughter of God.

Both grandmothers wanted to say a few words to our guests. Marlene began.

"This is a momentous day. We have four generations of women of my family here." Sadie, Robin's grandmother, and Marlene's mother was in attendance, along with Marlene, the firstborn daughter, watching Robin, her firstborn daughter, welcome Bailey, her firstborn daughter.

"I have to admit, when Robin shared with me that she met a nice young man, this was not how I thought the story was going to end."

There was laughter from the room.

"But as I got to know Rami and Mason and saw that Robin was happy with her decision to have a child this way, it reminded me that I was also a bit of a rebel. And, in the end, what we want for our kids is their happiness."

Next, my mother captured the attention of the room. She thanked everyone for being there, especially since this was not a traditional Baby Naming Ceremony.

"Like the rabbi said, this is strangers coming together to make a family. And all of the family and friends here are now part of this family."

My mother alluded to the difficulties she and my father had with my coming out, although she did not mention it specifically. What she did say was that there were years when she grieved the loss of a child for me, knowing how much I had wanted a family.

"Rami always had such a connection with children. He loved being a Hebrew school teacher. He loved being a camp counselor." She continued to praise my ease with kids, including my cousins and the offspring of my cousins. "But to come to Los Angeles to meet my third granddaughter, this is a surprise I never imagined."

She told us all that she was so surprised that we named our daughter after her mother, and not just in Hebrew, but the English name too. At this point, Mason and I looked at one another, wondering what she meant. Her mother's name was Bette. My mother told us it was one of the greatest honors when a child names their child after a relative who has passed away; it is another example of how we, as Jewish people, keep our history alive. Again, Mason and I exchanged a slightly cocked head and a bit of a squint, curious as to what my mother was referring to.

"And even though there are others in the family who have named their children after my mother in Hebrew, Batia, and in Romanian, Bette, now she will also have someone to carry the name that she loved because her mother called her this, Bailah."

In my thirty-seven years of life, I never knew that my grandmother was Bailah. I never heard anyone call her that, or refer to her that way. As Mason and I have often said, and as Rabbi Anat referenced earlier, certain things in life are inexplicable; they are simply *bashert*.

21
FINDING OUR RHYTHM

W e settled into a routine of sorts. After a few days in the hospital, Robin and Bailey went home to Robin's apartment. Bailey was a good eater and a good sleeper, but she was a newborn, which meant she cried a lot, ate a lot, and slept a lot.

Only that last one, the sleeping a lot, did not happen over one extended period of time, much to Robin's chagrin. Bailey was up every few hours, which meant Robin was up every few hours, including all those hours when the sun was down and the moon was in the sky.

Robin didn't complain, but every time I saw her or spoke to her, she looked and sounded tired. Robin's mother, who was still working, usually was home by midafternoon, which allowed her to help out by babysitting so Robin could rest. Marlene also hired a night nurse to come and assist for the first two weeks, offering advice and guidance to Robin as she settled into her new role as a mom. I gave Robin time to settle in without too many interruptions, but I was conflicted since I wanted to spend as much time with my daughter as I could.

I engaged in an early balancing act where I would wait for Robin to call me at some point in the day and let me know how things were going. Understandably but frustratingly, I often did not hear from Robin by midafternoon, at which time I picked up the phone and called her.

The conversation almost always took the same form. I apologized for bothering Robin. She said I was not bothering her, and she was sorry not to have reached out to me earlier, but she had a rough stretch of time with Bailey. It was at this point in that conversation that I was given details. She didn't sleep much during the night, she didn't eat, she was cranky, she couldn't be soothed and cry, or some other newborn behavior. I felt compassion for Robin for having to do this on her own, while feeling disappointed I was not able to experience these newborn activities for myself. Every day, I offered to come over and help out, and each time, Robin told me that she was okay. But if I wanted to go and spend some time with Bailey, I was always welcome.

That last offer, whether sincere or not, I took up. During those first few weeks, we agreed Bailey needed to find her own rhythm, so disrupting her routine by bringing her to my house did not make sense. I had Mason in one ear, telling me the sooner we brought Bailey to our home and introduced her to her room with us, the sooner she would adapt. In the other ear, I had Marlene, who spoke as if she were Bailey's other parent with Robin, telling me that she was happy to have me visit Bailey but to be sensitive to Robin's needs, so maybe I could limit the number of times I came over for the first while. Feeling split down the middle, I did what I so often did in my life and tried to please everyone. Since that was going to be impossible, I reached deep, deep inside of myself and asked what *I* wanted. It made sense to me that Robin was overwhelmed. It also made sense to me, and I hoped that if, or when, Robin or anyone else thought about the dad, not just the mom, they could see and understand *my* desire to be present for my newborn's life. I wanted to experience everything from the very mundane to the exceptional. After all, to a first-time parent, almost anything the infant does is significant, sometimes even amazing. To us, two adults who pursued an uncharted path to create a family, a gurgle, a wiggle of the fingers on one hand, an upright movement of the head, and many other seemingly inconsequential gestures were "firsts." We made of them what we wanted them to be, interpreting a hiccup as an attempt to say a word or the ubiquitous gassy baby to be smiling. We wanted that. We needed that. We longed to be parents, and now, here we were, just that. Parents. Only I was relegated to parenting from more than four miles away from my baby. It took many weeks before Robin was comfortable enough with leaving Bailey with anyone other than her mother.

Robin and her longtime friend Linda had Friday night season tickets to the Music Center, and the first of the plays of that 1999–2000 season was in the fall. While Bailey was only a few months old, she had not yet spent any protracted time at my house.

"I am happy to babysit," I said to Robin. I hated to use that term for my own child.

"Thanks, but I've got it covered," Robin said.

"Oh." I was surprised. What did that mean, I wondered. Not sure what else to say. I guess the silence motivated Robin to add some context to her short response.

"My mom's gonna watch Bailey. I'm going to drop her off there."

Marlene was the one who profited from Robin's minimal time away from Bailey much more than I did. Marlene also saw Bailey daily since she lived across the street from Robin, and already had a nursery set up at her house since she had other, older grandchildren. I was envious of that, but I completely understood that any new mom wants her mother close by for support. Robin was lucky to have that with Marlene, and as a result, Bailey was fortunate to grow up with her grandmother.

I was not happy with this most recent decision and decided that I had to stand up for myself. I specifically remember telling Robin weeks in advance that once she and Linda began their theater season, I wanted Bailey to be with me on those nights.

"Robin," I began, "I thought we had talked about this."

"What do you mean?" I heard a quiver in Robin's voice, the one that would present itself whenever Robin was uncomfortable.

"We discussed this, remember? That when you and Linda start going to theater this season, on those Friday nights, Bailey would be with me."

"I know. But the truth is, Bailey's not ready for that yet." She said hesitantly.

"What do you mean?" Now I was not only hurt but displeased.

"She needs to be in a familiar environment." Robin continued.

"Well, she will never be comfortable here until we start a routine of her being here. Just like you created a familiar environment for Bailey at your mom's house, it's time to do that at my house. Bailey's *other* house." I emphasized the fact that my house should be, and feel, like Bailey's second home, not Marlene's.

There was some more discussion, but no latitude from my side. I wanted Bailey to spend some time with me, in my house, in her bed, and the room prepared for her by Mason and me. On that Friday night, Robin, along with Linda, brought Bailey to my house. Robin was unmistakably tense and anxious, and I interpreted that as feeling vulnerable. I tried very hard not to take it personally.

"Here is the diaper bag," she said, handing it to me with her left hand while clutching a sleeping Bailey against her right breast. "There is breast milk in the side pocket, which should be refrigerated. I just fed Bailey before we left home, so she should be good for several hours."

Robin was running down the routine that she and Bailey had obviously created.

"Her blanket is here, and she likes to have it nearby, but not on her when she's lying in her crib."

"Great. Thanks. I will make sure that it's there for her." I said.

"I put a few diapers here, too, in case she needs a change."

Again, I was slightly insulted. Robin knew that I had prepared Bailey's room here with equal and ample necessities and extras, just like at Robin's house and just like at Marlene's.

"Thanks, but I have diapers," I replied, saying nothing else.

"I know, but she likes these particular diapers." Robin continued.

"Robin, I know." My tone emerged as one of compassion. "I've been over at your place often enough to know what diapers you use, and I have the same ones. As well as the same diaper cream. You've seen me play with Bailey, feed Bailey, and change Bailey, and you know I can do it. And that she is safe here."

Robin began to cry, still holding onto Bailey as if they needed one another to survive.

"I know this is a big step for you." I continued. "And it's a huge step for me, too."

Robin nodded, still tearful but seeming to be a tad less tense.

"It's a really big step for Bailey, too," I added. "This is one of the milestones that you and I had known would come for our child. It's here!" I tried to sound united in this, hoping that it would remind Robin that this was *our* child, not just hers.

"I know." She said. "I know."

As we stood in front of Bailey's bedroom door, near that back door of the house that Robin entered, I let a beat or two go by. Then, I reached out for Bailey, making sure that I was close enough for Robin to hand my daughter over to me but not seem aggressive in taking Bailey away from Robin.

With seeming reluctance, Robin loosened her grip on the baby and created some physical space between the two of them. I slowly raised my arms toward Bailey, but waited for Robin to begin the gesture of the hand-off. As she did, the tears came up stronger in stark contradiction to the softening of her grip. Finally, I placed my right hand under Bailey's slumbering head, and my left to create a cradle. Bailey was now fully in my arms.

"I have my pager on me if you need anything," Robin said, swallowing some of her words as she tried to hold back the tears.

"I know," I said. "She's going to be fine".

"And if you need to reach my mom, you know you can always call her. She can get here quicker than I can."

"I know."

"Okay, I'm going to go." As Robin said this, she leaned in to kiss Bailey on the forehead, after which our eyes locked.

"She's fine. You're fine. This is good, Rob." And with that, Robin turned around and headed back to her car, still idling, with Linda in the passenger seat.

Finally, Bailey was spending the night at her daddy's house. Mason and I were giddy with excitement. We made sure our dinner was prepared ahead of time so as not to take time away from fawning over the little angel in our presence. We had breast milk for Bailey when it was time for her to eat. Food-wise, we were set. We were prepared with the baby bathtub if we decided to give Bailey a bath. We had several books we might want to read to Bailey if she was awake and wanted some stimulation and engagement. We had music CDs poised for ambiance and enjoyment. Toys, stuffed animals, and rattles were placed around the room, welcoming Bailey to what would be her *other* home. I was very aware that with children whose parents did not live together, commonly, the mother's house was *home*, while the other was *Daddy's house*. I didn't want my house not to be Bailey's house; I wanted her to have Mommy's house and Daddy's house, both of which were also Bailey's houses. The crib we set up was Ben's old crib, only with new sheets, bumper guards, and a mobile. It was surreal, dreamlike, seeing Bailey, my daughter, who was asleep in her crib in our home as if this were the most natural thing in the world. Part of me wanted to stand there, quietly, just looking at her. Another part of me wanted to get the camera and document this moment, on the off chance it would not last. The level of nervous energy I felt in those moments seemed to start at my feet and rose through my legs, became butterflies in my stomach, caused my face to become flushed, and ended up tingling at my temples. All those years of planning and dreaming and hoping and wanting . . . they all came together here. My partner, in our home, with my daughter, was asleep in her crib. My family.

Several hours later, after we'd had our evening together, Bailey had eaten, burped, played, babbled, been bathed, been read to, had a few diaper changes, and was in jammies, asleep for some portion of the night. We heard knocking at the back door. Mason and I were watching TV, surprised by the light but distinct tapping. We both walked over to the door and saw Robin and Linda standing there. Surprised and somewhat taken aback, I asked, "Is everything ok?"

I didn't imagine Robin would come by and check on Bailey; my thought was that she would phone, or, in reality, I assumed she would trust everything was fine, and we would check in with one another in the morning. After all, none of us had any specific plans for the next morning. After asking them both in, Linda declined, saying she would wait for Robin in the car; she just wanted to say hello.

Robin came in and seemed rather nervous.

How was the play?" I asked.

"How's Bailey?" she asked, with immediacy in her voice.

"She's fine. She's great, actually. Fast asleep."

"Oh, good." She replied with an obvious exhale.

"How was the play?" I asked again, hoping to allay any concerns that she had.

"Oh, it was good." She said, distracted. "How was your evening? How was Bailey?"

I gave her the rundown of our evening, but it didn't seem to calm Robin at all. I led her to Bailey's room so she could see for herself that our daughter was asleep, safe from all the ills of the world. Still uneasy, Robin said, "I think it would be best if Bailey woke up in her own bed at home."

Ouch.

Why?" I asked. "What changed?"

"I think Bailey is still too young to be shuttled around from place to place." Robin began. "I'm anxious about leaving her, so maybe when we're all further along in this, and she's older, Bailey could spend more time with you, eventually sleeping over."

Agonizing shooting pains went through me. Being talked to in that way made no sense but also was incredibly hurtful. Very little in me at that moment could sympathize with Robin. I could not, and would not, accept that whatever postpartum hormones were surging through her, she was so unaware of what she was saying, and how it was sounding. I let Robin speak.

"Look, Rami, it's not about you. Not at all. This is what is best for Bailey."

"Robin, I understand what you are feeling, but what you are saying does not make sense," I replied.

"All the literature says that an infant should have consistency." She said.

"I completely agree with that, Robin. It's just that…" she cut me off as I was in mid-sentence.

"So if you agree, you'll understand why I want her home, with me, to wake up in her bed." She was now sounding more panicked.

"Look, Robin, the bed that Bailey is sleeping in now *is* her bed. She will get used to it, and it will become her bed more and more."

"But she's never slept in it before." She said. "I'm thinking of her. I'm thinking about Bailey." She proclaimed.

I stopped for a moment to reach deep inside and ask myself, 'Do I want this more for me? Is this in the best welfare of my child?' No. Well, yes and no. Of course, I wanted this for me. But nothing about Bailey sleeping the night at my house would in any way disrupt her schedule or jeopardize any routine.

"Robin, Bailey is asleep. If she weren't feeling safe, she would be awake and crying."

Robin looked at me, tearing up as she did when she dropped Bailey off earlier.

"I think it's you who is not feeling safe, which I understand."

"I feel safe!" she yelled. "This isn't about me. Think of Bailey!"

As much as I didn't want to upset her, neither did I want to give up our prearranged agreement.

I attempted to reassure Robin again.

"Bailey had a wonderful evening. We all ate together. I changed her diaper a few times. She was smiling and at ease when she had her bath. And now she's asleep."

"But she's never spent the night away from me!"

And that was the crux. This was not all about Bailey. It was also about Robin.

"Look, Robin, I know this is hard for you. I really do." I began, and as I did, so again did her crying. "We all have to get used to this. I've been looking forward to my daughter's first sleep-over ever since she was born."

Robin nodded, drying her cheeks with the backs of her hands.

"I have the monitor on in her room and am walking around with the other end of it in case she makes a sound. So far, she has been perfectly quiet." I held up the part of the two-way monitor that I was holding, proving to Robin that I was doing everything that I could to ensure Bailey's safety and comfort.

I also knew that many nights, Robin would take Bailey to Marlene's house, where Bailey would sleep in the nursery, and Robin would stay in another room. This way, Marlene would be there to share in the childcare while Robin replenished her physical energy. Debating whether to say anything about that or not, I opted to hold back. This was not a competition, nor was it a healthy way to start our co-parenting experience.

"I promise, Robin, I will take very good care of Bailey. If I sense at any time that Bailey needs you, I will call." "She's fine. You're fine. I'll see you in the morning."

With tears in her eyes, Robin nodded and ever-so-slowly moved toward the back door. I rubbed her back, both of us silent, and stopped on the stoop, watching Robin approach her car. I could hear Linda ask where Bailey was, but I couldn't make out what Robin was saying. Just before I shut the door, I heard Linda's voice, loud and clear, roar out the question: "You're gonna leave your child with that man?"

Fuck her! Who did Linda think she was? How dare she refer to me as "that man"? Linda, who had never married, had no children and was somewhat of a hard shell to crack, always seemed to like me. Or so I thought. We got along well every time we were together. As Robin's best friend, I understood she might be wary of Robin's decision to go ahead with this endeavor, but . . . but nothing! She spent months getting to know me. And Mason. And was included in all of the activities set up to welcome our rare family into the community of the world at large. Did she think I was facilitating all this for Robin and would then disappear once the baby arrived? Again, as with Marlene, it felt as if I were intruding on Robin's new life. *Robin chose me, people!* I wanted to scream. This is a *we* experience, not a *me* one. Not for Robin individually nor for me. Why was this seemingly so difficult for people in Robin's life to understand? Was it that she was telling them something different from what I was telling people? Did she talk about her alone having a child with a dad off in the distance somewhere? Or was she not mentioning me at all? I could not understand what was happening or why. But it hurt.

The following morning, shortly before 7, Robin was back. Mason, Bailey, and I were awake and dressed, already having started our day. Bailey had slept nearly seven hours straight, woke up, and ate, and while waiting for Mommy, we listened to music and danced. Bailey was happily cooing, going from my arms to Mason's and back to mine. Neither Robin nor I talked about what had taken place the previous night. I packed up the diaper bag, the one Robin had brought with her, along with Bailey's belongings from Mommy's house, and wished Robin a happy Saturday. I handed Bailey to Robin and helped them both out to Robin's car. I waved goodbye as they pulled out and drove away, feeling a wave of sadness.

Time seems to have a way of helping smooth out behavioral wrinkles, and it did so here as well. As the weeks and months progressed, Robin and I found our groove. The first overnight experience made it painfully clear to me that I did not want to be just a "sometimes" dad. I wanted to be, as Robin and I discussed before and during the pregnancy, a full-time dad with half-time physical caretaking duties. We were both the legal parents of this child. We had discussed how we would "share" her. I trusted that Robin would keep to her word. I wanted to avoid another situation that put me in the position of begging for my daughter to stay overnight at my house. It was as if this were a situation in which a favor was being granted, and a risk was being taken, leaving Bailey in my custody. As much as I had sympathy and compassion for Robin, why did she not seem to have any for me? I, too, went into this experience never having been a parent before, and I, too, had no hesitation about my abilities to care for a child. The sooner we established a routine, the sooner we would both become accustomed to it and know how to plan our days and our expectations.

It was then that I informed my workplace, where I was a paid intern gathering my hours for psychology licensure, that I was dropping my workload from full-time to three-quarters time. I would be leaving work Tuesdays in the midafternoon and taking all day Wednesday off. I assured my superiors and my clients that I could meet my responsibilities in the remaining days of the workweek, but at this point in my life, as a new dad, I wanted to have midweek time with my daughter as well as weekends. Robin and I arranged for a handoff on Tuesday around 3 p.m. Depending on where Robin was, either I went to her and collected Bailey, or she delivered her to me at work. We would transfer any necessary information as well as more breastmilk in the diaper bag, chat for a bit, and then say goodbye until Thursday morning when I would return Bailey to her mommy's house.

As for weekends, we opted for a division of time where one of us would have Bailey from Friday night until Saturday afternoon and then switch. This way, each of Bailey's parents had the opportunity to plan and know where we were expected as it related to our daughter. As the weeks and months progressed, the system became quite seamless. Robin and I talked on the phone during the week, sharing the new "tricks" Bailey was doing or the ailments we each needed to be aware of. To the extent that we needed to, we planned for weekends, so if Robin had theater tickets on a Friday, I would make sure to have Bailey then. If Mason and I had obligations or commitments on a particular weekend evening, then Robin and I could arrange where Bailey would be and with whom.

Robin was a good mommy. She not only showered love and attention onto Bailey, but she read and researched and provided whatever physical, mental, and environmental nourishment she could for her child. I, too, had read and researched, and learned as much as I could about becoming a new father. I implemented many of the current philosophies and values of the day, knowing that some would approve and others, many others, would have their say as to what I should do "better." Yet, intuitively, both Robin and I trusted our approaches to parenting, and it was working out well.

As with any couple, married or not, there are two distinct personalities. When those two individuals are parenting the same child, there will be apparent differences and, at times, a need to negotiate. Robin and I seemed to be doing that well enough. What we could not see was how our child was behaving at the other parent's house. We had plenty of opportunities to get together, the five of us, for meals and holidays and birthday celebrations and outings, and Bailey was always the focus. None of us had any issue with that. But for the most part, Robin, Marlene, and Bailey had their lives, and Mason, Bailey, and I had ours.

What a joy it was telling people at work on Tuesdays that I would be leaving early to pick up my daughter! It was as if I had waited most of my life to say that. "Yes, I have carpool duty." "Oh, so sorry I can't attend that meeting. My daughter has a playdate." Seemingly banal parental phrases tickled me. The pride with which I was now living my life was exponentially greater than ever before. No prior accomplishment could compete with this one: predictable paternal responsibilities. Where in some households, moms and dads negotiated their extraction from household chores and duties related to the kids, I yearned for them. I so enjoyed having Bailey's car seat strapped behind the passenger seat in my SUV. I proudly clicked the chair in and out as needed, carrying my daughter around from the grocery store parking lot to the cart as we sauntered up and down the aisles, collecting the needed items for the week. At the park, I happily withdrew the stroller from the back of my car and strutted toward the baby swings, where, most often, only mothers or nannies were attending to their charges. As the only man among them, I would receive smiles, nods, and the occasional question about my daughter, be it her age, if we lived nearby, who our pediatrician was, and almost always, where her mommy was.

That last query was a tough one for me. Of course, I knew where her mommy was—she was either at work or at home—but that was not really the question. What was, in fact, being asked was, *why are you here rather than her mother?* It was as if I was doing mommy a favor by taking time off during the day to babysit our child while mom was otherwise occupied. A part of me wanted so badly to say that today was my day to be with my daughter, that her mother and I have an arrangement where we each spend half the week with our child, and this was a day that I, along with my gay male partner, was on call. A voice inside me wanted to normalize for the world, or at least our little corner of the world that had a sandbox, a swing set, and monkey bars, that men, too, could be primary caretakers of infants. Not only that, *gay* men! Yet even in my head, it sounded angry and defensive, so I never said it out loud. Not unsolicited, anyway. My pride in having created my little family was not dependent on others' approval or praise. I swam upstream, against the current of popular culture, to be where I was, and now I wanted to delight in it, not to make this a cause célèbre. I did this for me, not as a statement against modern society. Just as Robin had opted for being a single mother by choice, I opted to be a gay dad. Of course, Robin was not, in fact, a single mother, a term that presupposes no father in the picture of the life of the child. She was more of a single woman who was raising a child with an involved dad. Again, it is not my place nor my responsibility to educate the populace around me as to literal versus figurative definitions of terminology as it pertains to my life.

Repeatedly, I was asked about my "wife" when others wanted to make small talk at the park, and it was then I chose to be direct. "Actually, I'm gay and have a partner." To my great satisfaction and pleasure, almost always, the response was one of excitement and praise. "Wow! That's great!" Or, "Congratulations!" I would smile, maybe even beam, and take it in. This was the undoing of all the years of internal negativity and external anti-gay sentiment, complementing the pursuit of exceptional and progressive thinking and actions. In my small way, I was a pioneer. Robin, too, was a pioneer right alongside me, not in the fact that she had a child as an unpartnered individual, but that she made the deliberate choice to create a child with a gay man. Knowing she was in a small minority, perhaps even a minority of one, she stepped outside the mainstream rubric and took a chance. Years later, in one of Bailey's more unhappy moments, she would refer to herself as a "social experiment," and perhaps she was correct. But that was never our intention. She had two parents who were willing to risk the norm to construct an atypical family unit, yet one that was deserved by all who wanted it.

Tuesday afternoon and evening routine became a source of pure fun and pleasure. Bailey and I often did some grocery shopping, played in the park, went to a children's museum, or met up with other friends who had children around the same age. We scoured the city for age-appropriate indoor and outdoor venues that catered to kids, like the now-defunct *Under the Sea*, an indoor play area set up as if all who entered it were living beneath the ocean. The walls were painted blue with fish, anemones, octopi, seagrasses, and other ocean-dwellers brightly rendered in primary colors all around us. There were "sea caves" to enter, in which educational videos were playing, with eerie yet soothing music accompanying the disseminated information. Did you know that of the more than one million species presumed to be living beneath the water, more than 90 percent of them are still unknown to scientists?

Since we would arrive home before Mason on Tuesday nights, I was usually in charge of preparing the meal. Ben was often with us on those nights, which allowed for a real family dinner. Mason and I had our routine in place, each of us knowing what we liked to eat and how to prepare it. Ben was a great eater, open to trying everything we made. When Bailey was eating only breast milk, it was easy; all we had to do was either feed her before we ate or at the table with us. Most nights, I would have fed her before Mason and Ben got home, and Bailey would hang out with us in her bouncy chair, propped atop the table. The four of us would converse, which mostly consisted of Bailey cooing or making other noises and Ben, Mason, and I responding to her as if she had asked a question or made an interesting remark. Between us, two adults, we made sure to engage Ben in conversation. As for Bailey, we would tickle her feet or simulate our forks as airplanes flying overhead. Ben vacillated between wanting to make Bailey laugh and pretending she was not there at all. Just like any big brother. Sometimes wanting all the attention for himself, other times seeing if he were able to get the heartiest laugh out of Bailey.

On the nights Ben was not with us, and it was just us three, we also had our routine. After dinner, it was bath time and story time. Each activity was in itself more than a treat; it was pure delight. From the time she was an infant through the next many years, there was singing, bath toys, silliness, and laughter. At first, bathing had the Goldilocks experience, making sure the water temperature was not too hot, not too cold, but just right. The appropriate shampoo, delicate soap for a newborn's sensitive skin, and the softest washcloth that cotton could produce were the only things we used on Bailey's very young, delicate skin. Mason and I converged as if we were in a long-rehearsed dance. With very little talking and planning, we each moved in and out of each other's way, one of us holding Bailey's head while the other gently yet efficiently ensured all the shampoo was removed. One of us played with her feet and made her giggle while the other soaped behind her knees, her little ears, and all the areas in between. We played lots of rhyming games, too. I became the king of word games, primarily for the purposes of distraction, but later on, because they were just plain fun. And silly. I always wanted more fun and more silly in my life since I was so often saddled with the responsibilities of someone older than my chronological age. This was the perfect opportunity to invite that in and revel in it.

Once all the washing and soaping and shampooing and playing and tickling and giggling were done in the water, Mason would announce that it was time for our little burrito to come out of the tub. One of us would grab the nearby towel and hold it open from end to end, with the longer side on the horizontal. The other one would scoop Bailey up, usually with a quick narrative of her "taking off" as a rocket might or "flying away" after saving all the rubber duckies from the raging waters of the bath, and maneuver her into the middle of the towel. There, she would be wrapped up first from one end, then the other, like a well-contained burrito, ensuring that none of the contents would fall out. And off we went to "Jammie-town."

From a very young age, Bailey seemed to enjoy stories, whether they were read from a book or told to her in conversation. She was eternally engaged. It seemed as if we were always in conversation with one another: Bailey, Mason, and me. The truth was, Mason and I shared stories of our days, of our clients, of our telephone calls with friends, constantly chatting with one another. When Bailey was around, she was included in the conversation. And when she was in another room, we still did so. When Bailey was older, she reflected on some discomfort at times when she was with me, feeling vulnerable, believing Mason and I were talking about her behind her back. What I pointed out to her, wishing she or Robin had shared this with me earlier in her life, was that Mason and I talked with each other all the time, including when she was not around. A circumstantial difference in Bailey's life became a factor in her belief system. When she was with Mommy, it was just the two of them. Either they spoke with one another, or there was quiet. With me, on the other hand, there was a third member of our family, providing an opportunity for conversation between two of the three, usually having nothing to do with the third. Sadly, Bailey grew up feeling apprehensive at times when she was with me, creating a narrative for herself that she was the focus of secrets or gossip.

In her younger years, story time before bed was a highlight in our home. We needed to allow ample time to read before saying good night. We started with picture books and books designed for infants and toddlers. Mason and I moved into position seamlessly, both of us seated on the floor, one of us holding her, the other within page-turning distance. We would either pick out some books from her shelf or ask her which stories she wanted. There were always at least two, often more. And, with each page, each inflection of our voices, every detail shared with Bailey from the book we were reading, she participated. Sometimes vocally with "ooohs" and "aaahs," later with actual words. And at times, quietly, but with her eyes. Bailey would look in front of her, at the reader, and then crane her head to the side, looking up at the face that belonged to the lap in which she was sitting. She needed to ensure we were all engrossed and absorbed by the same thing in the same way. Mason and I quickly learned that was a key element for our little girl: that we were all in this together. Stories and books were crucial for Bailey and are still to this day. They are the place to which she can retreat to disengage from life's everyday challenges.

Bailey was quite young when Robin, Mason, and I all noticed she was advanced in certain areas, especially vocabulary and reading. When we would sit with her and read a book, she, at the tender age of two, would periodically point at certain letters, or entire words, in the book and say, "What's dat?" At first, we weren't certain what she was asking: What letter of the alphabet was that? What did that combination of letters sound like together? How do words come together on the written page? Or something altogether different. To be consistent, Robin and I discussed what we were both seeing at both homes, so we agreed we would begin teaching her the alphabet and the sounds each letter makes. Depending on how quickly she took that in and if it held her interest, we would progress. I didn't want to be one of those parents who forced their child to be the valedictorian of the sandbox. I wanted Bailey to thirst for knowledge and then provide her with the nourishment she was requesting. I did not want to coerce her into reading before she was ready. But that kid was ready fast! Bailey had been given *The Berenstain Bears* by Jan and Stan Berenstain. This particular one was the B book. For obvious reasons, we all enjoyed it, and it gave us the ability to introduce Bailey to many words that all started with the first letter of her name.

"Big, brown, big brown bear, big brown bear, blue bull, big brown bear, blue bull, beautiful baboon blowing bubbles. Big brown bear, blue bull, beautiful baboon blowing bubbles, biking backward." Then, I would always add in with much gusto, "Bam!" since the illustration showed a collision that takes place as the bear, bull, and baboon are riding recklessly. We would continue to read the heavy-laden B book all the way through to "The End." We three delighted in that book, seeing if we could memorize it, which, after a million readings, we did. We also threw in a "bonk!" and a "boing" and other B words that could join the party, always laughing at the silliness of it all but equally always feeling somewhat sad for Baby Bird. One time, I remember seeing Bailey look particularly sad at the fact that the balloon popped, so I narrated as if continuing to read the book. "Beholding Baby Bird's busted balloon, big, bold Bailey bought Baby Bird a bright, burgundy balloon, making Baby Bird beam!" With that, all was right with the world.

Another one of Bailey's favorites was the story of Madeline. Author Ludwig Bemelmans created a series of books following the adventures of seven-year-old Madeline, who is sent to a boarding school in Paris and who lives with eleven other girls under the tutelage of their teacher, Miss Clavel. The casual rhyming patterns of the prose seemed to delight Bailey, and more often than almost any other book of hers, she would ask for this one specifically, even before she could fully talk. "Madewine!" So with that irresistible request, we would pull the book off the shelf, show the front cover to Bailey, and off to Paris we would go. It didn't take long for Bailey to know how to finish the sentences of the text itself, and with her young age and inability to yet pronounce all the letters of the alphabet correctly, it was just too cute not to indulge her. I think she and I enjoyed this equally.

"In an old house in . . ."

"Pawis . . ."

"All covered with . . ."

"Vines . . ."

"Lived twelve little . . ."

"Guws . . ."

"In two straight . . ."

"Wines."

On we would read, learning all about how these youngsters spent their days, with Bailey knowing how to finish each and every line of the entire book. Of course, this meant Mason and I also had to memorize the story so that on car trips or to redirect Bailey, we could instantly begin to "read" the book, regardless of whether it was physically nearby or not.

Teeth brushing was also a game in our house. We made many everyday activities into games. I know *I* enjoyed that, and from what I witnessed, so did Mason and Bailey. The perpetual camp counselor found quirky and unique approaches to chores and necessities so as to distract from the mundane. Once jammies were on, it was off to the bathroom and up on the stepstool so Bailey could see herself in the mirror, wash her face, and brush her teeth. Dr. Mark, Bailey's dentist, told us that a soft brush was the best, and we found that blueberry and bubblegum were two of my daughter's favorite toothpaste flavors. She was not a fan of mint, not then, anyway. At first, if she had things her way, Bailey would do a quick drive-by with the brush in her mouth and announce that she was "awwww done!" What did I devise? Counting! But not just any old counting. Counting to ten. But that could become boring too, so I decided we would count to ten in different languages! Bailey already knew how to count in English, so we added Hebrew and French. Mason stepped in with his knowledge of Spanish, and I added Romanian as a nod to Bailey's paternal heritage. Over time, Italian and pig Latin joined the rotation, as well as a made-up language of ten different animal sounds that might be heard on a farm. Moo. Oink. Neigh. Baa. Woof. Meow. Roar. Quack. Gobble gobble. Often, we would end with a quiet but funny sound that a snake might make by moving our tongues in and out of our mouths quickly, letting our tongues gently hit our upper and lower lips. While this regularly resulted in spitting out some of the toothpaste, it ensured we would laugh. And *that* was the goal. Laughter. Happiness. Fun.

Once in bed, Mason would play a quick game with Bailey by tucking her in, scrunching the blanket around her so that she could become his little burrito again, a bit of tickling here and there, a kiss goodnight, and then it was Daddy's turn. Even after several stories from books, Bailey and I had a ritual, one she would insist on, and I was happy to oblige. She would say, "Tell me a story from your mind." I don't know how she came up with that expression or what made her think I could entertain her doing this, but that was her request. Numerous iterations of various themes passed through her bedroom, but the one that stuck for years was *The Candy Forest*. Bailey would lie on her back, looking at me, sometimes seated on, sometimes kneeling near, one side of her bed. She would still be wrapped up burrito-style, but the intensity and seriousness of her gaze were palpable. It was as if she *needed* this next chronicle.

Once upon a time, in a faraway land, all the kids were very excited to be going on a very special trip. Everyone came together and sat on the bus, side by side with a buddy, looking from one to the other curiously, excitedly, wanting to know where they were going to end up. The bus rolled along, and one of the teachers stood up to give the students more information. "We are approaching a place like no other. Much of what you will see today will be new to you, so take it all in. Enjoy it. You are all extraordinary children, and you all deserve to have this very special trip." As the bus slowed down, all the kids looked out the windows, but all they could see was a tall, dark wooden fence. "Kids, behind these walls is a very special home."

One by one, the students stepped off the bus and gathered in front of the towering gates. The group was assembled in front of a huge golden-colored lock that looked impossible to open, keeping the children on the outside and all the mysterious excitement on the inside. "How are we supposed to get in?" "Yeah, we don't have a key!" Several other comments were made about the disappointment of not being able to see what they had come all this way to see when, all of a sudden, one little girl said, "Does anyone else smell chocolate?" "I do!" replied a couple of voices from the crowd. "Where's it coming from?"

The kids walked closer toward the gates, and one of them leaned in so closely that he figured out the answer. He reached up toward the wood and broke a small piece off. "It's the gate! It's made of chocolate!" At that point, all the kids ran up to the gate, pulled little pieces off it, and ate the delicious wood-looking chocolate. Before their very eyes, where the gate had been broken off, it magically became filled in again. They were not destroying the gate; they were experiencing the magic described to them by their teacher. "But the lock! How will we get inside?"

As a few of the kids moved closer to the big golden-colored lock, they looked at it more closely, and one of them realized it was not a real lock. "It's made of shortbread cookie!" Several hands moved onto the lock, broke off pieces of it, and ate it. And just like that, the gates opened, revealing a paradise on the other side. Trees made of graham crackers and mint-chocolate leaves. Streams of blueberry juice instead of water. A few houses made of gingerbread and icing. The roads were paved with black licorice, and the street signs were covered with edible glitter and sprinkles. Flowers of every color grew in the ground, each of them a different fruit flavor. Orange ones tasted of oranges, purple ones the flavor of grapes. Everywhere they looked, there was more to see, and all of it was a universe of goodies. "Children, welcome to the Candy Forest!"

Regardless of how much time I would spend with Bailey in the world of the Candy Forest, it was always worth it. This is what I wanted: to be a dad who, when it came time to get my kid to bed, would tell her stories, read her books, joke with her, tickle her back, allay her fears, and finally, tuck her in tightly, reassure her that she was safe, and be there as she drifted off to sleep. Some nights, this story went on longer, and I had to think on my feet to consider all the possible permutations of candy and sweets that could be made into everyday objects. On other nights, Bailey would be asleep before the kids realized that the wooden gates were made of chocolate. And some nights, Bailey would still be awake after quite some time inside the gates and exploring the Forest. Those nights, I would find a point in the story to tell Bailey she would be joining some of the kids who were visiting the Candy Forest at the Candy Forest School, so this was where I would say goodbye for now. It was her job to continue the story in her head, and in the morning, she could tell me all about what she did and what other treats she sampled, and we could add that to our story the next time we went there.

Wednesdays were "daddy-daughter" days. I researched what was going on around town and found various midweek activities that Bailey and I enjoyed together. World Music at the Hollywood Bowl was a fun six-week event every summer. Each Wednesday morning had a different theme based on the country from which we were going to make art projects and hear music and lore. One week, we made maracas using cardboard tubes with dried beans inside, taped shut on both ends, and decorated with stickers and glitter. That was for one of the South American days. On another day, we used wire coat hangers and tied different lengths of string along the base, with various shapes of sea life attached to the string to represent one of the island nations. Kids in front and parents in the back, costumed characters would tell the tales of the lands from which they came, all done with music and singing, always allowing for any instruments made that day by the children to enhance the production. For approximately two hours, we were whisked away, traveling all over the world, often with a CD as a souvenir to take home and enjoy.

Another activity Bailey and I enjoyed for many years together was Children's Opera. On designated Saturday mornings, Bailey and I would drive downtown to the Los Angeles Music Center. While L.A. is not necessarily known for its cultural arts but rather for film and television, quite a bit of theatre and music is offered to the residents of the city. The Dorothy Chandler Pavilion, the largest of the three theater venues, invites patrons into a ballroom fully outfitted with spiral staircases and shiny chandeliers, as well as velvet seats and phenomenal acoustics. Seating nearly 3,200 patrons on a popular night for children, certain modifications are made to introduce them, in an inviting way, to the world of opera. In the lobby, tables would be set up as "stations," each one providing instruction to the younger participants to learn something associated with what they were about to see and hear. Sometimes, it is a story, sometimes a crafts project, but always a very engaging adult holding the attention of those around them. Then, chimes would be heard, and someone in period costume from the upcoming show would inform us all to head into the auditorium.

Pillows were scattered on the floor, those being the children's seats, with folding chairs in the back for the adults. Popular operas were condensed both in time and language, so they were more graspable for the kids, with a few of the characters stopping throughout the performance to ensure we were all following the story. We were fortunate to enjoy *Aida*, set in the Old Kingdom of Egypt, which featured several makeshift camels and pyramids. One weekend, we laughed out loud while watching *The Marriage of Figaro*, where disguises and surprises led us from one silly event to the next. There was *Carmen* and *The Magic Flute*, along with a few others, all staged in a way that introduced us all to the different types of operatic voices, the music of the genre, and classic stories that could lead to infinite imagination.

Not only were we predisposed to music, but I was also delighted to introduce Bailey to new activities, ones in which she and Robin, for whatever reason, did not partake. When Bailey arrived, Mason and I already had our other children. There was Ben, of course, but our "firstborn" was Baron, a German short-haired pointer that Mason adopted before Ben was born. We joked that all three of our kids had names that started with the letter B. Baron was a sweet, gentle, and smart dog, and he loved children. He loved *our* children. But he wanted everyone in the family to know that he came first, and there were certain things he was simply not going to give up. Like walks in the neighborhood. When she was still a baby, I would strap Bailey into a backpack-like baby carrier, and when she was older, we would put on her "hiking shoes," as I called them, and we would go for a "hike." For some reason, going for a "walk" didn't excite any of us, but a "hike" was, well, more adventurous. More exhilarating.

When we walked, it was a stroll on the sidewalks around our house. But a hike that was off the beaten path. We might venture onto some gravel or dirt roads, where we would need to look out for uneven ground, wild plant life, and maybe even small animals. Truth be told, we lived in a community where we were never far from some trail, so going for a hike was just as easy as going for a walk. To see Bailey's excitement in knowing she could be an explorer, a traveler, and potentially a discoverer, that was the ultimate in parenting. What's better than seeing your kid's face light up, their imagination launched, and their desire to investigate the outdoors? We would put Baron on his leash, which Mason would hold, while I held one of Bailey's hands, and off we ventured.

On the days it was just Bailey and me when Bailey was nearing the age of three, I opted for new parks and footpaths, some with more difficult inclines, others near water, so long as we braved the unknown. With a fanny pack with some snacks and a small bottle of water always ready, we went off. Some days, I taught Bailey it was safer to "sidestep" her way up or down a sloped path to have greater traction with less possibility of falling. Using our hands to hold ourselves in place was something we did often, showing Bailey it was okay to get dirty; we could always clean up once we got home. Enjoying the outing also included listening to the different sounds of birds and insects, identifying different plants, and using our sense of smell to distinguish between sweet smells, acrid ones, and other natural odors. And one more thing was always a must: taking in the beauty of nature.

"Look!" I called out, pointing with my right hand as I held Bailey's with my left. "It's a bunny!"

Bailey's eyes followed my outstretched arm and was delighted to see a brown rabbit hiding in the bushes, all the while nibbling on some greenery.

"What do you think that bunny is thinking?" I asked her.

"Yummy snack," she replied with a smile.

"Would you like to eat some grass and leaves too?" I inquired, showing her on my face that I was kidding.

"Noooooooooooo!" she exclaimed. "Yucky!"

"I agree," I said. "We have snacks that we like better."

"Like goldfish!" Bailey said.

Talking was an integral part of our hikes. Real conversations. Whether the topics were what we were enjoying, why we were enjoying it, and how it might make a difference in our lives, observations, the weather, or even silly word games. Bailey and I would talk for hours, even when she was little. She was curious, and I was enchanted by her.

One day, when Bailey was about four years old, we were hiking. The sun was overhead, and we were following the dirt path beneath our feet as it snaked left and right amidst foliage and flora. As we walked, we noticed the shadows in front of us, all the while changing in shape, size, and the direction in which they were facing. Bailey asked me about that, wondering how shadows were created. I was no expert on this topic, but from what I understood, the sun was always shooting its rays onto the earth. That creates light. When people or objects get in the way of that light, it causes the light to cast the image of that object or person onto a surface nearby, and that image is the shadow.

"So, is the shadow of me what I look like?" Bailey wanted to know.

"Sometimes it is, but only the outline of you."

"But when I bend down to try and touch it, it doesn't look like me anymore."

She was right. Bailey wanted to make contact with her shadow, but when she leaned in its direction, the rays of the sun folded the image onto itself, and it no longer looked like a person's outline at all but rather a multisided blob of a figure.

"Look. when you and I are standing next to each other," I continued, "and I hold my hand out toward you, and you do the same toward me, it looks like our shadows are holding hands." Bailey was mesmerized as she stood and moved her hand only slightly in different directions, seeing the images she was creating on the ground. She stood in one place, and one small movement at a time, she watched to see what she was creating. Moving her right leg forward and to the right to make it look like her leg was crossing over mine. Raising one hand overhead to see if she could make it look like she was touching my head. Little movements gave her such pleasure, and while I didn't know what she was thinking as she was doing this, it made me think about shadows. For so long, I had been chasing what were elusive dreams and shadows to me, wanting them to look like my fantasy. Yet for so long, each time I pursued them, it was as if they folded in on themselves, like when Bailey bent down to try and capture her image. I had been chasing shadows, trying to make them into the image I wanted. In reality, I had to wait until a certain moment in time when the sun would shine in just the right way, and I would be in just the right spot. Then, and only then, would the image I had been waiting for materialize.

After a while of Bailey enjoying her shadow etch-a sketching, we moved on, knowing that moment had passed, but we had plenty more to discover. To this day, there are very few things that put the same smile on my face as remembering those early days with Bailey. Walking into her room on any given morning, I saw her standing in her crib, fresh from a night's sleep, with tousled hair and sparkling, inquisitive eyes. Her first words to greet the day were, "Hike today?"

Life continued as it did, and the fulfillment of my routine was vast. I finally had a career I was enjoying, one from which I received considerable accolades. Mason and I were a happily partnered couple, navigating, as all couples do, the hiccups of life but, overall, enjoying each other's company and our life's adventure. I was back in contact with my parents, who were much more accepting of my lifestyle and my life and eager to get to know their West Coast granddaughter. Robin and I were co-parenting well, addressing issues as they arose. It quickly became apparent to me that Robin and I had created similar lives for ourselves. I had Mason, who, for all of his wonderfulness, could be domineering and intractable. Plenty of times, I had to remind him that he was not the only one who got to make decisions. There were others to consider. Robin had Marlene, whose personality was, in some ways, very similar to Mason's. She was often overly assertive, wanting what she wanted when she wanted it. That left Robin feeling pulled between wanting to please her mother and wanting to be fair to me. From time to time, Robin and I would joke about how similar our "parenting partners" were and how, in the end, she and I had to hold the line, knowing what *we* wanted, even if it meant disappointment for others.

In addition to deferring to Robin on many decisions, I was, if I say so myself, an easy and accommodating parenting partner. Marlene wanted to see Lisa and two kids in San Francisco and invited Robin and Bailey to join. Within the first two years of Bailey's life, she must have traveled by plane more than a dozen times. Of course, I was saddened to miss out on weekends with my daughter or weekdays when they would be gone. Yet each time, I reminded myself this was all for Bailey: enhancing her life by being closer to her family, which included her extended family. I knew that at some point, I would want to take Bailey to Toronto to meet her Canadian family, and I would hope Robin would be as gracious and receptive as I had been all these years.

In reality, Robin had a difficult time thinking about letting Bailey go for a week with me, but when Bailey was about three, that time came. We discussed that Bailey was comfortable with me, safe with me, physically and emotionally, and I would do whatever I could to help Robin with her anxiety, but the time had come. One year earlier, I had learned that my dad had a cancer diagnosis, and I wanted to see him before he went into surgery. I wanted to take Bailey with me, just in case the outcome was not an optimal one. Robin was so shaken by the thought.

"Oh, Rami, I don't think Bailey's ready for something like that!" Robin said.

"Something like what?" I asked, already sensing that once again, we would have to go through one of Robin's anxious moments about being away from Bailey.

"Bailey being away from me for such a long time."

"Robin," I continued, attempting to stay measured in my tone and response, but quickly feeling relegated, again, to the sidelines of parenting my daughter. "Bailey will be fine. Bailey *is* fine. When she is not with you, she is happy. She is confident. She is her same amazing self."

"No, I know, but..." Robin trailed off. "I just think it's too long. She's never been away from me for more than a couple of days."

"I know. And she has come back fine. None the worse for wear." I said, hoping that this would help create the image for Robin that Bailey can tolerate separation from Robin.

She suggested that she and Bailey come together to Toronto, and they could either stay with my parents or at a hotel, but Bailey needed her to be there.

"Robin, I have to say, both personally and professionally, this is not a healthy message you are sending to Bailey." I tried this route of reasoning.

"What do you mean?" she asked.

"By you coming to Toronto, you are saying, through your actions, that Daddy is not safe or capable of taking care of Bailey and that Bailey *needs* Mommy to keep her protected."

After several attempts at negotiating this, I gave in to Robin, telling her that while I did not agree with the decision, I would go along with it. This time. But at some point in the not-too-distant future, I *would* be taking Bailey with me to Toronto without Mommy.

The summer before Bailey's third birthday, my father's prognosis was excellent—he was cancer-free—and I had not been back to Toronto since his hospital stay. I was booking our trip. I prepared Robin in advance, giving her the dates I would be going along with all the phone numbers and addresses of my family and close friends whom she had met. Robin was hesitant, but to her credit, she acknowledged that Bailey would be fine, and it was she who would have a difficult time with the distance. I asked her what might help because if there was anything she could think of, I wanted to ease her discomfort. We promised we would talk on the phone every day. Robin said she would give me a small gift to give Bailey every day she was gone so Bailey would have something from Mommy every day. I promised Robin that if Bailey was so upset that it might help her to be home earlier than the original return date, I would consider coming back early. The professional therapist in me knew this was anxiety, driven by an attachment that might not be the healthiest, but I was not Robin's therapist. I was the co-parent to our child and reminded her that she had chosen to have a child with me. She has seen me parent and care for our child for nearly three years. She knew who I was and how Bailey was when she was with me. These were all facts Robin had witnessed, and they were not in dispute. In the end, we were going.

On our way to the airport, Mason, Bailey, and I were talking about Toronto and who she would be seeing there.

"Remember Debbie and Mark?" I asked.

Bailey looked up at me and nodded. "He has the long beard that he braids."

"That's right!" Mason said, smiling at me, that Bailey was associating physical traits with the people she was recalling.

"Well," I continued, "We will see them. We're also going to see Anita and Elliott. Anita and I have known each other since we were kids. And now we both have our kids."

"They came to visit us too!" Bailey stated.

"Yup," I responded. "And you'll also get to see the people who we've spoken to on the phone. Like my brother, your uncle, Gil."

"And Dana," Bailey added my sister-in-law, her aunt.

"And just like you have your cousins Benjamin and Rachel in San Francisco, you have two cousins in Toronto, Alana and Natalie."

"Are they bigger than me, or am I bigger than them?" Bailey wanted to know.

"Alana is four years older than you; Natalie is two years older than you. You are the youngest." I explained.

"I guess I'm the youngest cousin of all my cousins." Bailey was doing the math, calculating that she was the third cousin who came along on both sides of her family.

There was also Mason's family, again, some of whom had been to visit us in Los Angeles.

"Is the food different in Canada?" Bailey asked.

"That's a really interesting question. Why do you ask?" I was curious where that came from.

"I don't know. I was wondering if I would know the foods there."

"Savta will be making some food for us that she made when she and Saba came to visit in Los Angeles. The meatballs she made…"

"I *love* Savta's meatballs!" Bailey interrupted me, gleeful at the thought of my mother's meatballs. "Will she make her potato soup too?"

"I don't know, but I'm sure if you ask her, she will. Maybe she'll even let you be her sous-chef."

The thought of helping her grandmother in the kitchen must have taken Bailey back to a memory that took place in Los Angeles. My parents had been visiting, and as my mother was busy cooking away, Bailey was intently watching her. At one point, my mother brought over a step stool for Bailey, and the two of them worked tirelessly side by side.

Bailey asked about the weather; she wanted to know what activities we were going to do there. She asked all appropriate and legitimate questions. We answered them all, and Bailey was happy.

I was aware that I was nervous and excited, at long last, bringing my daughter to the city where I grew up. Introducing Bailey to family and friends would be easy; Bailey and I had an easy rapport with one another. I knew when she was tired, when she was hungry, and when she was uncomfortable, and how to address each of those situations. What I was also aware of was how much luggage one needs when traveling with a toddler! Ordinarily, I would pack my carry-on bag with enough clothes for one week, knowing that if I needed to, I could do laundry wherever I was staying. This time, we would all be housed with my parents in the home where I grew up, but they had none of what was familiar to Bailey. In addition to the car seat that we needed on the plane, there was a big suitcase filled with some of Bailey's favorite books, board and card games, clothes, and, of course, the presents from Robin. My brother and sister-in-law could offer us things from my nieces if we needed them, but because this was Bailey's first trip to Toronto, I wanted to make as sure as I could that she had familiarity with her. This way, in preparation for future trips to Toronto, she would hopefully have positive images and recollections. After we loaded up the cart with all of our gear, including all the snacks and games for the plane, I stopped for a second. Who was I? Who was this person who travels with so much stuff? I did not recognize myself. It was not burdensome, nor was it difficult. Simply unfamiliar.

We walked into the terminal toward the ticketing counter where our passports would be needed. There were a few odd looks at a gay couple traveling with their child. It was apparent from the documents that Bailey and I were actually related, but when we were asked who Mason was to us since we all stepped up to the podium together, we had to take a breath, and explain. Mason and I were a couple. This was my biological child. She was *our* daughter. We were going to Toronto to visit family. *Our* family. This was in the early 2000s; a gay family was not at all typical or commonplace. Our luggage went off, and hopefully, it will be found on the other end. And off we went, through security, and finally to our gate.

We still had some time before boarding, so Mason and I took out some of our "travel games" to entertain Bailey. This was going to be a long trip for a three-year-old. Nearly one hour in the car. It takes another 45 minutes to get from the entrance to the terminal all the way to the gate. Now, another 45 minutes or so until boarding, then 30 minutes or so until take-off, and then five hours to touch down. We were in need of considerable patience. We played I Spy for a while, then on to a card game where we had to match the animals. After that, we built a story, which involved making silly stories, each of us taking turns. I started with, "Once upon a time, an elephant was looking for his glasses because he wanted to read a book." Mason continued, "But the elephant could not remember where he put those glasses. He looked high and low." It was then Bailey's turn, and without skipping a beat, she pressed on. "They weren't in his tummy because that would be silly. They weren't in his bed because he would crush them." And on we played. There was also time for some goldfish crackers, a couple of books, and a "last potty break before the plane," where I took Bailey to the bathroom "just in case."

While we sat and amused ourselves, two Air Canada employees came to the gate, turned on their computers, and pressed a few buttons to open up a locked clear door, presumably the passage to get to the plane. They announced they would be starting with boarding shortly. That was our cue to pack up as much as possible, leaving only the bare minimum out for Bailey, with the rest in satchels and carry-ons that we were hauling over our shoulders. One of the agents began her announcement, informing all passengers that early boarding was commencing. She was inviting all those who needed additional assistance with boarding to come up to the door, showing their passports and boarding passes. Several elderly folks stood, two with walkers and one with a cane, and there was an Indian woman in a full Indian sari and headdress seated in a wheelchair with an attendant. These people all inched their way forward while the rest of us sat nervously and impatiently, ready to spring forward at the second our rows were called.

"And now we invite all those families traveling with young children who need a little extra time to board to come forward." And it hit me. This was me! *I* was finally a family! I was partnered. With a man. Whom I loved and who loved me. I could be honest, not only with myself but with the world, about who I loved. And we had a child!

The wait was over. I had created my life's vision. My goal to have a family was achieved. I was now providing a childhood for someone completely different from the one I had. I was showing a child what childhood *should* be like. Playful and silly and light. No more hiding. No more chasing the dream. We were here. I stood up, threw one strapped bag over my shoulder, picked up Bailey's travel car seat in my left hand, took Bailey's hand in my right, looked over my shoulder at Mason, and said to him, "Come on. Let's get our family on the plane."

EPILOGUE

———❧———

As the clock ticks on…

It has been many years since the first flight that I took with my family. In addition to Toronto, where Bailey met her extended family, our little family of three also created memories closer to home and abroad. We traveled with Mason's cousin and her daughter, Gaby, who is just a few weeks younger than Bailey. The two of them put their heads together to create dance routines, sleepover activities, special food concoctions, and other pastimes that kept the rest of the world out of their private little corner. They devised a short rap that had accompanying hand choreography to explain who they were to one another. "We're second step cousins-in-law, twice removed, sort-of by marriage, outlaw-ish, in-law-ish, reddish, pinkish, bluish green!" When they did this, it often reminded me of my childhood, those days in the bomb shelter in Israel, when I would get lost in watching my twin cousins pass the time in a very similar way. Only this time, rather than feeling on the outside, longing to feel connected to them, I celebrated the fact that I *was* on the inside. It was me who created this happy, loving, convoluted mess of a family, one that reveled in its exceptionality. The girls, just like my cousins, beamed as they performed the requisite movements, sometimes not reaching the end without one of them, if not both, laughing to the point of folding themselves over in half with laughter, falling to the ground.

We, as a larger family, along with Robin and her mother, sometimes with her sister and Bailey's San Francisco cousins, also spent time together. An Alaskan cruise, long weekends in the mountains, and some calendar holidays all seated around one large table. Of course, just as Mason and I spent time with Bailey without Robin, Robin and Bailey traveled and created a life together independent of us. The goal seemed to be achieved: we made a family for Bailey. Robin was sort of a single mother, but not really, since Bailey had a dad. I was a sort of step-parent to Ben, who had Mason and the mommies. Bailey was a sort of sister to Ben, but only part-time. Welcome to this new world of families! Bailey always knew that she had a mommy, a daddy, and a Mason. Once, when she was about seven years old, she was showing a friend our house, and this was part of the description.

Bailey: This is my room.

Friend: Ok.

Bailey: This is my dad and Mason's room.

Friend: Who's Mason?

Bailey: He's my daddy's partner.

Friend: Ok.

Bailey: And this is Ben's room.

Friend: Who's Ben?

Bailey: Well, Ben is Mason's son, so if Mason is my daddy's partner, he is my half-dad, and Ben is his son, so Ben is my quarter-brother.

Bailey was figuring it all out. On her own, in her own time, and we were all thrilled. She was the glue that was holding together our ragtag family—disparate people from disparate places united by the courage and pluckiness of Robin and Rami.

It's now 25 years since Bailey was born, and so much has taken place. The good, the bad, the ugly. As well as the thrilling, the exotic, the mundane, and the novel. Bailey and I had our Daddy-Daughter days, as well as our special times to read, play, hike, sing, and create together. I was able to do so many of the "dad" things that I had eternally longed to do. Bedtime, bath, and reading. Teaching her to ride a bicycle. Teaching her to swim. Giving her the opportunity to stand up on ice skates and rollerblades. Helping with homework. Bailey sous-cheffing in the kitchen as she learned to cook and bake. Bailey cheffing in the kitchen, with me being the sous-chef so that she can try out her new skills. Extra-curricular activities like dance, gymnastics, choir. Piano lessons. Guitar lessons. Visits to the library and the bookstore to explore the newest publications as well as the classics. On the days that Bailey was with me, I drove her to school and picked her up. That was a commitment that I made to myself in becoming a parent; I wanted to do as much as I could of the everyday activities since I would only be spending half the week with my child. And it was my pleasure. Starbucks on the way to school in the morning, for a frothy or iced something-or-other for Bailey. Sometimes, a stop or two on the way home for makeup, clothes, toiletries, or whatever else she wanted. It was all glorious. For me, everything from the ordinary to the extraordinary was the latter: extraordinary. I loved it all.

As Bailey grew and we grew as a family, life was good. Of course, we dealt with the goings-on of any family system, incorporating Ben into our family of three, but that was only possible one evening per week. It was nearly impossible to be a family of four, given the impediments of time and schedules. But, on Tuesday nights, we were that family. The four of us at the dinner table, discussing the activities of the day and the past week.

Looking back at this past quarter century, the image that comes to mind is one from cartoons I used to watch as a child or the black-and-white movies of yesteryear, where the hands of a clock race around the face of that clock, showing time moving swiftly. Day after day, week after week, month after month, season after season. How did we experience all of these life-cycle and calendar events in what seems like the blink of an eye, all of them now in our collective rearview mirror? Yet, this is the most natural and ordinary of things to happen: life.

During these turns around the sun, we lost Mason's dad. He had been ill for quite some time, and although he had lost most of his ability to speak, he and two-year-old Bailey had a language of their own. He would smile and wiggle his fingers at her, and in response, she would smile and wave back at him. She did that little kid wave, where she held up her hand and moved her fingers up and down at the knuckles, imitating an arcade claw. He would then motion for her to come closer to him, and she would comply. Once within touching distance of one another, he would again wiggle his fingers, this time on her head. She would laugh, claw-wave goodbye, and move on. Seeing Mason's father's smile linger every time this occurred left us with a highly poignant memory.

My mother was diagnosed with Alzheimer's Disease. The progression was not particularly rapid at first, which enabled both of my parents to attend Bailey's Bat Mitzvah. She wanted one. She wanted it to look like the ones she had attended. She wanted to learn the prayers, lead the service, and have a big party with music, dancing, food, glitter, friends, and fun. Which, in the end, she accomplished. Valiantly. She worked weekly with a come-to-the-house rabbi, Rabbi Faith, who understood Bailey, and together, they created a booklet unique to Bailey's beliefs and integrity. In addition to the long-established prayers, there were poems, readings, thoughts, and reflections as part of the service.

It was bittersweet to see my mother in Los Angeles. This would end up being her second-to-last last trip ever, the last one being from her home in Toronto with my father to a memory care facility, where she would spend the next several years of her life, such that it was. But, she attended the Bat Mitzvah, and even with the slightly vacant expression on her face, not quite sure what was taking place, she found herself grounded during the ceremonial passing of the Torah from generation to generation. At that moment, she was "home." I remember her whispering, presumably to Bailey, *"Mama Shayna."* No sweeter nor more significant and heartfelt words could she have tendered her granddaughter, namesake of her mother, from generation to generation.

It was during these past years that Mason, too, had his health crisis. Shortly after his fiftieth birthday, Mason's heart began to malfunction to the point where the medications he had been on throughout his life were no longer achieving their requisite responsibilities. Mason had a pacemaker-defibrillator installed in his chest, and that, too, provided nominal results at best. Then, one unfortunate night in November 2009, Mason was not well. After multiple and time-consuming arguments, he finally agreed to let me take him to the hospital. En route, he collapsed in the front passenger seat of my car and was technically dead upon arrival at UCLA Hospital. I was on emotional auto-pilot myself, pulling up to the Emergency Department and calling out for help, which came in the form of an orderly with a wheelchair. The two of us propped Mason from my car onto the chair, and he was rushed through the waiting throngs into a triage area, where his shirt was cut off, and the paddles were applied—five separate times. Mason regained consciousness, and from there, he was put on life-support machines for more than four months until he was physically ready for a heart transplant. Gratitude does not begin to express the feelings I have for the poor soul who died and applied the pink dot to his driver's license, allowing his organs to be donated to other needy individuals. Sorrow does not begin to communicate the feelings I have for the family of this young man, losing a loved one at the dawn of his adult life. Still, the events took place as they did, and since that auspicious day in April 2010, one day before his 54th birthday, Mason returned home intact, ready to continue the life that he, and we, had worked so hard to create.

Throughout those months, taking care of Bailey on my Daddy-Daughter days was a respite. A refuge. Robin and I both talked to Bailey about what was happening to Mason. Bailey and I maintained our schedule, school pick-ups, and drop-offs, making dinner at home, homework, bathtime, and endless amounts of conversations. Laughter was always a part of our time together, for which I was so thankful. Bailey had no idea how loved she was, especially during the time when I might have been losing the family I had worked so hard to have. Not loved as a life preserver but as a beacon. Bailey represented to me the next generation. The hope. The idealism. The innocent naivete. All the things that were in direct contrast to the grim realities that were feasibly just around the corner. That first Tuesday night dinner in April 2010, with Ben, Bailey, Mason, and me, seated around the table after a punishing hiatus, eating one of our go-to meals, stir-fried chicken and veggies, brown rice, and a salad: there was no better family dinner.

Middle school. High school. Then, setting her sites on college, Bailey, Robin, and I journeyed to various colleges and universities that Bailey wanted to visit, all in the hopes of finding her "home" for the next four years. We flew back east to survey a myriad of small- and medium-sized liberal arts colleges and arrived in New York in an unanticipated April snowstorm. I grew up in Toronto, so I was comfortable with walking in boots, layered clothes, a coat, scarf, hat, and gloves. But Robin and Bailey, less so. As we trudged through snow and sleet toward the end of our first day there, I asked Bailey if she could see herself living in weather like this.

"I've never lived in snow, and I don't want to be afraid of it. This might be the best way for me to overcome that fear."

A dozen or so colleges later, we returned to Los Angeles, and Bailey filled out her applications. If you believe, as I do, in the concept of *beshert*, defined as "destiny" or "preordained," Bailey ended up exactly where she was supposed to be. She had her four years away from home, and, to no one's surprise, graduated from a prestigious university.

Time has marched on, not only for me, but for all of us. Throughout these years, the world has changed. While not everywhere, there is a much greater definition of and acceptance of what family means and looks like. No longer is it as difficult for the LGBTQ+ community to have children, and to live more of a mainstream life. For this, I am thankful. I am also thankful for the life experiences that I had in my less-than-easy expedition to the building of my own family. Ups. Downs. Conflicts. Resolutions. As the calendar pages continue to turn, there is more to learn. More to do. More to ponder. More to overcome. In other words, there is more life. I don't know anyone who survives life without some emotional battle scars. Living with those scars makes the reward of family, and of life, that much sweeter.

I was recently involved in a car accident that could have been a fatal one for me. Surviving it emboldened me and reassured me. There is more life to be lived. The patience I have needed to show myself in the healing from this accident is my reminder, once again, of perseverance and determination. The hard work of physical rehabilitation, as slow as it is, is representative of my dedication and drive to heal, and to move forward. Things do get better. I had lost my parents for a time, but worked to ensure that it would not be forever. It looked like I was going to lose Mason to illness, but through his tenacity and my dedication, we are together today.

In addition to perseverance, I believe in, and have, patience. I have learned that patience is not inaction; it is hope. We don't always know *when* something will happen, but we have to trust, and work as if, it will. I have heard it said that you regret the things you don't do more than the things you do. Therefore, no regrets. March on, no matter how challenging the hardships might seem. There is value in the fight, and satisfaction in the efforts made. We have today. Today is an opportunity to do. And, if we are lucky enough to get through tonight, and have a tomorrow, that will again provide us with a new today, another today, to keep pursuing our goals.

All those years ago, I unconsciously set myself a goal: to have a family. To have my own, biological child. As the goal rose through the sub-conscious into the very active conscious, I pursued it. Many times on that journey I was disappointed, disillusioned, deflated. But, it was all worthwhile in the end. I became the dad I wanted to become. It has been the amalgamation of all the things I ever wanted and never dreamed of.

I think back to Anita's wedding all those years ago. I remember the dimmer switch. All these years later, I see that my time did come to turn light out of darkness, order out of chaos, something out of nothing. And I celebrate. Every day.

Acknowledgments

———⟁———

I t really does take a village. So many people have been directly and indirectly involved in this project. There are a few specific individuals who have been instrumental in moving this book from my head onto the page.

To Jennie Nash, my first memoir professor, thank you for your encouragement, tough love, and guidance. To Victoria Griffin and Elizabeth Oliver, immeasurable thanks for helping me edit this manuscript over and over and over again.

To my longest, not oldest, friend in the world, Anita Stern Weidman, thank you for always being my voice of reason, whether I want to hear it or not. To Debbie Smith, my second longest friend in the world, I thank you for always letting me depend on you, for anything, no matter the scale. To Sharon Glassberg, my third longest friend in the world, I thank you for a friendship that came about so randomly and has endured through the unthinkable. And to Judy Falb Mizrahi, my fourth longest friend in the world, I thank you for the safety and love of being the first friend I came out to, and the one who guided me into my own therapy. You four women continue to inspire me.

To my parents, who do not realize it, but it was through your steely resolve and relentless resilience that I am who I am today.

And to Mason Sommers, my Boni, the man I choose to be with every day. Thank you for teaching me so much about myself and allowing me to teach you about you, which ultimately makes "us" the "we" we are today.

And to Auggie, the cutest doggy in the world.